Dedication

Thank you, Hashem.

I dedicate this writing to my Mother's many fine teachers and friends:

Jimmy Porter, Jim Kennedy, Don Pritts, Big Frank, Scott Hunter, Marty Slattery, Ann Walls, Dottie Edgar, Roger Grandy, Lynn Byron, Jackie Clark, Bill Wilson, Bob Smith and all the others from that anonymous fellowship who now attend the great meeting in the sky.

And also to those Fellowship friends of Mom's still living, and who walked Mom's journey with her over the years.

My special thanks to Rose, Sherry, Mary, Barb, Rabbi Yossi Serebryanski, Rabbi Buz Bogage, Robert B. and Wayne M. They helped me stay relatively sane while seeing my duty through to its end. Thanks also to Robert Boggess for creating the artwork for the book's cover.

And I dedicate this writing to two of my own best teachers:

Maximo Corrada
Walter Goldberg

May they both rest in peace. They made our world a better place

As a professional, I would be remiss if I did not first warn all who are considering being a SOLE caretaker that it is an extremely demanding task, one that I suggest people do not take on. However, as a human and as a friend, I understand that there are circumstances where a person makes the decision to dedicate a portion of their lives to providing "end of life" caretaking for a loved one. Aaron's story is such a story.

In this incredibly honest book, Aaron shares his decision. He covers the suddenness of the onset of his mother's illness, his struggles to understand what has happened and the gift of love he gave to care for her. He writes openly about his mistakes, some of the lessons he learned, and many of the things that he did incredibly well. His pain, as friends disappeared, as his life experiences shrank to the narrow window of his mother's final years are found throughout the book.

This is a book for those who either are considering being a sole caretaker, or who are in the midst of caretaking for a loved one. His journey will help you understand that you are not alone in many of the experiences that you feel, or may feel. There is not "something wrong" with you because of your feelings. Sole caretaking is simply that difficult of a task.

This book gives you help in making your decision and support on your journey. I applaud Aaron's gift to his mother and his gift to you, the reader.

Melvin J. Wernimont, Ph. D.
Greenwood Village, Colorado

PRELUDE

I send you all love.
I send you all peace.
I beg your forgiveness as I make these amends.
I did the best I could at all times.
Please forgive me for having thought ill of anyone.

Shalom,

Aaron Ainbinder
aaronainbinderbooks@outlook.com

TABLE OF CONTENTS

TABLE OF CONTENTS
(continued)

Just Before The Stroke Of Seven

Journey of a Solo Full-Time Caregiver, Whose Mother Had a Stroke Which Led to Dementia

FORWARD/INTRODUCTION

In the time it takes for a blood clot to travel from my Mom's heart to the Wernicke's area, left rear part of her brain, my whole life changed, as did my Mom's. As the reader goes through this writing, he or she will learn about the changes in Mom's life. In a nutshell, she will no longer be able to call her AA partner-sponsors every day, or regularly attend AA meetings, or go anywhere by herself. Mom will no longer be able to safely be by herself at any time. Mom will no longer be able to easily communicate in sentences which are consistently, or even very often, clear, and which convey information. Mom's whole language center in her brain will no longer function properly.

Stop and think for a moment, if you will, all of the well-organized and categorized words that are in nifty little files in your brain. Try to imagine taking all those nifty little files that hold those well-organized and categorized words, and dumping those files onto a large conference table. Then try to imagine understanding something that is said to you, or constructing a clear sentence in order to share some information with another person. This is a snapshot of how, in the time it takes for a blood clot to travel from her heart to the language center of her brain, my Mom's life changed. And it does not take but a second or two for that blood clot to make its way to the brain. It is not a great distance to travel.

And how did my life change? I am my Mom's youngest son and I moved back into her house, the house that I grew up in, 7 years ago. Mom had gotten to an age where the house was too much for her to take care of herself, and I was not making much money in my line of work. When Mom's stroke hit her, on Friday evening, March 29, 2013, just before the stroke of 7:00, I went from being, among other things, a full-time paraprofessional (teacher's aide) in a middle school, working with severe needs special education students with hearing impairment, to being a full-time caregiver for my, at the time, 82-year-old Mom.

For the prior seven years I had enjoyed working in special education. I had found a niche that fit me well, and the skills that I gained from this work are proving absolutely invaluable and indispensable. In the time it took for that blood clot to travel its path, my daily and weekly routines and activities were no longer feasible. No more working in special education, going to the gym just about every day, playing bass in a band or two, going to shul (synagogue) on Saturday mornings with Mom, and regularly attending Alcoholics Anonymous (AA) meetings, either with her or on my own.

In my search for direction and guidance, following the stroke, I found nothing, and I mean nothing, that I could use for reference, instruction or direction as to how to be a caregiver for someone who has gone through what Mom has had happen to her brain. The stroke-related web sites that I searched through all pointed to the direction of hiring in-home care. At roughly $22 to $30 per hour, this is not an option for us. The most recommended local agency charges $22/hour. I would need 9 hours a day while I was at work. This is about $1,000/week. Mom and I would burn through all of our financial resources before the end of the next school year. And then, we would be right where we are now, but with no cash in the bank. I made the choice to leave my employment so that I could provide the care that Mom needed every day and every night.

I offer up this treatise/book with two goals in mind. First is that it will be helpful to someone else who unexpectedly finds themselves in a solo full-time caregiving situation, similar to mine. Second is that enough people purchase copies of this work so that I can provide some funding to other caregivers who leave their gainful employment to take care of a family member, so that when their caregiving role comes to an end, they do not find themselves to be in financial difficulties.

I have no family here in Denver other than my Mom, and she has no one other than me. My choice was obvious and my decision came to me naturally, easily and with never a second thought. I am not a tzaddik (Jewish saint, sort of) but this is just how and who I am, and in keeping with the relationship I have developed with my Mother over my lifetime. There is no way that I couldn't not do this.

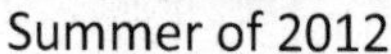

Summer of 2012

November 8, 2018

Bedtime – March 28, 2019, Thursday.
What a fine, full and significant day!! Blessings, Love, all around.
Mom.

'Twas a fine day indeed, Mom.
Love Ya!! Aaron

Friday 3-29-2019
Here's to Friday Good Life –
We are blessed. ♡, ♡, Mom

Just Before The Stroke of Seven

The First Stroke

On the previous page is the last entry to a daily log that my Mom and I kept on the kitchen table. We used this log to leave each other messages and words of encouragement. I also used the log to remind Mom of plans that we might have for any given day. As she has gotten older, her memory has naturally been somewhat affected, and these log books helped to remind her of things. I doubt that Mom will ever be able to keep such a log again in her life.

Just before the stroke of 7:00, Friday night, March 29th, 2013. Mom and I were watching Louisville playing Oregon in the 2012 men's NCAA basketball tournament. I told Mom that I had Duke in the next bracket and Mom bet me $1 that Louisville would win. She said that I needed to make the next game interesting, since I had filled out a bracket this year, but had not entered it into a pool. Last year, we both filled out brackets and I put them in a pool at the school I worked at. It only took a short time to explain to Mom what an NCAA bracket was, and how to fill it out. Mom is 82 years old and enjoys good sports. She always has. Baseball is the sport that she most enjoys, having watched, and listened to, the New York teams back in the 1950's, when she and Dad lived in Brooklyn.

We took a break to light the Shabbas (Jewish Sabbath) candles, and walked into the kitchen. The Shabbas candles are on the counter in our kitchen, next to the stove, as they have been for years. As Mom reached over to pick up the book of matches, she slowly started to lean into the counter and looked over to me with a faraway look in her eyes and a blank look upon her face. I held her up, to keep her from falling.

"Mom! What's my name?" – No response.
"Mom! Stick out your tongue!" – No response.

Her eyes focused up at me with a look that I will never forget, and which there are no words to describe.

I reached my left hand into my pants pocket, grabbed my cell phone, and dialed 911. Mom had had a stroke. It was 6:57pm and in the time it takes for a blood clot to travel from Mom's heart to the left posterior (rear) quadrant of her brain, our lives had just changed in a most profound manner.

The details of that evening read like a textbook scenario of what can go "right" after someone has a stroke, if "right" can be used in this type of medical emergency. I am still on the phone with 911 when I hear sirens outside of our house. We live a block and a half down the street from a fire station. I am still on the phone with the 911 operator when I ease Mom into a kitchen chair so that I can let the firemen into the house, hoping that she would not fall out of the chair during the few seconds it took me to get to, and open, the front door. An ambulance arrives within 5 minutes of the firemen. It is now just short of 7:10pm.

By 7:25, Mom is at Rose Hospital and 20 minutes or so later, I am there to sign the paperwork which allows the doctors to begin administering TPA, a blood clot busting drug. This must be done within that crucial "golden hour" after a stroke occurs. We were 17 minutes under the wire. On the way out of the house, before I drove myself to the hospital, I grabbed Mom's will and the papers that grant me medical power of attorney for her in the event that she becomes incapacitated. That event had occurred.

The doctors then had me, via an audio/video computer link, talk to a neurosurgeon at another hospital that specializes in neurosurgery and stroke. That surgeon had already seen a CT scan that showed a blood clot in Mom's brain and he explained to me that if they air-lifted Mom to the other hospital and removed the clot, further damage might be minimized. He needed me to make that decision immediately so that they could get a helicopter prepped and ready to fly. An immediate decision on my part was necessary. Long before this stroke hit, my Mother had reviewed her Advanced Medical Directives with me. Mom's desire for DNR (Do Not Resuscitate) and her desire for no extraordinary mechanical means of keeping her alive now had to be weighed by me before I made any choice as to what to do with or for her. An immediate decision on my part was necessary. No time for much pondering or weighing choices, was there? I made the decision to let the doctors treat her as they saw fit to do at another hospital.

We flew her to the other hospital and so began a one-month stay at a hospital stroke center, here in Denver, Colorado. I was later to find out that a close friend of ours lives across the street from Rose Hospital and she saw the helicopter arrive at the rooftop landing pad, and then take off a few minutes later. She said a prayer for the person, whoever it might be, that was being loaded onto the helicopter. Only later did she learn that it was Mom taking flight that evening. Again, that was on March 29, 2013, and it all began just before the stroke of 7:00.

WHY THIS BOOK WAS WRITTEN

This book/treatise began as a way for me to keep my notes from being scattered on my desk. I kept notes on little note pads during the times I spent in the hospital with Mom, talking with doctors and nurses and doing what needed to be done here at home before Mom was discharged from the hospital. When I saw my note pile getting out of hand, I began typing them into a Word program on my computer, with the thought that over time it would be beneficial for me to look back and remember things that I would probably forget. It is now 6 years since the first stroke, and I am editing my writing, preparing it for publication. It is my sincere hope that what I share with you, Dear Reader, is helpful to you and/or to someone you might know.

April 29, 2013 -- One month to the day, following Mom's stroke, I took her back to our home. And then the real work began.

I took the next day, April 30th, off from work, so that I could stay with Mom at home. I returned to my work at a local public middle school the next day. An old friend of Mom's was hired by me to stay with Mom while I was at work. She was here from 6:30 – 3:30, Monday thru Friday until the school year ended in the first week of June. Since then I have, quite literally, been with Mom 24 hours a day, 7 days a week, with the rare exception of a few hours when I hired the same friend of Mom's so that I could get out for 2-3 hours. We only did this a few times before I ended that situation and I have been on my own with Mom, as her full-time caregiver, ever since.

Occasionally, some old friends have come to stay with Mom for a few hours while I went out, but the times that has occurred are few and far between. I remember a case manager at the hospital, who told me that it is often the case that friends of the stroke victim will disappear. I confidently told her that I did not expect that to happen, since Mom has been in Alcoholics Anonymous (AA) for 41 years and has a host of friends who love her, many of whom had already let me know that they are ready and willing to help out any way that they can. Sadly, the case manager's words are proving to be true. My cell phone rarely rings with friends offering to help out, and our home phone rings even less often. We are fortunate to have one or two close friends who stay in touch, and one of them has come by several times to visit, which allows me to bug out for a couple of hours. I will deal with this part of caregiving later in this writing, eventually with a softened perspective which took a lot of work and a very long time to develop.

Suffice it to say here that without a spiritual approach to the isolation, there is no way that I could possibly be an effective caregiver for my Mom. No way at all. The resentment would eat me alive. Through the avenues and approaches of spirituality, AA program and Judaism, I have come to not only be "o.k." with the isolation, but I have come to see the great gift of being a full-time caregiver. Again, more will be written about this later in this treatise. I ask the reader of this writing to understand that the spiritual and/or religious approaches and practices that I will be writing about are what works for me. Everyone has their own ways of dealing with whatever challenges come their way in life.

I am writing these notes in November, since I did no writing back in May. I was too busy just trying to figure out how the heck to do this caregiving thing. I kept my notes either on pads of paper or on my home computer. The approach that I took was similar to that which I utilized in my work with special needs students who had very limited language skills. Since the effect of Mom's stroke was Wernicke's aphasia, this suited us well for the month of May. I already had several sets of word and picture cards which I've used over the years, so I began using them with Mom. A/apple, B/ball, C/cat, etc., was the extent of our work, and Mom struggled mightily. I have recorded many of these sessions and it is with a smile on my face now, as I write these notes from memory some six months later, to think of how far Mom has come in her recovery. I intuitively knew not to wait for direction from some case manager or outside person, since we would lose valuable time. Even while Mom was in hospital I either brought word/picture cards with me or I had a set of them in her hospital room. And I worked with her there in the hospital.

Wernicke's Aphasia – The Wernicke's area of the brain is one of two areas which is involved in speech and understanding of language. When the Wernicke's area gets assaulted, with a blood clot in my Mother's case, it is akin to taking all of the neatly organized words out of their file folders, so to speak, and spreading them out on a conference table. The result is that the patient will have great difficulty both in understanding what is said to them, as well as in expressing themselves in meaningful sentences. The patient will be able to string lots of words together, but in ways which convey no meaning. This is known as "Word Salad." This form of aphasia is also known as "fluent aphasia" and it also severely impairs reading and writing.

WERNICKE'S APHASIA TRANSCRIPTION

The following is a transcription of a conversation that Mom and I had on October 12, 2014 and it is a good representation of what is meant by "Word Salad." It is probably obvious, but "A" is for Aaron (your humble author) and "M" is for Mom.

A – Mom, we just had dinner and you have your cup of tea. You were looking around for something. What are you looking for?

M – It was very basic simples but heavy duty core from their main, and here I am. And I thought, I wonder.

A – Are you looking for something to eat?

M – I don't think so. No, I couldn't find them, and I couldn't get them through showing me. You know, whatever I did, I did something mistaken whatever there was.

A – Try and describe the thing you are looking for.

M – What else was left from something that was pecked in. And, um, so that's been something with any of these smaller ones or clearing of some kind. Maybe that something like this be something else.

A – That's chocolate.

M – Still, some of these paying off now that they are smaller for me, for us.

A – You are looking at your TV tray here. You had a bowl of soup. Is that what you are looking for? You ate your soup. Do you want me to heat more for you?

M – Yes, it could be. I don't think so. There is something in there that I had been a little more than I could handle, with big couple answers, you know? And, uh, for quite a while I had gotten to a place of being anything further to be paying attention to big stuff. Whatever it is, I'm off on any of that.

A – I can't imagine what you are looking for.

M – Foolish. What a foolish man.

A – You're not foolish. A little mixed up.

M – Yeah. Yeah. Does it also look what any of these are bigger than they look smaller when they just something like this?
*** End of Transcribed Conversation **

There was absolutely no direction that was given me in the hospital, other than a list of the medicines that Mom needed and a general suggestion or two from the physical therapy folks. There was, and still is, no case manager of any sort, from any of the medical providers or from the hospital. When Mom was discharged from the hospital, it was fortunate that the Walgreen's next to the hospital was open until 6:00. Mom was to be discharged at about 4:30, when I got there after school let out, and the hospital had none of the prescriptions that we would need. They suggested that I go by a pharmacy to get them filled. I would have Mom with me, in the car after she had not been out of a hospital for one month. To leave her in the car while I went in and dealt with filling a number of medications seemed preposterous to me. I asked the discharge nurse about this and she appeared quite incensed by my questioning her actions, or lack thereof.

The whole scene was simply unbelievable. It was as if the hospital had never dealt with this sort of situation before, and they are known to be a highly regarded Stroke Center. I was told by the discharge nurse that Mom's blood thinner medicine, Warfarin, was to be given at as close to the same time as possible each day. It was now about 4:45 and I asked the discharge nurse what time the Warfarin should be taken. She said, "5:00." I pointed to the clock and asked her how I was supposed to do this, as the prescriptions had not been called into a pharmacy yet, let alone had they been filled. In the end, I had the nurse give Mom her 5:00 Warfarin and I had the nurse keep Mom in her hospital room while I went next door to the Walgreen's, after I had to ask the nurse call in the prescriptions that we would need. She finally told me that there was a Walgreen's next door to the hospital, which was open until 6:00. Honest to G-d, I had to give this nurse step by step instructions as to what needed to be done before I would allow her to discharge this patient and before I would take Mom out of the hospital room.

I'll not go into any more details about the patient discharge process here, and I hope that I have painted a sufficient image as to how insane this discharge process was. Extrapolate this scenario of being ill-prepared, and you will easily see that there was absolutely no direction or support given to me as to how to take care of my Mother, who was an acute care stroke patient. Add to that my lack of experience as a full-time caregiver, and you have a bit of a picture of what it was like, and what I was thinking about, as I drove Mom home on April 29th.

I will share one incident here, and then let it go. It was the evening of April 2nd, five days after Mom's stoke, and her first night on the Neurology Ward. She had been transferred out of ICU/Critical Care late in the afternoon. This was the worst, most nightmarish, most difficult and most regrettable night of Mom's stay in the hospital. I was in Mom's room, sitting by her bed while trying to calm her as she continued to try to sit up and get out of her bed, over and over again. The nurse in her room told me that it was really critical for Mom to lie down and stay in her bed. Mom was fighting this to an extent that was just terrifying to me. She kept trying to sit up by working to put her legs over the side of the bed. I kept putting her legs down. "Why are you doing this to me?" Mom cried. "Why don't you love me?" Mom cried out. Over and over, again and again, this repeated itself. She would try to get out of bed and I would push her back down. The nurse was of no help other than to tell me that she had to keep Mom lying down and in bed. Then the nurse (who was, it turned out, a rookie that had only been doing this work for a few months) called for a POSEY Bed. And then she administered a drug to Mom that calmed her down a bit. That drug turned out to be Haldol, an extremely powerful antipsychotic drug, and I believe that she was given a lot of it.

There is a contraption called a POSEY Bed, which is a bed that a patient is put in and which that patient cannot get out of. It is covered with soft plastic netting and it zips closed from the outside. It is used for patients that will not stay in bed. The nurse and several other nurses and aides put Mom on a transfer board and slipped her into the POSEY Bed. Then they zipped it shut with Mom inside, protesting all the while. Mom was reaching for the mesh netting with her weakened hands and making soft, animal-like, moaning noises. If I remember correctly, it was by then about 2:00 in the morning.

I finally went home to feed the cat and sleep for a couple of hours. When I came back to Mom's room she was catatonic in that bed. Absolutely non-responsive and not waking up. Her breathing was labored and her pulse was extremely slow. The rookie nurse was in the room and doing nothing but typing notes on her computer. The drug that this rookie nurse had given Mom was Haldol, an antipsychotic drug that is used to treat schizophrenia and bipolar disorder. Mom must have been given a tremendous dosage of this powerful drug, or several doses during the hours that I was gone, because she was absolutely catatonic. I told the nurse to call the doctor immediately. I did not ask her, I told her. I ordered her to do so. The nurse looked at me nervously, and she had a right to be nervous. Something was dreadfully wrong and I was going to hold her pretty little toes to the fire.

The head of Neurology came in, got Mom out of the POSEY Bed and attempted to get Mom to respond to her. There was no response. The doctor sent Mom for a CTI scan to see if she had had another stroke. Mom had been overdosed on a powerful drug by a nurse that did not know what she was doing. And the nurse had gotten the administration of the drugs approved by the doctors that were on duty. When Mom got back to the room later in the morning, it was determined that she had not had another stroke. The staff that I talked with were nervous and vague about what might have occurred. I kept bringing them back to the Haldol. They were cornered.

Later that evening, as the drugs wore off and Mom "came around" some, I was sitting in a chair next to her bed and Mom sat up. I rubbed her back for a minute, and Mom said, "That feels nice." It was then that it dawned on me that perhaps all she needed, and wanted to do last night, was to get off her back for awhile. I asked her if she would like to stand up or sit in a chair for a bit. Her response was an emphatic "Yes!" I helped Mom to stand up and a nurse brought a large chair next to the bed and we helped her into it. Mom let out a big sigh of relief, and all was well.

The entire episode of the night before had been totally unnecessary and the hospital staff should have known it. I wish I would have known it. They had the experience. I did not. To this day (November 16, 2013) I think of that night as one where I failed Mom as her son and as her caregiver. Even though I know, rationally, that I had no way of knowing that what the nurse and doctors were doing was wrong, I still am hard on myself for missing the obvious. All Mom needed was to sit up. Her back hurt. She was not having a psychotic episode of any type at all. Her back hurt. That was all. And since she had had a major stroke and could not tell me, or anyone else, what was going on, she acted out in a way that the hospital staff found disruptive and disagreeable. <u>What the heck is a stroke patient who has Wernicke's aphasia supposed to do? How are they supposed to communicate even their most simple and basic needs?</u> Figuring out the communicating piece of this puzzle was a baffling task.

While I was in the room that horrible night, I had complete trust that the doctors and nurses knew all about stroke patients and what was best to do for them. I was dead wrong. One would assume that a Stroke Center would have learned that any patient who has been on their back for several days will reach a point of discomfort, and all that they need is to stand up or sit in a chair for awhile in order to ease their discomfort. That was all that Mom needed. All that I needed to do for Mom that night of April 2nd was to help her out of bed and into a chair for an hour or so. No need for heavy drugs or a cage-like bed. But, sadly, I did not know what to do, and I trusted the nurse that was supposed to be caring for my Mother. As I type out this terrible story of this terrible night, I can feel that my blood pressure is way up and there is great sadness in my eyes and in my heart. The only comfort that I have is that Mom remembers none of it. On April 3rd I had the rookie nurse removed from Mom's room and I gave the doctor instructions that she was never again to have anything to do with my Mom's care.

It is, Dear Reader, contrary to my nature to speak in such a manner, or to make such demands. That the doctor heeded my instruction tells me that he knew that the hospital had really screwed up. It is only because I have neither the time nor the inclination to do so, that I do not sue the hospital for such an unprofessional, dangerous and unnecessary treatment of their patient. I have absolutely no doubt that a similar occurrence has happened to other stroke patients. This is the end of the story of the POSEY Bed episode.

I spent the entire month of May just getting through my days at work as the school year worked its way to a close. I did not do any writing exercises with Mom and I kept no notes. As I mentioned a few pages back, during the day while I was at work, I paid a friend of ours to stay here at the house with Mom. I would occasionally leave school a bit early so that I could get some grocery shopping done. I would get home around 3:30 and Mom would be in bed for the night by 6:00 or 6:30. For the 2-3 hours that I Mom was awake after I got home from work, we would talk a bit and I would then fix us a light dinner and get Mom into her bed. Trips to the bathroom were frequent. Since Mom could not communicate her physical needs, I took her to the bathroom a couple of times before she went to sleep.

On the weekends we spent the days here at home, sitting in the living room watching sports, or sitting on the back porch. I had not yet figured out how to get the routine and mundane things done, like grocery shopping or getting to the gym. That would come more naturally over time. On the weekends, I took Mom to the bathroom every couple of hours. At night, I never slept more than a couple of hours at a time. I would hear Rosie, our cat, or I would hear Mom tossing and turning in her bed and I would come upstairs to settle things down and take care of whatever needed to be taken care of with Mom. May was a very long month. I regret that I was not at my best in my work at the school.

The writing exercises, which begin on page 21, and my notes about them, are specific to the Wernicke's aphasia that occurred due to Mom's stroke. The reader might benefit from some of the particular tactics and skills that I used during and around these exercises, and I make some comments about other caregiving that I provided to Mom during this time. If you, Dear Reader, are caregiver for someone who does not have language deficits to the extent that Mom does, you still might pick up a pointer or two, or at least know that some caregivers deal with one thing and other caregivers deal with different things. All that I can write about are my experiences and, again, it is my hope that by writing about them I can be of service to someone else.

June 6, 2013 -- This is the first day that I had Mom start to work on writing words and sentences. While in the hospital, it was recommended that I not have Mom do any writing. The speech therapists' view was that it would just be too hard for Mom to do and it might be detrimental to her recovery. Contrary to what my intuition was telling me, I listened to their advice, but if I had it to do over again, I would have started Mom to writing as soon as she was out of intensive care. I must admit that I had Mom try to write some letters and words a couple of times, about two weeks after her stroke. She was only able to make some straight lines, and then the speech therapist gave me the above advice. I should have stuck with it. Writing and journaling is something that Mom has been doing for several decades now, and it is my belief that the sooner that someone in her position, having had the type of stroke that she had, returns to attempting to do what is most familiar to them, the sooner those neuro-pathways will begin to rewire themselves. We have lost two crucial months, but there is nothing to be done about that now.

It is only in hindsight that I am able to see that the hospital "experts" who worked with Mom on the rehabilitation floor used a generalized approach to their patients. This type of approach may work in the college class text book, but in real life, the speech, physical and occupation therapies are most beneficial when specifically tailored to the individual whose skills have been compromised. Perhaps this can only be done in a one-on-one situation. I am sure that the therapists at the hospital did the best that they could, given the number of patients that they each have on their case load, and the relatively small amount of time that those patients are under their care. And, I am grateful for what I learned from watching them as I visited Mom in the hospital. Much of what I learned was what not to do. Here at home there are no rubrics or protocols which I have to fit my Mother into. It is the other way around. Apparently, such is not the case in a hospital.

In my experience working with special education students, I often worked with colleagues who hold the belief that difficult tasks should be avoided with the most severely afflicted students. I wholeheartedly disagree with this paradigm. My job as an educator was to challenge the students and to facilitate their ability to succeed in learning to the highest degree that they were capable of. I hold the same belief in my work with Mom. My way is to raise the bar, not to lower it. My job is to figure out ways to enable the person who is in my charge, to get over, or close to, the bar that I set.

The following pages are from the writing exercise spiral notebook that I use in working with Mom on her writing skills, which include reading, writing and comprehension. I have cropped out any full names that are on the pages, other than Mom's and mine. One thing that I found interesting on the first page is how Mom substituted numbers for the names of her children. Substituting numbers for words/nouns is a common occurrence since her stroke. I also note that while I wrote her name as "Marcie", she wrote her full and proper name, which is "Marcille."

Throughout most of the writing exercises that are copied into this treatise, the reader will see that I write a sentence and then draw a blank line underneath it for Mom to copy what I have written. There are also notes on the bottom of many of the pages of our exercise book. These are notes that I made during the day, or during the exercise itself. In this writing, the reader will see that I will sometimes expand on what these notes represent to me, since they are often short and may lack clarity to someone who is reading them. My penmanship is also occasionally a bit of a trick to read.

On some pages, Mom is let loose to write whatever she chooses to write. Or, as often has happened, Mom could not focus in on my instructions to copy just the words that I have written, and she just wrote what she could, or what came to her. I encouraged all of her writing, and did very little correcting or redirecting when she was not following my instructions to just copy what I wrote. As long as the pen in her hand was moving, we were making progress. I often reassured Mom, "This is just practice. It is kind of like exercising." Sometimes, however, I did a great deal of redirecting, reminding Mom that it was not that she had done something wrong, but that the primary purpose of the writing exercises was to help her brain to focus in on single tasks and instructions. Much reassurance was, and continues to be, needed for my Mom.

NOTE: It is now the middle of October and I am scanning some of the pages of our writing exercises into this book/treatise that I am writing. Some of the notes that I wrote in our exercise book I will expand upon from memory. Some of the pages are self-explanatory. It was not until July that I thought about writing this book/treatise, and the reader will notice a change in style and form from that date forward.

NOTE: It takes 15-20 minutes, and sometimes a bit longer, for Mom to do her writing in most of the writing exercises that we do. I usually sit in a chair in front of her and point to the word or line being working on. I do not use a finger to point with because a pen points more precisely to individual letters that I want Mom focusing on. During the writing, I do not talk much, and never do I talk about anything other than what she is writing. Even words of praise from me for her accomplishing the writing of a word or sentence are kept to a minimum. Extraneous words and talking are distractions, and Mom's brain needs all of its resources to concentrate and focus on writing just 5 or 6 simple sentences. This notion of extraneous talking presents itself in many aspects of working as a caregiver and also when working with special needs students, as I have done for the last number of years. Those of us with normal functioning brains often tend to talk too much. It is a difficult habit to change. And it is necessary to do so if one wants to be an effective caregiver to someone in my Mom's situation.

PLAN AHEAD BEFORE GOING OUT

IMPORTANT: In many of the writing exercises, and throughout the rest of this book/treatise/thing that I am writing here, the reader will see that Mom and I regularly go out of the house to do our grocery shopping, go to the Jewish Community Center (JCC) arthritis swim classes, doctor's appointments, visiting friends, etc. The time and planning that is required before leaving the house is something which requires thoughtful attention on my part. Here are just a few of the things that I try to keep in mind:

- Does Mom want to be going where we are headed?
- When has Mom last eaten, and when is she likely to need to use a bathroom? Do I have the necessary bathroom supplies with me?
- When is Mom due to take her next medications? Our situation is pretty easy here. Mom takes her pills three times a day – breakfast, dinnertime and bedtime. Other caregivers might have a different scenario. Plan ahead and have the medications with you.
- When is Mom going to need to rest?
- Have I left enough time to get where we want to be, without trying to hurry Mom? Hurrying in anything is simply not an option. It cannot be done in our case.

I share with you here a lesson that I was taught by one of the physical therapy (PT) guys at the hospital. It is, in fact, the only useful bit of instruction which I received, and it is extremely useful and important. I suggest that the reader pay attention here and carefully consider the variety of implications of this lesson. Going out of the house requires a careful thought. I cannot overemphasize this point enough.

The PT guy was taking Mom for a walk down the hallway and up a flight of stairs, so that I could get some practice using the gait belt that is put around Mom's waist when we walk. This also provided Mom with some more practice using her walker, with me having a hand on the belt for support and to catch her if she started to fall. Use of a gait belt is suggested so that the caregiver does not overly support the care recipient by grasping their arms. I was told that old bones break or come out of the joint very easily, and shoulders in particular are susceptible to being damaged. We got to the stairwell and I was encouraged to help Mom up the stairs. The PT guy did not say much, so I left the walker at the bottom of the stairs and Mom and I successfully got up the flight of stairs. Success!! Yay!! I certainly showed the PT guy how good a caregiver I was going to be, didn't I? And then he said, "Good job. But now your Mom's walker is at the bottom of the stairs and you two are at the top of the stairs. What are you going to do now? Assuming that you went up a flight of stairs to go somewhere, like into your house, you are going to be stuck."

He was, of course, absolutely correct. If I let go of Mom and the belt, to go down and get the walker, we risked Mom taking a fall. And to fall down a flight of stairs would not be a good thing. Lesson learned by me, and learned well. The PT guy knew that best way to teach me this lesson, and I am profoundly grateful to him for doing it just like he did. He was not a particularly friendly man, but I give credit where credit is due.

WRITING EXERCISES

So, Dear Reader, the following pages are copies of some writing exercises that Mom has done. Again, in many of them you will read that we went somewhere and enjoyed some sort of activity. Getting to these activities, and back home again, requires much forethought. Since we have done these excursions for a while now, (remember that I am writing this in mid-October) the preparation has become second nature to me. And still I forget something now and again, but I try not to.

NOTE: As I edit my finished writing, in May of 2019, I think back fondly of the relative ease of the care my Mom required in the first year or two. As the aphasia progressed to dementia, my skill set had to grow and my patience had to expand. Dementia is a cruel disease, and it "progresses" in one direction only, and that direction increases in difficulty for all involved. To bear witness to my Mother fading away, here but not here as she was, a shell of the woman she had grown to be, is to bear witness to the passing of a life and a soul. The early years of caregiving were relatively easy, when compared to what was to come. In balance, both sets of time were beautiful, sometimes only seen that way in hindsight and not at the time.

June 6, 2013

My name is Marcie.

~~Marcille~~

Aaron Darryl Larry Amy
211 ~~2/2~~ ~~322~~ 222

Aaron, Th Th is my name is

Television

Marcille
Marcille G. F. [illegible]

Mrs. Grossley
[illegible] Marcille

Al B — piano
~~6/25~~ – Tu 6/18 – 1:30 Higgins Plaza
14th + Detroit

Michael hooked up cooler and sprinkler

Sally has a toothache

Jean came for a visit

June 8, 2013

Morning - visit Carla and Melinda
On the way home, we stopped to
helpeda blind lady cross a street.
Morea and Arcela
Recenda and catela
With a creat cathela Cafa
Recentent Leadst Recoat heath dalbal

Rose came to visit
Piast Canthela
in the came cane seeth

Watching Rockies vs. Padres - Mom read "COORS FIELD" and
said "~~What a~~ "COORS FIELD - what a beautiful place."

Dinner - Soup, ice cream, pie

June 8, 2013 -- We were watching the Colorado Rockies vs. San Diego Padres baseball game. Out of nowhere, Mom read "COORS FIELD" and said "Coors Field – what a beautiful place."

June 9, 2013

Tomorrow we go swim.

We ate pancakes today.

We talked with Larry.

We talked with Larry.

LARRY

Reading

Hearing

Speaking

Writing

= Language

My name is Marcie.

My name is Marcie.

My name is Marcie

Dinner – chicken sandwich, pickle and pie.

We did Rosie's water treatment.

June 9, 2013 -- It is interesting to note the difference in Mom's writing from one sentence or word, to another. Note the clarity of "Language" and "My name is Marcie" as opposed to the confusion in the rest of her writing.

We had a long talk about "language" and the diagram that I wrote on the exercise page. This is a diagram that Mom wrote out for me several years ago while we were talking one night about teaching children who struggle with language and its components. Mom was a 2nd grade school teacher for almost 30 years. When she saw me write out the language diagram, she brightened up and was very, very focused on what we were doing. Mom had wondered why I wanted to do these exercises with her and what the point of it was. She did not express these thoughts quite that clearly, but I was able to decipher what she meant. The familiarity of the diagram is well-noted by me, and I will return to it many times in the weeks and months to come.

June 11, 2013

Dinner time: A) Do you want some more?
M) Yes. I have had enough.

Morning - We went out so Aaron could get his hair cut.

We stopped at the bank.
→ ~~We stopped andgandaiAig~~

We gassed up Aaron's car.
→ ~~We two allAp AadAAA~~

Mom and Aaron made beanie weenies.
→ ~~MO/\ omnAaron and Bonnie slarry~~

June 11, 2013 -- Note the "Dinner time" entry at the top of the page. I asked Mom, "Do you want some more?" and she replied, "Yes. I have had enough." The language deficit that Mom has is pronounced and, at the same time, random. If I were to ask again, "Do you want some more?" it is likely that I would get a completely different answer from Mom. People have asked me if there is rhyme or reason, or a pattern, to Mom's word substitution. There is not. Also note the complete lack of clarity or ability in Mom's writing today. Her ability to write, or copy, correctly is also completely random.

June 12, 2013
13, 21, I 27, 13

Today is Marcie's birthday.
201 I'll very [illegible] today today
Do not Your today today
When [illegible] to a new one nice
Today is today a good one please
I am today today today nexday daytoe
I am a [illegible] able to [illegible] to
be able to a [illegible]
I [illegible] another agouther
Todasy to a [illegible]

2:20 Back from JCC - Mom read the door sign
"Please do not ring bell. Knock Only"
Could not read it 3 weeks ago.
Told me the "U" sound, when I held up an
umbrella, Could not come up with "umbrella"
but said "when it rains."

Morning writing - record

June 13, 2013

June is (13, 2013) → hand on hand.

We called Rose to say hello.

We called Rose to say Hello ← hand on han

We called Amy to say thank you.

are call p Anthone tee Berthethy

Marcie read her birthday cards.

[illegible]

Amy, Jean and Jim, Phil Lamphier, Aaron

[illegible] Aaron

All sent Marcie birthday cards.

[illegible]

Morning - Did Rosie's water treatment.

* AARON - watch your penmanship!

* Reading "When we retire at night..." with Mom, as she gets into bed, "Were we thinking of ourselves most of the time.." I said "Too much of the time". Mom said "Well, that's something for us to pay attention to." A good "Mom-ism". Clear as a bell! Thank You, G-d. for her gentle ways.

* Before heading to bed, Mom was able to let me know that she wanted tomorrow to be a simple day without any "extra people or stuff." I had to decipher what she was saying - After she ~~said~~ said a simple swim at JCC "that would be nice."

June 13, 2013 -- Elaborating a bit on one of the notes above – "When we retire at night…" is from page 86 in the book "Alcoholics Anonymous", which we refer to as the Big Book. This is the 11th Step and the line is from a paragraph frequently read at the end of the day, before heading to sleep. After 41 years of continuous sobriety in the AA program, I would wager that Mom has read this paragraph thousands of times. Any time that I read Big Book stuff to, or with, Mom, a sense of calm comes to her like no other time. She knows that book well. Even with her stroke-damaged brain, the AA and Al-Anon recovery memories are, if not readily accessible to her to converse about right now, they are at least still in her brain.

The second set of notes, in my less-than-legible writing, were interesting to me. This was the first time that Mom had expressed her desire for particular activities, or the limiting of them. She requested "a simple day" without "extra people or stuff" and though it took a while, I was able to figure out what she was trying to tell me. I have been done with the school year for about 10 days now, and have been spending full days with Mom, finding my way as we go. What should she be eating? How much sleep does she need, and when? How much activity she can comfortably handle before tiring out and needing to sleep? How do I tend to personal needs in the bathroom? This is a learning curve for both of us.

FAMILIARITY IS IMPORTANT

The need for familiarity is paramount when working with someone in my Mom's condition. Wernicke's Aphasia makes taking it very difficult, if not impossible, for the person to absorb new information, organize it and figure out what to do with or about it. That sort of higher level brain function is greatly impaired with this malady. Keeping things at hand which are familiar allows the person to more easily make their way through each day. As with most all of us, familiarity breeds comfort and a sense of ease. Avoiding anxiety-producing scenarios is of great importance with my goal of being a loving and effective caregiver for my Mother. Note this, Dear Reader.

June 18, 2013 -- I once again wrote some sentences about our day. I asked Mom if she was up for writing a few sentences. She said, "I'm really not in great shape. Do you mind?" And she said this spontaneously and as clearly as a bell.

We gave Rosie, our cat, her water treatment. Rosie is very old and has renal (kidney) failure. Every three days we put Rosie up on a stand and give her a subcutaneous water injection. Using an 18-guage needle, which is pretty big, about 75ml goes into her, under her skin and above the muscle. We have been doing this for over 4 years.

After Rosie's water treatment, Mom handed me the towel that Rosie was on, and said, "If you would shake this out." Mom may leave a few words out of sentences, but it is wonderful when she is able to string enough appropriate words together to convey information, or a request, to me.

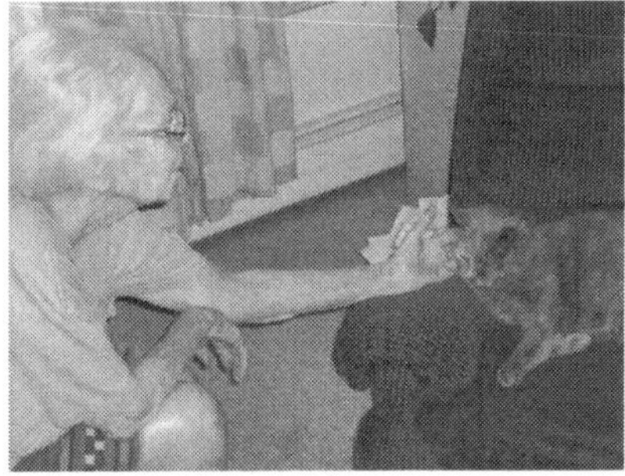

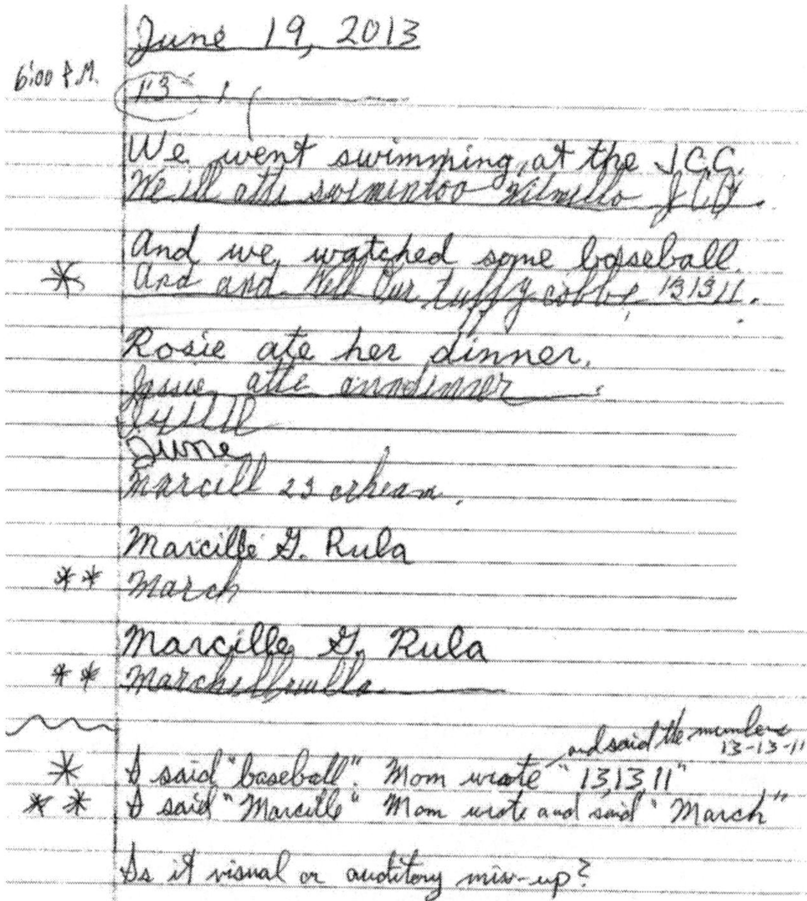

June 19, 2013

6:00 P.M.

We went swimming at the J.C.C.

[illegible]

And we watched some baseball.

* [illegible] 131311.

Rosie ate her dinner.

[illegible]

Marcille G. Rula

** March

Marcille G. Rula

** [illegible]

* I said "baseball" Mom wrote and said the numbers "131311" 13-13-11

** I said "Marcille" Mom wrote and said "March"

Is it visual or auditory mix-up?

June 19, 2013 -- I have no idea where the "131311" came from. Some neuron in Mom's brain is, perhaps, talking to me in code? I doubt it. Mom is oftentimes not aware that she is using the wrong words or, as in this case, numbers instead of words. Her brain has a lot of rewiring to accomplish. Or perhaps she had the 1311 York Street AA club in mind.

June 20, 2013 -- Mom remembered that schools have "summer off." Prior to this, I had talked a bit about schools as we drove by some elementary schools in our neighborhood and also as we have driven by East High School, which Mom attended when she was high school aged. At those times, it was apparent to me that what I was saying was not registering with Mom. I remember asking her, "Mom. Do you know what a school is?" And her answer was, "No." Mom was a 2nd grade school teacher for almost 30 years. For her to remember that schools have summer off is a sign either of the healing of her brain or the randomness of the damage that has been done.

June 21, 2013 -- This evening I was doing some physical therapy with her, tossing a small soft ball back and forth. I said to Mom, "Very nice throw." And her reply was, "One smile laughs one." Go figure it out...

June 24, 2013 -- 10:30pm – Mom woke up and joined me in the living room. I was playing my string bass to some Grateful Dead. We then watched the end of the Giants vs. Dodgers baseball game. I asked her, "Giants vs. Dodgers, both from New York. Who do you root for?" Mom's reply was, "Not only do they come out little, they come out small." Mom enjoyed it when I put NCIS on the television. We used to watch that show quite a bit, and I was surprised that Mom stuck with it, since, other than sports, television shows are language-based and with her aphasia they are very much impossible for Mom to follow.

June 29, 2013 Saturday
Ain-Rula Sunday Monday

Rosie would not eat any chicken.
Rosie would do not soch etlech

But Rosie did eat a green pea.
But Losie dos eat cashy

Mom and Aaron made soup today.
each eatch at mom

The soup is split green pea.
If your soap is plean guan Cealea

The soup has onion, carrot, mushroom, celery.
The Soup is a soup is a carrot of a mushtoom
The through ofthrough are sough
I though seemed Thought
I clear my daghs – daighte
My safe to Aaron throught.
Why are note clear of my tonight

Lesson recorded

Dinner - Asked Mom, "What is this?" She said, "I don't know." Great! Sentence!

* 1st - Mom, on phone with Larry "O.K. honey, here's your brother" 1st time.

June 29, 2013 -- I recorded this writing lesson on my hand-held digital recorder. So far (As of October 25th) I have about 30 hours of recorded material, going back to when Mom was in the hospital. Below the last sentence in the exercise, "The soup has onion, carrot, mushroom, celery" are five sentences that Mom wrote on her own.

BRIEF INTERLUDE AND CHANGE OF SUBJECT: I am writing this on October 25, 2013 as I read through the writing exercise book that I use with Mom. I have not read back through this book until now, and feelings of sadness, joy, melancholy and disbelief are rising to the surface in me. I have been working solo with Mom, 24 hours a day, 7 days a week, for almost 5 months now. Except for a few times when, for a few hours at a time, I hired the person that stayed with Mom here at the house back in May, while I was finishing the school year, Mom has not been out of my line of sight or hearing for almost 5 months. Reading back through this book brings up memories that are energizing and poignant and deeply life-changing.

July 1, 2013 -- 11:00pm – Mom was sitting up in bed. She was confused and afraid and worried about all the "new people" and "new places" around her. I explained to her, once again, that she had had a stroke and that her brain had been injured. "Of course" she said. I tucked Mom back into her bed and headed back downstairs. As I got down the first couple of stairs, I thought not to assume that Mom knew what a brain is. I went back to her room and asked her, "Mom, do you know what is a brain?" (I often will phrase questions with the subject as the last word. It has been my experience in special education that the last word that some students hear is the one that they pay most attention to.) She did not know what a brain is. I offered Mom a simple explanation and let it go at that.

We keep a bag with a variety of small bite-sized Hershey's chocolates here in the house and I often use them to settle Mom's nerves or to break whatever tension she may be feeling. As upset as Mom was when I first went in to talk with her, I thought to offer a piece of chocolate to Mom. She said, "I don't think so. I think not. I'll just have 2. One of these, and one of these." She was completely unaware of the contradiction. And then she enjoyed the chocolate and went back to sleep.

July 2, 2013 – Empathy and sympathy sometimes just rip at my heart. I have a video monitor set up so that I can keep track of when Mom gets up from resting or sleeping. Last night, around 10:30, I saw her sitting up in bed, just looking around. When I went in to check on her, the bewilderment and sadness on her face was profound. We talked for a bit and I reminded her that "it was a stroke thing" that was going on. I talked her through what had happened to her. She did not remember that she had had a stroke and that her brain was injured. Once again, giving Mom the information calmed her down and explained why all the "new people" were around and why "everything seemed new and strange." The words in quotes are hers.

Mom sits a lot in our living room and opposite her chair is a book-shelf wall that is filled with stuff from the 50 years that Mom has lived here in our house. Dad's fraternity beer stein, my Bar Mitzvah Chumash (bible), clay sculptures made by my sister in high school, a crystal vase from my great grandmother. These are just a few of the items which, this morning, evoked strong emotion and fragmented memories for my Mom. We had a long and intense conversation this morning as, once again, she gestured a lot toward the book shelf wall and talked about "him" and "they" and other misplaced pronouns, the references to which I have only been able to guess. This has been going on since Mom came home from the hospital. She often points to books on the shelf and makes reference to people whom, I have thought, only she could see.

This morning, it came to me that the items on the shelves were evoking strong memories that were confusing Mom. I deduced that she knew that certain items were important to her, but she did not know why, or where the items fit into her life. She finally came out with "Who am I? I am feeling in a place of being nervous and afraid. And I don't know what to do." I knew that I had finally figured out the puzzle of that wall of fragmented memories, and what she was trying to tell me, or whoever was sitting with her. We talked for awhile longer and I, once again, explained the effects of her stroke. I explained that her memory and her words/language had been injured, and that the items on the book shelf presented a visual reminder to her that she had lived a life that she could scarcely remember, and which was greatly upsetting to her. I then suggested that we had talked for a pretty long time already this morning and that it would probably be best to stop talking for now, particularly since her language center in her brain is what has been damaged. We both are people of strong faith in G-d, and we both have placed ourselves unreservedly in His care. I told her that we both needed right now to remember that and to have faith that we are o.k.

July 3, 2013 -- Morning – Mom said, "It's like being young and not knowing what to do."

July 5, 2013 -- Morning – Mom said, "Honey, how come I get so lonely?" I replied, "Do you mean when I leave for a few hours?" (A friend of hers had come over to give me a break.) Mom said, "Uh-huh." She had a real sad, child-like look on her face. I'll leave it at that...

July 6, 2013 -- In our writing exercises, I asked Mom to give me a sentence and I would write it. We had had an enjoyable time in the pool at the Jewish Community Center (JCC) and Mom came up with the following sentence: "We worked with our physical affairs." In part of the writing exercise, I wrote "Colors" and "Animals" and underlined those words, and numbered five lines below each word, so that Mom could, hopefully, come up with words in specific catagories. For "Colors", Mom came up with "blue, green, red, yellow and orange." For "Animals", Mom could not come up with any names of animals, so I dictated them to her. She wrote: "duck, rabbi, cat, squawl (squirrel) and dog." (She frequently uses "rabbi" when referring to a rabbit. After all that writing, Mom said, "Mom's dog is ready for sleep!"

July 8, 2013 – In the morning, Mom was looking sad, and while talking with me, she said, "I'm just realizing that I am a wounded woman." Later in the morning, an old friend of ours came to the house to fix one of the sprinklers in the yard. Mom said, "Oh, Michael, what a joy you are." Name recognition for Michael was there, which was not the case three weeks earlier.

July 11, 2013 Thursday
Redurosew 2323 Thursdew

Today Marcie washed the dishes.
I wash to fulfil dishwasher.

Today Marcie washed dishes in the club.
Today I washed [illegible] [illegible] [illegible]

Dinner was soup and carrots.
Dinner was soup for one carrots.

Dishes My Four Children

1. Wash her washer.
2. I was watking for cleaning [illegible] cleaning
3. I was alking for food cleaning.
4. My walking clean things.
5. Washing my clothing [illegible] cleaner.

Amy Larry Darryl Aaron
[illegible] Larry [illegible]
[illegible] Darryl Aaron
Marryl

3:30 Afternoon Leaving pool @ JCC – Appropriate reciprocal response, unprompted "My name is Joy" "My name is Marcie."
1st time unprompted reciprocity.

The second sentence, "Today Marcie washed dishes in the club" was one that Mom partially came up with. It does not matter that the word "club" makes no sense. For the underlined "Dishes" and "My Four Children" I had asked Mom to come up with names for different dishes that we had washed, and for her to write the names of her four children. Obviously, she went on to write other things, but write she did. The note at the bottom of the page makes note of appropriate and unprompted reciprocity when talking to someone else.

LOSING ONE'S SELF TO CAREGIVING ROLE

Edit on July 27, 2019 – It is poignant for me to think back on this, and other writing exercises which I did with Mom. Only in hindsight am I able to see how much of myself I put aside, dismissed and/or lost as I gave 100% attention to my caregiving. Reading back through, and editing this book/treatise again, preparing it for publication, I am more easily able to see why my caregiver burnout is producing, in large part, some depression and inability to get, and keep, myself in gear, with any forward momentum.

My Mother was a very intelligent and educated woman, living a simple life in many ways, totally focused on the world of recovery (AA), but she was not stupid, and yet during the writing exercises, as well as when she and I engaged in conversation, Mom could rarely string together words in a meaningful manner. She could rarely see something written, and copy it accurately. Rarely could Mom verbally express herself and convey intelligible meaning.

My thinking was 100% occupied with endeavoring to understand her intent, and then to figure out how to facilitate what I though she either desired, or what would be best for her to engage in. For anyone to do this 24 hours a day, 7 days a week, for what turned out to be about 5 years was a herculean task. I do not note this in any attempt to state what a grand fellow I was, and am. It is, however, the truth of the matter that anyone doing solo full-time caregiving will be entering a world in which there is a very high risk of burnout, of depression presenting itself, and an even higher risk of losing oneself in the process. Just now, Dear Reader, as I am typing this, I put on a Robert Goulet CD which Mom and I listened to countless times. Since Mom died, I've not played it, or any other of the crooners' music which

Mom so loved. Right now there is a smile on my face as I think back over the years that this book covers. I am grateful for the memories!

July 13, 2013 -- We had breakfast with a couple of neighbors this morning, at a restaurant not far from home. My brother, Larry, was in town and the neighbors enjoyed interesting and varied conversation during the meal, and as Mom asked what they were talking about, I filled her in, albeit in slower and simpler words than were being used by everyone else. Mom took it well, and enjoyed herself, the company, the outing and the meal.

I cried when we got home. Really went into my bedroom and then into the bathroom downstairs, and had a heavy cry. I was weeping for what has been lost to me and to Mom. Her ability to participate in general social conversation is lost now, and the odds of it coming back are not odds that I would bet on at this point in her recovery. I must give some thought as to what kinds of social engagements we are going to participate in, and accept invitations to. Mom is not stupid. Her brain has been injured. Thinking back to last night's conversation with her, when Larry and I returned from being out for a few hours, I know quite well that Mom is aware that she is different now and that some things, skills and abilities that she once had, are now gone.

I generally do not allow myself pessimistic moods, but sometimes it cannot be avoided, particularly when the situation is so glaringly stark. Being a full-time caregiver for someone I love is not a clinical job. It rips at my heart. Part of me wants to control even more the circumstances, situations and activities that Mom is exposed to. Part of me also knows that I am not in control of her recovery, most of the time, if even at all. And yet, I am the decision-maker for her in almost all areas. This is a strange dichotomy and it is a difficult road to navigate.

We went to the JCC again this afternoon with Larry. When we were done swimming, and after getting her into dry clothes, our conversation turned to Larry and the fact that he leaves on Monday afternoon. As I got Mom out of the family changing room and back into the wheelchair, to sit for a bit while I went back into the room to change into my dry clothes, Mom asked me to stop for a minute. She said that it just dawned on her that Larry was my brother and that he did not live with us. She was still fairly mixed up about Larry, his wife, Janet, and where they live, and what a "visit" was, but she was struck by her ability to realize that Larry was my brother. Mom also remembered that she and Larry talked regularly on the phone. She had not remembered that they did so. Time sequence and days of the week are still mixed up for Mom, but she was saddened by the thought that Larry would soon be gone from her. And she was also sad for me that my brother would soon be leaving. She asked me when I would see him again. I had to tell her that I did not know, but that it would probably be quite awhile until he could come out for another visit. Tears came to Mom's eyes. There was nothing that needed to be said. What words can I use when the stroke-damaged word-center in her brain is the reason for Larry's visit? Another poignant and heart-wrenching aspect of caregiving for an aged parent.

After the JCC, we went to King Soopers so that Larry could go inside and get some fixings for dinner. An odd conversation between Mom and I ensued. Mom's words: "Given out a swooping of the void, but I was here and it was real." Mom began to cry. "I lost your brother's recall, but I'm getting it back."

When we got home, and as Larry was preparing dinner, I helped Mom with her bathroom needs. Mom continued talking quietly to me about her realization that Larry would be leaving, though she mixed up the days or time sequence. Again, her eyes filled with tears and she said to me, "Honey, I'm going to miss him enormously." I hope that my brother Larry reads these pages some day.

We had dinner, played some music upstairs, with me on my string bass. Then we went downstairs and I played a few tunes with Mom on plastic egg shakers and me on my bass guitar. After a couple of tunes, Mom just sat and listened while I played a few more. 10:00 and time to help Mom get ready for bed.

It is 1:00 Sunday morning now. Sleep eludes me as Rosie, our cat, cried out at 12:15 and Mom called to me. I hit the "talk" button my monitor downstairs and told her that I would come up and take care of Rosie. By the time I got to Rosie a minute later, Mom was sleeping again. I am not. I will spend another night on the couch upstairs, ready and handy to tend to Mom and Rosie's needs. We will get up later this morning, and do it all over again.

Larry and Mom

In the morning, Mom said the following to me: "Larry is your brother, right? He really does live in a different part of the country, doesn't he? Last night I thought about that he'll be leaving, and I started to cry."

July 18, 2013 -- As Mom's brain is coming more and more back online, the memories are bringing some depression and fear to her. Yesterday morning, she told me that she was "a wounded woman" and was very afraid. We had a lengthy and heavy talk. What Mom is remembering is some very, very unpleasant emotions and feeling from her difficult and violent childhood, and she does not have the words in her head to sort out the feelings. She just has the feelings.

Mom wrote some sentences with me this evening, and I showed her pictures of the people that we are going to see tomorrow. This helps, in that just using people's names does not provide enough information for Mom to comprehend and be comfortable with the plans for the day. Little by little, I am building a notebook of pictures of familiar people and places that we are around. I keep in mind that verbal instructions are often misconstrued. Do not over-narrate while working with Mom. Too many words cause confusion.

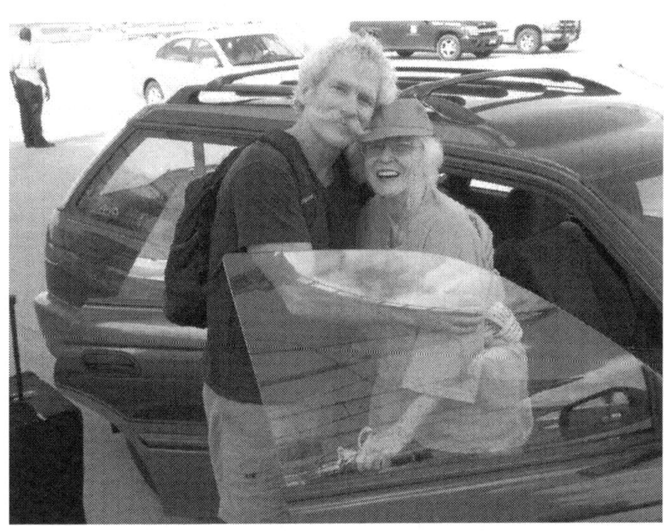

July 19, 2013 Friday

Friday, May July

Dr. Rubenstein is so good.

Dr. Doctor is good for my [illegible]

Delicious Dr. Rubenstein for our

safe Dr. Rubenstein For the [illegible]

safe doctor giving.

Safe save giving giffing

Mom looked at the picture

Mom looked at the [illegible]

and remembered Dr. Rubenstein's name

and our [illegible] next need better

Here are Her Dr and her call.

Dr. Rubenstein good doctor are present.

Dr. Rubenstein is here for her helps great health.

1st Time! Mom came up with a sentence. NOT Aaron

Evening Pills: "Give me the bigger ones first." ← 1st Time!!

Afternoon: Mom remembered where the handicap placard was when we got to the ICC. Got it out of glove box and hung it up. Mom, "Hey! I remembered where it was." Before that, she said "Wait. Don't tell me. Let me think."

There are some interesting notes on this day's writing. The first three sentences are the first ones that Mom came up with, totally on her own. The notes on the bottom of the page are little things that I look for. When giving Mom some of her evening pills, she said, "Give me the bigger ones first." That was the first time that she spoke up regarding taking her medicine. This afternoon, Mom remembered where the handicap placard was, which we keep in the glove box of my car. One of her jobs is to take care of putting the placard up and to put it away when we leave the parking space. Mom said, "Hey! I remembered where it was!" Before getting the placard out, she said, "Wait. Don't tell me. Let me think."

July 20, 2013 – Today, Mom wrote two pages of sentences. The first one was our usual sentences encompassing a basic review of our day. The second page was unexpected, but Mom was completely engaged in writing and talking, so I flipped the page and encouraged her to continue. Our talking got kind of heavy, and I wrote the line, "Mostly I'm a blank" after Mom had talked to me for awhile about how she was feeling. I then prompted her to write about anything that was important to her. Out came "integrity meaning very beautiful" and I wrote that down. We talked about both of us focusing on what we can do and not on what has been lost.

The note at the bottom of the second page of Mom's writing says, "lost – that I can never get it. I'm really gone from thousands of days." To a great extent, Mom knows what has been damaged by stroke. She also knows that some of her thinking and memory has been lost due to her age. These are heavy talks to have with one's Mother, and they are the kinds of real heart-to-heart talks that build the ties that bind Mom and I to each other. She has nobody any more to talk to at length and at great depth. I believe that she had some "partner sponsors" that she could talk with somewhat like this, and I believe that she sorely misses them.

July 20, 2013 Saturday

~~July the 20 July July the Sat~~

pancake
The Pancake

We made pancakes this morning.
We made ~~paper thick pancakepakes~~

Strawberries were in the pancakes.
Stf were in the The exchare

Peanut butter, jelly and maple syrup
Peanut Hub jelly and ~~our papyr~~

went onto the pancakes.
Our best to the pancakes

Rose called and will visit this afternoon.

Our calles and the visit this afternoon
Our are calles are the visits is this afternoons

This ~~cons~~ squarels at our
the visit
squirrel A the squarel is seen at our services

20, 2013

July 20, July 23,

Mr M.S. with Mrs July and
Inn a last night

~~Ms~~
Mostly I'm a blank.

write ~~whright~~ caught

integrity meaning very beautiful

focus on what we can do, and not
The Lost art wait we ~~We do not~~

to focus on what has been lost.
To the on the Have the Lost ~~of the Been very~~
Marcie Matcie Nalcie Risting

Marcille G Rula
Marcille and The Rubusteen

"lost" — that I can never get it.
"I'm really gone from thousands of days.

July 24, 2013 -- Mom came out with the word, "gigglery" today. Gigglery is a great word, and very descriptive. As I have done in much of our writing exercises, I encouraged Mom to write whatever she wanted to in the bottom half of the page. She really went at it today.

July 24, 2013 Wednesday

~~I Res Reading~~ ~~Wednistly~~

Mom did some reading today.

~~Mom did somee the reading today.~~

There were young people at the pool.

~~We were at the young people at the~~

The Rockies played baseball.

~~The yourt Rock at the Play at the~~ Baseball.

Ruth Ambrose came to visit.

~~Aesthetic Rembro came to visit~~

The Remember Reading to next soon

To do tomorrow reading and do them to you.

I can set somecute aire yay!!

I can set my hair cut now.

easy My hair is cute ~~easy~~ is early seem

My hair is helping and ~~helping~~ helping.

Rose is cute from our ~~cat~~ care

sips Rosez Rosie ~~see~~ us see her help fun.

Rosie slipe a fun one for from!!

We do having a good frey!!!

gigglery

July 27, 2013 -- Leaving the JCC, Mom was speaking with Allison, who works the front desk. Allison has always been really friendly and supportive of Mom and I, and she is a real bright spot in our forays out to the swim pool. This is part of what Mom said to Allison: "If you make a decision and later find it is not for you, you can make another choice." Mom had strung together 4-5 sentences, which made sense and which were clear as a bell.

Evening – "Progress" – Mom was washing the dishes. I reminded her that when she first came home from the hospital, she could not remember how to wash dishes. I asked her, "Do you know why I tell you that?" She said, "To tell me progress."

July 28, 2013 -- It rained last night and this morning. Mom said to me, "Look. The thing back there looks burned out." She was talking about the next door neighbor's fence. When the fence gets wet, the wood gets really dark and does, indeed, look like it has burned.

Leaving the JCC, Mom told Allison, "You are a rare beauty. There is just a glow about you." She said this clear as a bell. Just beautiful to hear Mom speak clearly and coherently.

TECHNIQUES FOR HANDLING ONE'S OWN EMOTIONS

August 1, 2013 -- This is a series of surrenders, this caregiving thing. All too often I beat myself for not being "perfectly" serene and patient at all times. The patience, effectiveness, perspective, all comes from surrendering to the current situation. One of Mom's old sayings was "They aren't doing it to you. They are just doing it." Mom is not choosing to be forgetful or language-challenged.

Edit on August 6, 2019 – Throughout my writing you will read that my emotions periodically got completely off-leash. I hit the wall several times, figuratively and literally. I acknowledge that up front, and I take full ownership of when I fell short of the mark. It does not make me a bad guy, just a man who did the best he could at any given time. You will also read that I have promised to be honest in my writings, even when my honesty reveals my failures and shortcomings. I am not embarrassed by anything that I reveal in this work. I am not a tzaddik (Jewish saint, sort of), nor was I a caregiving guru.

The entry from August 1, 2013 has this line in it: "The patience, effectiveness, perspective, all comes from surrendering to the current situation." It also has a great teaching which Mom lived by, and shared with many people, and it is worth repeating here: "They aren't doing it to you. They are just doing it." Handling one's own emotions, while engaged in 24/7 caregiving can be a real challenge. Staying on top of this is crucial for the well-being of the caregiver and the care recipient. Note this, and note it well, Dear Reader. Some techniques I worked diligently to keep in mind were:

- Surrender and surrender again to the current situation.
- Remember that you chose to take on this job.
- How important is it, (whatever the situation at hand) anyway?
- Step away, even for a few minutes, when agitated or upset.
- Say a quick prayer, asking G-d for patience.
- Say a quick prayer, asking G-d for more patience.
- Bring to mind the love that drove you to take on this duty.
- Accept the things you cannot change.
- Change the things you can – that will probably only be you!
- Call someone, even if only for a couple of minutes that duty might allow.
- Remember that giving 100% of one's self to the care of another person will most likely make one's perspective skewed.
- Expect nothing from others. I failed a lot at this one.
- Know that others would help if they could. We cannot expect people to do what they cannot do. I failed a lot at this one too.
- When your caregiving recipient gets upset with you, think of how you might feel having to be taken care of with all of your needs, at all times and every day. Conjure up empathy!

At the back of this book/treatise is a section titled "Important Caregiving Things To Remember And Do Not Forget" and I suggest you remember to refer to it regularly, particularly when you are beginning this journey. I was not at all perfect at remaining patient and effective at all times, but my batting average was pretty darned good. Another of my Mom's sayings/teachings was: "We have a pretty good batting average." If I was a professional baseball player, my average would have been about 950. I have given too much power to the 5% of the time I screwed up and fell short of the mark. Note this, Dear Reader, and go easy on yourself. Put down that stick that you are, or may be, whacking yourself with. Life and caregiving will beat you up enough, without you piling on more whacks!

August 2, 2013 -- I wonder if Mom is requiring more care due to an increased reliance upon me, since I have been with her 24 hours a day, with no breaks from friends, for more than two weeks now. Or, is the increased care just another phase of her stroke recovery? Or, is it a sign of decreasing mental and cognitive acuity? I don't know the answer to this scenario. There is no rule book that I can reference. The whole task of caregiving is coming to me through experience, day-by-day.

Bright notes after swimming today at the JCC. Mom allowed me to shampoo her hair, which is something that she is not fond of doing. Something about a shower makes Mom quite nervous. But she said that she trusts me and that she knows that it is important to do. I assure her that I will only take a minute or two to wash her hair, and then it will be done. After washing her hair, I towel-dried it and jokingly mussed it up into a frizzy and fuzzy "doo." When Mom saw it in the mirror, she just loved it and decided not to brush it out straight, like she is used to doing. As her hair dried, it curled up nicely and she was quite pleased.

As we were getting ready to leave the parking lot, Mom asked if we could go by the Blodgett's house and show Jean her new hair. Of course, we did so, and the two ladies enjoyed a nice conversation while Mom and I sat in the car on their driveway. NOTE: Mom referred to Jean's husband as "her" and then immediately self-corrected to "him." Jean and I both noticed the correction. This was the first self-correction of a pronoun for Mom. Mom then mentioned the nice dinner we had with Jean and Jim, her husband, last night. Jean and I both noted Mom's remembering what we did last night.

As caregivers, we must look for the little things that show progress in the person who has had the stroke. Sometimes, the things that we are shown are very small, such as a single word used for the first time, or the self-correction of an inappropriate word that was used. And all of these things are encouraging to me. I also am careful not to point out to Mom too often when she has used an inappropriate word, nor do I always point out when she self-corrects or uses the correct words. This is by feel for me, and there is no set rule that I go by. It is a gut thing.

August 9, 2013 -- Interesting changes in this last week. When Mom has gotten confused or concerned about her mixing up words, or not being sure what to do, I have been taking the time to remind her that she had a stroke and that what she is going through is perfectly normal. A couple of days ago, Mom got real upset with me and was able to communicate that she felt I was ashamed of her and that I was embarrassed by her weakness in some areas. It took a lot of staying calm, a few tears that came to my eyes, and a whole lot of remembering that she has an injured brain that is mixing up words and feelings. I have stopped reminding Mom that she had a stroke. I have back away from "shadowing" her whenever she gets up out of a chair or out of her bed. Mom is getting to the bathroom by herself several times a day now, and when she wants or needs my help in there, she is calling for me. I am even "letting" Mom use a paring knife to cut up strawberries for our breakfast cereal in the morning. This relative independence that she now has is, I believe, allowing Mom to be more relaxed as she has entered into yet another new phase in her recovery from stroke.

IMPORTANT: Remain sensitive to the person who has had the stroke, in terms of what kind of relatively safe activities they can begin to participate in on their own.

IMPORTANT: While cooking with Mom a few days ago, I had her doing what I thought was a relatively mundane part of the cooking. I casually used the words, "You know how to do that." This was upsetting to Mom, and it hurt her feelings. She was able to communicate to me that she really does not remember how to do some things. Do not assume that "You know how to do that."

This is quite a mystery in terms of what to do, or not to do, for Mom. Though I am constantly on guard and thinking several steps ahead in terms of her safety, I need to be growing into surrendering to the fact that I am not in complete control of her safety and recovery. Being over-protective with an adult who has had a stroke can be as detrimental as being over-protective with a child.

August 9, 2013 -- 7:45pm -- Just put Mom to bed for the night, after a restful day for both of us. We enjoyed going again to the indoor pool at the JCC. I am lost sometimes in the mistaken thinking that if only I do the right things with Mom, we can reverse the damage that her brain sustained, and she will be back to how she was, prior to having a stroke. This will not happen. I will not write that "it may happen", because I do not believe that to be true. Mom appears to have had another "event" either yesterday and/or today, in the form of a smaller stroke of some type.

HOW WE DID MUNDANE TASKS

And so this went, Dear Reader, day after day as the days turned into weeks, and the weeks turned into months. Many of the days, or large parts of them anyway, were quite enjoyable for me. Parts of some days were otherwise, but the days remained pretty much the same and we got through the summer as well as could be. I believe that I have painted a clear enough picture of what we were doing. The following is an outline of how we did some of the mundane, but necessary tasks.

Regarding getting tasks or day-to-day business taken care of, I again suggest that other caregivers ask themselves, "How important is it, anyway?" You may find that when in a caregiving situation, priorities either change or are changed due to circumstances.

Below are some activities that Mom and I do together, and some ways that we accomplish those things. The underlying principle is Mom's inclusion in the activities and the decision-making. Perhaps some of the logistical details will be helpful to someone who is reading this.

IMPORTANT: I have found that a choice between two options works best. Any more than two gets confusing for Mom. I found this to be true in my work with special education students as well. And for some reason, having three choices was the most difficult for the students. That has proven true with Mom as well.

GROCERY SHOPPING -- Mom is in the wheelchair, and we put a shopping cart in front of her. Her two canes go in the cart. She guides the cart with her hands, while I push the wheelchair. So far, we have yet to knock over any end caps or product displays. And with me helping in the turns, by inconspicuously sliding the wheelchair a bit, we make out just fine. I encourage Mom to pick out the fruits and vegetables while I hold the bag, or vice versa. Be sure to allow an extra chunk of time for the shopping, and learn to enjoy the experience. People are generally real friendly, and I notice a whole lot of elderly shoppers that look like they wish they had someone to help them in such a manner. Several have come right out and told us that. I have often wished that I had a sidecar on the wheelchair, so that we might help someone else who is challenged with mobility and shopping.

COOKING – I do the chopping and then put the chopped items into a cereal bowl, which Mom then puts into the pot or the pan. I hand Mom the spices and encourage her to add them to the item that we are cooking. I also encourage Mom to tell me the name of the item, or read the label of the spices. Mom enjoys being helpful in our preparing and dishing up all of our meals, though on days (or nights) when she is particularly tired, or her legs are "talking to her," she also enjoys it when I bring her meal to her. Again, providing Mom with choices is the key.

NOTE: In the last sentence, I originally typed the word "giving" and then changed it to "allowing" and then changed it to "providing." This is the attitude shift that I work to continually be aware of, and to practice. The thought pattern and belief system behind "giving" and "allowing" is control-oriented, and I am endeavoring to view things differently. Providing is more along the lines of the motive that I want to come more naturally for me – providing care, i.e., caregiving.

DRESSING – I give Mom choices of what she wants to put on. I limit the choices to two of any given piece of apparel. More than two choices in most anything just causes confusion. I assist Mom as needed, averting my gaze as necessary. There is no reason to ever verbalize a feeling of being uncomfortable helping another person with their needs. We abandoned the use of a bra while Mom was in the hospital.

EXERCISE – This is wide open in giving Mom choices of even wanting to swim (our primary form of exercise), the time that we go, or if she even is up for it on any given day. She also knows (having learned through numerous times in the water together) that when she begins to tire out, all she has to do is tell me. And I have learned to monitor the amount of time we are in the water. I generally ask her how she is feeling about 40 minutes into the pool. I gently check with her a couple of times before that, but I am conscious not to hover and to allow Mom time by herself or with the other seniors that are in the arthritis water class.

NOTE: Oftentimes, when there are not many people in the water, Mom will make her way over to where I am in the pool, just to chat for a minute or more often just to touch base for reassurance. It is really quite touching when she does this. Kind of like a young child that comes to a parent now and again, just to make herself certain that all is well. I am not a parent, but my empathy is enough to sense this in Mom. Quite touching to know that she views me as a source of safety and comfort.

WATCHING SPORTS – Baseball has been our most-watched game thus far, though the football season is now upon us. The rules and objects of both games are not at all clear to Mom, but she has always been a sports fan and enjoys watching a game. I am mindful not to over-narrate the game, and not to over-explain the rules, innings, strike zones, downs and yards-to-go, etc. I am looking forward, G-d willing, to watching basketball with Mom. That is something that will probably be most easily understood by her, and it is a game that we have watched a lot over the years. In fact, it was the Louisville vs. Oregon NCAA tournament game that we were watching on the night that Mom had her stroke. I will not mention that to her.

NOTE: Watching anything other than sports on television is not comfortable for Mom. Television shows and movies are all language-based, and that is the part of her brain that was damaged by the stroke. We have tried and it usually does not go over well.

WRITING – In a spiral notebook, I write the date, underlined and with a blank line drawn underneath. I then write a few sentences that are relevant and pertinent to that day. Again, with a blank line drawn underneath. The blank lines are for Mom to copy. I generally leave the bottom half of the page blank, and if Mom is in a writing mood, I encourage her to write something that she wants to write. Mix it up and keep creative in the writing suggestions. I have tried categories of words, such as colors, animals, foods, etc. Mom is not yet able to do those comfortably or well. We are edging back into categories, but we are doing it verbally for now.

PICTURE/WORD CARDS – Great to use for reviewing the alphabet, letter sounds and familiar words. Many boxes of these types of cards are available in categories of types of words. Keep the cards handy, and keep it fun.

MATH -- We have attempted doing simple math addition just a few times, with very mixed success. With Mom's Wernicke's aphasia, numbers and words get really mixed up, but with the months going by, this is something that we will spend time on, G-d willing, this fall and winter.

CALLING FRIENDS – The telephone works both ways, as a close friend reminded me just a few days ago. I often remind Mom that she used to call a small number of her close friends on a regular basis. We are doing that now, and when I dial the phone for Mom, I endeavor to have handy a picture of the person that we are calling. When I prompt Mom with something like, "Mom, you use used to call so-and-so when it rained, just to see that she is doing o.k. Let's do that now, alright?" And if I know that a friend of hers is going through something challenging, I will prompt Mom about that as well.

NOTE: Mom's phone rarely rings. It is my hope that with Mom calling some friends, they might get over their fear and apprehension of calling her.

Mom has a wonderful and old friend of 40+ years, Mary S., who had a traumatic brain injury (TBI) many years ago. Mary has telephoned me, and Mom, several times and left messages of warmth and good wishes. Because of Mary's TBI, she talks very fast and nonstop, her brain injury making it difficult for her to be conscious of what she is doing. Mary is aware of this and she is also quite aware that because of Mom's TBI, Mom operates at the other end of the spectrum with regards to language. The sensitivity that Mary has shown in limiting her conversation with Mom, hard as that is for Mary to do, is a level of sensitivity that just makes my eyes misty. We just got off the phone with her, and I take a moment here in my writing to acknowledge Mary's restraint when on the phone with Mom. Thank you, Mary S.

September 14, 2013 -- Mom awoke fairly early this morning, apparently after having some sort of disturbing dream about being all alone with nobody around. She also awoke being confused about a number of little children being around – I'll assume that this was part of what Mom was dreaming.

To awaken from a disturbing dream, nervous and feeling alone, is a hard way for Mom to start her day. Such a sad and lost and forlorn look is in her eyes and on her face this morning. Sitting on the back porch in the cool morning air, Mom said to me, quite clearly, "It's just hard." It is mornings like this that bring front-and-center to my mind that no matter how challenging this is for me, it is always most difficult for Mom. Sometimes we are given an opportunity to show some kindness, even if for just a few minutes, by stopping our busy lives and agendas, and sitting down to chat with a wounded person.

CHANGING CLOTHES AND BATHROOM NEEDS

An old friend of mine at the JCC asked me, in a sensitive manner, just how I managed to help my Mom with getting to swim and exercise in the pool. What he obviously meant was how do I deal with getting her into and out of her swim suit? Perhaps this would not be such a sensitive question, if it was a man for whom I was providing care. So, I will address it here.

The first time that I needed to help Mom use the bathroom I was a bit nervous about how to do so while preserving Mom's dignity and maintaining a sense of appropriate modesty. Fortunately, in my work with students in special education I have had the opportunity to help both male and female students with bathroom needs. I employed the same methods with my Mom. A body is just a body, poo is just poo, and pee is just pee. It is no big deal.

Mom is able to take care of most of her own needs in getting onto and off of the toilet. She requires reminders as to what toilet paper is for, and how to use it after she urinates. Mom is able to wipe herself after she pees. When she has a bowel movement, I put on a glove and wipe her from the back. Men reading this may not have thought about the importance of wiping a woman from front to back, so as to not draw fecal matter into the vagina. This is followed up with the use of a wet-wipe, so that her bum remains nice and clean. I do not narrate to her what I need to do, but I do ask her to lean forward so that I can help her. I always say, "Pardon my hands, Mom." I say the same thing when she has wet herself during the night and I use wet-wipes to clean her up, front and back. This occurs just about every morning. Mom steps out of the wet pull-up and wet shorts while she is standing next to the toilet. I then use a wet-wipe to wipe her down and keep her fresh and clean. She then sits down and finishes whatever toilet business she has. I help her into a new pull-up and new shorts or pants while she is sitting on the toilet. If her shirt has gotten wet, we then replace the shirt.

There is no embarrassment to Mom or me. She is oblivious to it, for the most part, and I do not make a big deal out of it. Like so much else in life, the more that we focus on something, talk a lot about it, get excited about it, or make a big deal of it – that is when that "something" becomes a big deal and can get uncomfortable for everyone concerned.

In the bathroom, the wet-wipes and the glove go in the small waste basket that is kept next to the toilet. To flush them will eventually cause problems with the sewer system. Any clothes or bedding that has gotten wet, I just bundle up and take downstairs to be washed. If Mom needs clean and dry shorts and/or shirt in the morning, and if the bedding needs to be changed, I get these things ready while Mom is still sitting on the pot. I keep two or three disposable protective liners on top of the mattress. These absorbent sheets are waterproof and disposable, about 2'x3' and I place them under the area where Mom sleeps. Plan ahead and avoid a wet mattress.

CHANGING SHIRTS/BLOUSES

When helping Mom to change her shirt or blouse, I hold the new shirt or blouse in front of her, with the neck area open and ready for her to put her head through it. Fortunately, Mom is able to take off her own shirt and all I have to do is avert my eyes in order to help her preserve her dignity and modesty. I occasionally remind her that I am doing this, and this helps us both to remain comfortable.

IMPORTANT: Always travel with a bag containing clean short/pants, shirt, pull-ups, gloves and wipes. I use a book bag with a shoulder strap. I also make certain that I have a water bottle with me to make sure that Mom drinks water throughout the day. Not drinking enough water can cause problems with bowel movements.

GETTING MOM INTO HER SWIM SUIT

I make sure that I am in my own swim suit, our gym bags are packed, and that everything is ready for us to walk out the front door as soon as Mom is suited up. We have found that it works best to get Mom into her swim suit right after she uses the toilet at home and while she is still sitting on it. Mom wears a one-piece suit. Her shoes, shorts/pants and pull-up come off first. Her shirt remains on at this time. We put her feet through the leg holes first, then her shorts/pants and then the sneakers that she likes to wear in the swim pool. I then have Mom stand up and we hoist the suit up to her waist. Then her shirt comes off. As it happens to be for Mom and me, she is fairly short, at just about 5 feet tall. I am a full foot taller than she is, and this works to our advantage. We take off her shirt and while Mom leans her head against the bottom of my chest, for balance, I reach over and around her and pull the suit up as high as I can. I then hold the arm holes open for her and she puts her arms through and adjusts her bosom so that everything is in the right place in her suit. I fasten the suit in the back and we then put on the t-shirt that Mom likes to wear in the pool. And off we go...no big deal and minimal narration on my part.

After swimming, Mom and I use one of the family changing rooms. The one that we usually use has a warm air hand dryer on the wall, right above the bench that Mom sits on. Mom really likes the warmth of the blower, and this makes the changing experience something that she is comfortable with. I give Mom a towel to hold up to her chest while I undo the hook on the back of her swim suit. This allows me to lower the top part of the suit while Mom keeps her bosom covered and her modesty intact. The shirt goes on, and then she stands up while I pull down the bottom of the suit. She then sits down and I take off the suit and her water shoes. I put a folded towel under her feet so that they can get dry and stay warm. Then on goes the pull-up and the shorts/pants, socks and shoes. Mom puts on her lipstick, glasses and hat, and out the door she goes, to wait in the wheelchair while I get myself dressed.

I have written the above as a fairly clinical narrative, and this is the attitude and mind-set that I maintain while I am helping Mom with her personal and bodily needs. Remember that the more that we focus on something, the bigger it gets. And with a care recipient that has had a major stroke, whose language center has taken a serious hit, one must always be cognizant of the effect of heavy focus and over-narration. Keep it light, understated and simple. And it becomes light, understated, simple and natural. This sure makes both of our days much more pleasant in just about every way imaginable.

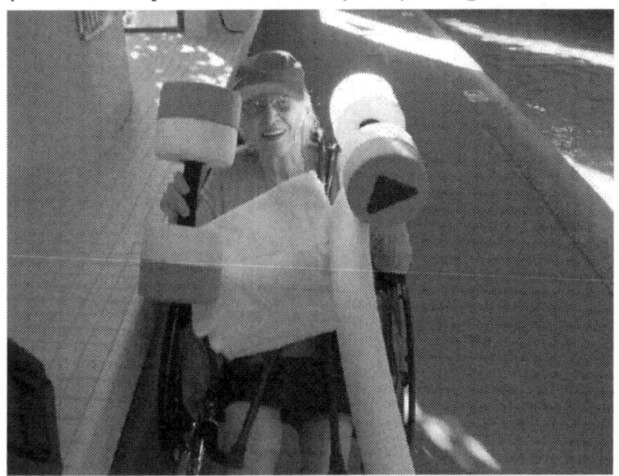

Mom before a swim

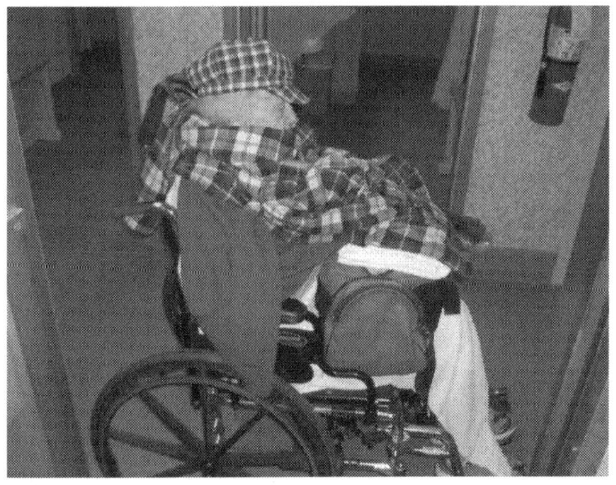

Mom resting after a swim

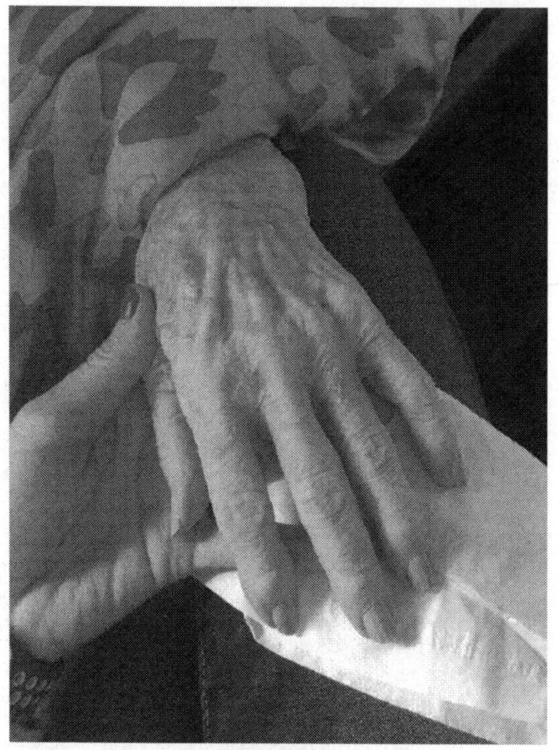

5 years later.....
Stephanie Connell
Painted Mom's Nails Pink
November 3, 2018
Stephanie knows the rest of that story.

September 26, 2013 -- In the arthritis water class today, I was chatting with a lady whose husband is now joining us in the water. He has Alzheimer's and I enjoy being able to work a bit with him while I still keep an eye on Mom and her water exercise participation. Speaking with the lady, our conversation drifted into my perceptions, as well as some of my questions, about her husband's and my Mom's abilities to lay down short term memory. After just a few minutes of our talking, the lady said something that struck me to the core. To paraphrase, she said, "Just getting through the routine of our day is enough for me." Wham! I felt at last that I was not alone in that thinking.

SEPARATION ANXIETY

MOM'S COMFORT ZONE WITH ANYONE COVERING ME

As time goes by with me being around Mom 24 hours a day, I am often struck by the separation anxiety that Mom exhibits when I talk about my need to occasionally be away from her so that I can tend to some things that I must do by myself. This comes up when I tell Mom about different appointments that we might have, such as dentists, doctors or banking. Most of the time, Mom asks me if we will be together to do such-and-such, or when we are going to see so-and-so. Out of the blue, she will get that "scared little girl" look on her face, and she will ask me if I am coming back.

Whether this is separation anxiety, since we have established a daily routine of my being around her 24 hours a day, or whether these are abandonment issues from her childhood -- who the heck knows. But it is present and it is a real part of my position as her solo full-time caregiver. And for anyone else who is a full-time caregiver, this issue may also be presenting itself. Every day, I seek the positive aspects and ramifications of this scenario. Yes, Mom's dependence on my presence creates a difficult environment for me to get away from for a while, which I must do for a variety of obvious reasons.

At the same time, her dependence on me allows me to have a great degree of her trust, so that when I tell her that we need to go do something and that it will make sense when she sees it, we are often able to avoid long and unproductive verbal explanations of what is at hand. Mom trusts me to a very, very high degree. And since I am responsible for virtually everything that she does each day, this trust keeps things peaceful for us. This level of trust also allows Mom to be generally compliant with my decisions and directions. Finding myself in such a position is often not comfortable for me. I am not by nature a bossy person, nor have I ever sought out positions of management.

Others in my family are, by nature, more suited for such things, but not me. And yet, it is what it is now, and I must do the job I have taken on.

The only situation where separation anxiety or abandonment issues never comes up is at the JCC while we are in the water. I will regularly leave Mom in either the class instructor's care, or with the lifeguard knowing that I am going to the Men's area for a steam and a shave, and I will be back in 10-15 minutes. If we are at the pool in the afternoon and not in an arthritis class, and I ask Mom if she will be o.k. for about 10 minutes while I go take a steam, she always asks me to go tell the lifeguard before I go.

Mom does not inquire about anyone, either by name or otherwise. I have mentioned this to her a few times, but have learned to just let it be. It is my belief that she does not have access to the part of her brain which allows her to recall people by name, if at all. When I show Mom pictures of her friends or her other children, she often kisses her fingertips and then touches the picture, but she does not say their name or tell me any stories, memories or thoughts that she has of them. She knows them when she sees them in person, though. No doubt about that.

October 21, 2013 -- Evening – "Is everything there stretched out or elongated? It looks funny to me." My pulse went up and I thought that maybe Mom was having some sort of brain episode that was affecting her vision. What it turned out to be was that I had turned the TV channel to some basketball, and the tall players…

October 22, 2013 -- Once again, Mom was crying a bit when I came into the bathroom to help her finish up. For the last several weeks, Mom has become more and more aware of her age, frailty and limitations -- physically, mentally and emotionally. She has said to me many times how she just does not know what to do and that she feels that she wants to help me and others more, but just cannot do it. The sadness that is on her face when these feelings arise, is an image that is burned into my heart and into my soul.

One day, after a swim at the JCC, we got home and Mom wanted to dig up some dandelions that have been growing in the grass near our front door. In years past, dandelion "hunting" has been the part of yard work at the house that Mom has always done. She used to call it "picking her daily dozen" and she would go to the back yard and dig up a dozen or two, put them in a bag, and then go inside for a nap. In the last several years, as Mom has gotten older, it was a source of pride and accomplishment that Mom would show me her "daily dozen" on the back porch picnic table. What a gas it was today to have Mom tell me, for the first time this year, that she would enjoy digging up dandelions and that she wanted to do it right now

We have some close friends that have invited us to their house for Thanksgiving at 4:00. I have no doubt that they are having the gathering early for our benefit and out of respect for our needs. And I am extremely grateful to them for their thoughtfulness and kindness. Thank you Mel and Anne.

(Edit on February 7, 2019 -- Below are pictures of these two wonderful friends, pictures taken on February 16, 2014. It gives me pause as I type this edit, seeing my Mother as she was just about five years ago. G-d bless you, Mom. I met with Mel in November 2018, and he shared some thoughts and perspective with me, particularly regarding how I had not directly asked for help. Mel's words have helped me greatly in releasing resentments, gaining understanding and having a kinder view of others. I may write more on this later, or perhaps not, as it was a deep and personal conversation we had. Thank you, Mel. In hindsight, I wish I had done what you suggested. But sometimes only in hindsight do we see as clearly as we might have wished for at the time.)

Mel, Mom and Anne

(Anne's Father, Walter Goldberg, was one of my best teachers, as I noted on the Dedication page. He taught by being an example of how to be a mentch.)

Rose and Mom

October 28, 2013 -- Rose, a dear and old friend of Mom's, called to see how we were today. I have been working a bit with Mom on her phone etiquette, and Rose proved to be a beautiful chance to have Mom practice what we had talked about. Mom has a habit of immediately starting to talk when I hand the phone to her, saying, "Blessings, blessings, Love, love..." and then handing the phone back to me. She hardly allows the other person on the phone to get a word in edgewise. To be honest, Mom has had this habit since long before her stroke, but it has been more pronounced since the stroke. Why Mom has this habit is an issue which is beyond the scope of this piece of writing. I have talked with Mom about allowing back and forth conversation, since a couple of her friends have told me that they feel like Mom is giving them the bum's rush on the phone.

The part of the conversation that I stayed in the room to overhear was a beautiful and appropriate back and forth sharing. I stayed within earshot just long enough to ascertain how it was going, and then I stepped away so that the ladies could have their private conversation. I have always done this since living with Mom. She is a closed-mouth friend to the women that she works with and does program (AA) with, and I respect their privacy, intimacy and confidence that what they share is kept confidential.

Rose is an amazing woman and her ability to be around Mom, and to have Mom be at ease with her around, is truly a gift from G-d. Rose commented to me that she doesn't know why other people have problems talking with Mom. Yes, some words are mixed up, but Mom is quite capable of being understood by someone who is understanding, patient, calm and who allows time for Mom to talk.

ENTERING A NEW STAGE

Our days continued much the same for many months. Many small strokes occurred, each one taking away a little more of my Mother, the dementia slowly presenting itself more and more, and the people we both knew presenting themselves less and less. "What can I do for you, Aaron? What can I do for Marcie? How can I help?" These are sentences that I heard from some few friends in the weeks while Mom was in the hospital, and I have not heard these sentences since that time. To be sure, there have been a few friends that have come over to spell me from time to time, more so in the first few months that Mom was home, and I am grateful to them for having done so. All but two of them have disappeared, and one remaining friend lives a good distance from us and does not get to Denver very often. The other has her own physical challenges and her own difficult aging and infirm family matters to deal with.

The more that I focus on our relative isolation from old friends and family, the more often I find myself heading down into a dark hole of depression and resentment, and this is not where I want to be. I have written about this in previous pages, and my hope continues to be that I will reach a state of surrender that is permanent.

One nice thing that Mom talked with me about was that there is no arguing that goes on in our house. We may not always agree about things, and sometimes one of us says something that hurts the feelings of the other, but we have learned how to talk our way through the hurt feelings without escalating the situation. This is a skill, and a conscious choice, that the two of us have made over the years. Both of us come from families where this is not normally done. Mom had hers in growing up, and I have mine.

Since Mom and I live together, it is a good thing that we are able to work our way through the "bumps in the road" as I call it. I suppose that most families have their own dysfunctional workings. The point with my Mother and me is that we chose to change the habitual patterns we both had found to be unhealthy. It can be done. It really can if two people want clean communication.

My original writing has countless episodes noted, of small strokes, setbacks and successes in day-to-day caregiving. I am keeping my original writing, but have cut out a lot of the day-to-day narrative here, lest this work become unwieldy for you, Dear Reader.

DNR (Do Not Resuscitate) CONSIDERATIONS

My Mother is 100% DNR and this is in her Advanced Medical Directives, in which I am authorized as her Power of Attorney to make certain that her medical and health wishes are followed. More than once I have given thought to what I will do when, or if, Mom has another major stroke. I believe that it is a matter of when, rather than a matter of "if", though obviously there is no way of knowing. My belief was proven to be correct.

If I call 911 again, and Mom is taken to a hospital in grave condition, just how long do I allow her to remain in the hospital? How much critical care do I allow the hospital to provide for her? If the event is quite serious and death is imminent, do I discharge Mom and take her home so that she can have her life end in the peace and comfort of her own home? How do I accomplish this? How much help will be available through Mom's Medicare policy? These are thoughts that I ponder now and again.

I have considered not calling 911 if Mom has another major stroke, but I have discarded this option. I believe that it would be unethical, and possibly it might be illegal, for me to make such a decision, even though I have both her medical Power of Attorney and her general durable Power of Attorney. I believe that there is a Jewish commandment or directive to seek medical attention when needed, even in an extreme case. What to do after the doctors make the evaluation is, however, well within the ethical realm of what is mine to decide. Knowing Mom as well as I know her, I will do my duty and honor her wishes. While Mom was in the hospital I had to remind the doctors and nurses, several times, that my Mom was 100% DNR. I eventually had them put a DNR wrist band on Mom.

Preparing dinner with Mom is heartbreaking at times. One evening, Mom's job was to cut up some grapes and then make some toast for us to have with tonight's soup. Mom was at a total loss as to what to do or where to begin. She told me, "I'm sorry, honey, but I just went blank." She says that quite often these days. She was doing so well, and progressing so steadily, until a few weeks ago. Keeping in mind that the process is more important than the product, is helping me to relax when Mom is not sure how to cut up grapes, or make her bowl of breakfast cereal, or any other of a myriad of daily things that Mom struggles with. It is the process, not the product, that is, for me, what this caregiving is all about.

Earlier in the summer, I was able to fake my calm demeanor when occasionally I got uptight. Now, I do not have to fake it. It is just there, and I am grateful that it is, because Mom is quite perceptive of my moods and attitudes and she knows when I am uptight. I am glad, for her sake and for my own, that I am not uptight too often these days. And I am well aware that this is something that I need to stay on top of. It is dangerous to rest on one's laurels.

My Mother's cognitive capabilities are fading. This is an emotionally difficult, and spiritually beautiful, thing to witness. I confess that many times I have had to pause and cry a bit, while away from Mom of course, when I ponder how much she is fading these days. I often sit under a tree in the back yard and just sob. The things that were, just a month ago, relatively easy for her to do herself, are now much more challenging for her. Sometimes Mom will come to a complete stop and sort of freeze her movements. She will tell me, when I ask her what is going on, that she forgot what she was supposed to be doing. This happens in the living room, in the bathroom and in the car.

Editing my writing on February 9, 2019, 5 ½ years since the above was transpiring, I wish I had a family member I could call and talk with right now as I read back through this stuff. These old memories about what the work with Mom was like are just gut-wrenching. End of Edit.

While there are, indeed, some parts of each day where Mom is alert and involved, much of the time she is quiet and seems to be seeing a dimension that is hidden to me. She sees beauty in everything and often pauses while we are walking to or from the car, and just says, "Wow, how beautiful." And oftentimes, when I look at her eyes, they are getting older and older every day. When Mom gets tired, she gets particularly "faded" and I am not shy about suggesting that she lay down and take a rest. What was a 30 minute or one hour nap, or rest, is now a couple of hours. This may be due to the change in seasons and the shorter days. I don't know, and it does not really matter. It just is the way it is.

Mom got really dizzy this morning as we were getting her dressed to head to exercise classes at the JCC. We were in the bathroom and she was finishing up brushing her hair and putting on her lipstick. I had her sit on the toilet seat and she took several slow breaths until the dizzy spell passed. When Mom looked up at me, there was a look in her eyes that was most peculiar and beautiful. I believe that yet another piece of her stroke-damaged brain said: "Bye-Bye."

She looked old and tired and peaceful. After the JCC, we went grocery shopping at King Soopers. Mom was excited to be going shopping with me. The last few times there, she wanted to just sit in the car and relax, but today she was looking forward to helping me with the shopping. When we got home, there was a rabbit sitting on the front lawn and Mom stayed in the car to watch the rabbit while I brought the groceries inside.

I share the above mundane details because perhaps another full-time caregiver will be reading this work of mine and be comforted to know that for someone else in this unique position of caregiving, routine activities are all just part of the deal.

At the water classes, David Faingold is the instructor on Wednesday. David is always very encouraging and supportive of Mom, has been teaching the class for many years, and has gotten to know Mom well. Last week, I asked David if he would be a pall bearer when Mom died. He said he would be honored to do so. I have great respect for this man and his character.

David Faingold and Mom

All of the Arthritis Foundation teachers at the JCC are wonderful people. Mom and I look forward to going to these classes. "I'm grateful that we know each other so well, and for so many days." This is what Mom said to me one evening in late November 2013, after I helped her to brush her teeth and get ready for bed. I am a lucky man, a fortunate son and a blessed caregiver.

November 27, 2013 -- This evening begins our Jewish holiday of Hanukkah. I lit the candles on our menorah with Mom, and she sang along with me for the blessings and a tune that we traditionally sing each night of Hanukkah. Although the Hebrew words were beyond Mom's capabilities, she faked them as best as she could, and she sang along quite nicely with the melodies. I then gave her $1 in Hanukkah gelt (money) and she put it on the table, saying, "We can just leave it there." I suggested to her that she could use the dollar to buy some cookies the next time we are at the JCC. She enjoys nibbling on two cookies, or crackers, after we change her out of her wet swimming clothes. Mom liked that idea. That evening, Rabbi Yossi sent me the following in an email:

"Addiction recovery Rabbi Shais Taub says the miracle of Chanukah was that people weren't discouraged with only one day's worth of oil. Instead of divvying up eight portions, they lived in the moment and used the full amount without letting the seemingly bleak future disparage them. Live in the moment and stop letting a seemingly bleak future discourage you and good things will happen! Happy Hanukkah!!!"

I am including this teaching from Rabbi Taub because it is pertinent to what goes on with me, and perhaps other full-time caregivers, as well. The faith and courage to believe that we are enough, have enough and will have enough, is something that is regularly in my mind. I try to keep it that way, anyway. I have been doing this gig for/with Mom for almost six months now, and I wonder if I have another six months in me. Or another year, or two years, or whatever time we are given. I do not allow my thoughts to go there for too long, since it is pointless and counterproductive. But my thoughts do, indeed, occasionally go there. This faith and courage is the opposite of fear, and is necessary in order to be an effective caregiver each and every day.

SELFISHNESS, DISHONESTY, RESENTMENT, FEAR

Edit on July 27, 2019 -- Below is a synopsis of what Roger G. would share in our AA meetings and when talking with me when my world became unmanageable. He was an old friend from Mom's recovery days, and whom I was blessed to get to know. Roger is now gone to the great meeting in the sky. Most everything, Roger taught, boiled down to selfishness, dishonesty, resentment and fear. One day, when Roger and I were sitting and talking, I told him that it was not enough for me just not be in the midst of those things; to not have those feelings and emotions. I knew that I had to replace them with something, but I did not know what to replace them with. I could expound on what is typed below, but I will not do so here, as it is beyond the scope of this writing. Suffice it to say that on the right side of each of those words is what I was taught the replacement feelings and beliefs could be. Any time that I found myself falling short of the high standard of caregiving, which I endeavored to hold myself to, it proved to be true that one of the four words below and in bold letters, on the left, was in play. Any time, and every time, this proved to be so.

There is a piece of paper with these teachings written on it, taped to a kitchen cabinet, above where we did (and I still do) meal preparation. These teachings are always in view, though all too often not always in action:

Selfishness ---> Love
Dishonesty ---> Truth and Wisdom
Resentment ---> Acceptance and Gratitude
Fear ---> Faith and Courage

Editing this writing on July 28, 2019 – It comes to my mind that the above synopsis may not be easily and clearly understood by someone who is not familiar with recovery program lingo. Here are my thoughts on the matter, as it relates, in hindsight now, to the caregiving

I was involved in. I am going to keep each explanation relatively short, though each one deserves being deeply delved into. I strongly encourage and suggest that other caregivers pay special attention to the thoughts below. It may make your life, and the life of your care recipient, much more tolerable and enjoyable. Some of what I share below may sound "preachy" to people who are not comfortable with "G-d talk" but I ask those people to not pass by the principles laid out below. Put aside, or skip over, the mention of G-d if you need to. That's o.k. But if you are a caregiver, I suggest that you consider the general notions below and not throw out the baby with the proverbial bathwater. Caregiving will challenge us all, so it cannot hurt to have some extra tools in your tool belt.

Selfishness ---→ Love

Most of the time, I truly enjoyed what I was doing with, and for, my Mother. The spiritual and emotional fulfillment was incredibly rewarding. But on occasion, and all too often for my liking, I found myself wanting desperately to escape from the duties I had so willingly taken on. This would happen when I was tired, frustrated, overwhelmed with responsibilities, and generally isolated from the life I had. My job, and my responsibility, was to turn my thoughts away from selfishness and towards love. Love for my Mother. Love for the opportunity I was presented with, to be of maximum service to her at her time of need. I would most likely have plenty of time for my own pursuits when my Mom's life ended. My sense of duty and responsibility runs deep in me. And I am human, so sometimes I just wanted chunks of time for my own needs, wants and desires. As our situation was, however, I had scant few hours to myself.

Dishonesty ---→ Truth and Wisdom

When I felt abandoned, unloved, discarded, etc., by the people Mom and I used to get to see, I endeavored to turn my thinking to a truthful perspective, and I prayed for the wisdom to be able to do so. The truth is, and was, that this was my duty and not theirs. The truth is, and was, that we all have limits as to what we can do for others. This held true for all other thoughts which plagued me, such as thinking that I was incapable of making the correct decisions for my Mom; that I would fail as a caregiver; that I was not enough ________ (fill in the blank as fits you, Dear Reader.)

Resentment ---→ Acceptance and Gratitude

Any time that I became resentful about my situation as caregiver, I was in resistance to life as it is, and as G-d wanted it to be. That remains true to this day. When, as a caregiver, my resentments presented themselves (and that happened more often than I wish it would have happened) the quality of my caregiving immediately plummeted. It is said, in an anonymous little fellowship, that resentment is the #1 offender. This proved to be true with me. I regularly kept myself on guard for resentments, turning as quickly as I could to thoughts of acceptance of circumstances as they were, and gratitude for the many blessings, spiritual and material, which Mom and I had. Resentment – not accepting people, places and things as they were – was the #1 issue I had while caregiving. I wish I had been stronger, more of a guru, more of a spiritual giant. But I was, and am, just me; a human being, a son doing the best he could for his Mother who had had a stroke and required fulltime assistance. Here are just a few examples of when resentments regularly cropped up with me:

When I got to feeling resentful about having given up my life as it was, prior to Mom's stroke;

When I got bored with our familiar daily routine. Familiar daily routines are what proved to be necessary for my Mom to be able to know, to the extent that she could know, what she was to be doing and what to expect throughout each day;

When I got angry and hurt by the absence of people we knew;

When I got frustrated with Mom's inability to do anything on her own, needing me to facilitate just about everything, every day, every week, every month...

My #1 resentment, for a few years, was when I got hurt by feeling stuck, since I could not come up with a contingency plan, should anything happen to me. I chose to limit the time and distance away from home – away from Mom when she was occasionally in someone else's care – because of the lack of a plan, in case I got hurt in a car wreck or some other accident. There was no family member willing to even be on the joint checking account, let alone to be a successor agent should I have found myself out of commission or dead. The couple of friends still in touch with me had their hands full with their own ailing family members, so I did not ask them. This lack of a contingency plan added a huge load onto my shoulders, and added tremendously to my caregiver burnout.

Fear ---→ Faith and Courage

There must be 100 forms of fear, it has been said. Any time that I found myself in fear, I was taught to ask G-d to remove my fear, and to turn my thoughts to what He would have me be -- A man of faith and courage. Faith that all is, and will continue to be, taken care of, though perhaps not as I envisioned. Courage to keep on keeping on, moving forward and doing the best that I could do at any given time. Courage to know that my best was all that was expected of me by G-d, by my Mother and, hopefully, by myself. Some of the fears I had were:

Fear of losing my mind from 100% caregiving focus;

Fear of running out of money;

Fear of running out of patience;

Fear of some day having to put my Mother in a facility, selling the house to finance it, and finding myself financially broke* after giving my all to taking care of my elderly Mother;

Fear of committing suicide – what kept me from that sometimes was the guilt I would bring onto myself for having left my Mom with nobody to take care of her and see to her needs.

*NOTE: One of the goals that I have in writing and publishing this work is to sell a zillion copies of it and set up a philanthropic source of funding for other solo full-time caregivers, so that when their duty comes to an end, they will have some funds sitting in a bank account.

Further on in this work, Dear Reader, you will read about how I fell short on many occasions in the areas of Selfishness, Dishonesty, Resentment and Fear. I have been brutally honest in my writing, even with the times I failed completely. Know this, though – every time I fell short of the high standard I set for myself; every time I blew it with Mom; every time I lost my cool, raised my voice, or the couple of times that I punched a wall, I took ownership of my actions and words, apologizing and making immediate amends to her. I am not a tzaddik (Jewish saint, sort of) and I proved that too many times. I gave this caregiving, this solo full-time caregiving, my best shot every day. That is all that I can ask of myself. Even now, however, with my Mom gone almost 9 months, I too often beat myself up with self-recriminations. But that is another matter, for another writing, at another time.

December 2, 2013 -- It is almost 1:00 Tuesday morning now, and I just spent half an hour or so sitting on Mom's bed, talking with her. I had been in the living room, playing my string bass for an hour or so, and in the video monitor I saw Mom sitting up in bed, looking at the clock that is across her room. She thought it was just after noon and Mom was wondering if she needed to get up and help with anything. I told her that it was past midnight and she was astounded. "Really?" she said. I held open the curtain for a moment and showed her that it was really dark outside, and I reminded her that at noon the sun was out. "How peculiar" she said. "How peculiar. I really am getting goofy."

Mom then proceeded to talk and her word usage was much like it had been back in May and June. Many, many words were used by her, disconnected and conveying little to no coherent information. Wernicke's aphasia at its most pronounced representation. Sadness has been replaced by deep compassion, with a dose of sadness remaining in the mix. And yet, the compassion that I feel now, as her son and as her caregiver, is the relief that Mom is relatively content and not fighting, as she put it tonight, "the things that she has lost." Mom is well-aware that there are great holes in her abilities and awareness these days, and that she is not able to understand most of what is going on around her. With one exception, she told me, and that exception is me. She reiterated to me, once again, that she knows how much assistance she needs, and she again told me how grateful she is that I am here to assist her. Mom told me that she feels that she has "enough" even with the deficiencies and deficits that she knows she has.

I do not know what is bringing about this regression, as I think it to be, back to the first couple of months after Mom got home from the hospital. I do not know, and it really does not matter. It is not something that I feel compelled to figure out. We did, in fact, get an appointment this morning at her doctor's office, to get her INR checked, and I told the nurse about Mom's dizzy spells and her cognitive regression. The nurse told me that she would pass her notes on to the doctor and that he would call me.

December 3, 2013 -- This is one of those days that calls on all kinds of skills, experience, patience and faith from this humble caregiver, with a long period of dizziness for Mom in the morning. We did get to the noon JCC water class, and Mom enjoyed herself quite a bit. Talking with the class instructor, she told me that she has noticed the regression, or slipping, with Mom in the last week or so.

When Mom and I were to light the 7th night of Hanukkah candles, I telephoned my brother, Larry, and put my phone on speaker, so that he could join us from San Diego while we "did Hanukkah." Mom enjoyed this immensely. She was really quite emotional, in a positive way, after we hung up the phone with Larry.

Nice evening....and then things got challenging.

A MINI-STROKE HITS

After helping Mom get into bed, around 8:00, I was looking at the video monitor around 9:00 and saw Mom tossing and turning some. She then called out to me, "Honey, can you come talk with me?" As I was sitting on her bed, quietly talking with her and holding her hand, she had another of the seizure-type episodes like she had back in June. It was intense, but it passed really quickly. You would be amazed at the strength in her hands and arms when these things hit. The hand of mine that she was holding was now held in a vice-like grip. I reached out and took her other hand so that she would not whack it against the headboard of the bed. Strong grip of hers there, too.

I stayed and talked with her for quite some time and she finally got settled down and turned over to go back to sleep. An hour or so later, in the monitor I saw that Mom was sitting up in bed, so I went back to her bedroom. She was quite confused and talking much like she was 5 months ago - classic Wernicke's aphasia. After 10-15 minutes or so, I helped her get into, and use, the bathroom.

Back in the bedroom, we were sitting on the edge of the bed, talking some more, and Mom just blacked out. Her eyes rolled back in her head and she sort of mumbled, "Oh my..." Fortunately, I had my arm around her shoulders and caught her as she tipped over backwards. The episode only lasted 30 seconds or so, but Mom was noticeably weaker and more confused. I don't know if it was just blacking out or another stroke. Over the next 15 minutes, she was kind of in and out of it, but not so completely blacked out.

It is now 2:30am on the 4th of December. Time for some sleep. Who knows what kind of a day is to come. All that I can do is trust G-d that we will be given whatever we need in order to take care of whatever comes our way.

December 4, 2013 – At 6:00 this morning, I helped Mom take care of her bathroom needs. She was cheerful, as usual, and did not appear to have any memory of last night's events. I certainly am not going to remind her of them, or talk to her about the seizure or her blacking out. As her caregiver, it is important to keep things on a positive note.

December 7, 2013 -- Old friends came to our home tonight to play music. We all played in a band named "The Human Beams" for several years. A good time was had by all. Mom was at numerous gigs we played. She did well at watching over the tip jar.

Paula, Dan, Mom, Marcella, Wayne
and your humble author

December 10, 2013 -- I miss having back-and-forth conversation with my Mom. The following is what transpired while we were watching a basketball game.

Aaron: "One team is in white. What color is the other team wearing?"

Mom: "I thought it was 18."

When I focus on deficits and what has been lost, that is all I see. Mom and G-d are giving me the opportunity to expand my line of sight. It is up to me to make use of the opportunity at hand. When I take each person within the confines of what they are able to give, then I do not have the conflict of expectations. It takes me a lot of conscious work, mindful work, to keep the above thoughts in mind. This is hard, folks!

December 31, 2013 -- It is 10:00ish New Year's Eve here at home. I tucked Mom into bed at 8:00. At 9:00 I saw that she was sitting up in bed, so I went in to check with her. Mom had no idea that it was evening and that we had had a nice dinner just a couple of hours earlier. No memory of it whatsoever. An hour later, I again saw that Mom was sitting up on the edge of her bed, just looking around. This time she asked me for something to eat, so I brought her some wonderful cake that a friend of ours, Rose, had made for us. That, and a few grapes, some gentle conversation and Mom was tucked back into bed.

Most of the people that Mom has known for decades in AA have not been heard from by us. Those that were around in the early months, after Mom had a stroke, have almost all disappeared. And Mom knows it. She is not stupid, but she is very forgiving and understanding. Even so, she is hurt and pained by their absence. And this is the single most potent source of my discontent, resentment and disgust. The rabbis do not visit or call on the phone, and the foundations I have contacted do nothing more than direct me towards complete government dependence and Medicaid. The idea of "Honor thy Mother and Father" seems to be nowhere to be found in their practices.

Yes, Dear Reader, I have some spiritual work to do here. There are good people in the synagogues and Jewish foundations, and they do a lot of good work. They simply are not meeting my needs or my Mom's needs. Pastoral work is not what they are capable of doing, and I do not understand that. And I am finding nobody in positions of power and influence who will take the time to examine our situation, which is such a core part of honoring one's Mother and Father. I cannot believe that we are the only two people who are in the situation that we are in, and I cannot understand why they are all turning a deaf ear to us.

There is something that I am missing, and I have nobody to go to for advice, guidance or direction. The two people that I would normally call upon, in a different situation, are my AA sponsor and my rabbi. But these two men are each a part of the two groups that have me all riled up. Where am I to go? The people I, and Mom, miss in our lives are good and decent people. Our needs right now, and mine in particular, just seem to be beyond their comfort zone.

From Psalm 146 – "Do not rely on nobles, nor on a human being for he holds no salvation."
From Psalm 147 – "...the outcast of Israel He will gather in. He is the Healer of the broken-hearted, and the One Who binds up their sorrows."

I C E (In Case of Emergency)

2014 – In case I am incapacitated, and in the event that we got into a car wreck, I keep the following always on me:

- I have a piece of paper taped to the back of my driver's license. Printed on it is information which would let a first responder know who I am, who Mom is, what her medical condition is, her doctor's contact info and the names of a couple of my friends who have keys to our home.

- In my pocket I always carry a flash drive in a zip-lock baggie, bound with a rubber band. On the drive are copies of all legal documents pertaining to Mom and her care.
- When we go to the gym, or to the doctor's office, in the gym bag or shoulder bag I carry, there is an envelope with printed copies of the POA (Power of Attorney) and Medical Directives pertaining to Mom and her care. Also in the bag, of course, are items which are necessary for Mom's personal care. And lipstick! I never traveled without having Mom's lipstick at hand. She is, after all, a lady.

Lacking a contingency plan, this is the best I came up with. What would be done in case I am out of commission is beyond my ken. I also text Roberto, a friend of mine, four times a week, letting him know that I am up and around. As our phone rarely rings, Mom would be in a tough spot if I dropped dead here at home. She would not know how to use a phone to call for help.

NOTE: After about two years of texting Roberto like this, I chose to give it up. It was too depressing.

<u>The backup plan. A contingency plan. A "what if something happens to Aaron" plan.</u> Another person who could sign checks, pay bills and have the legal authority to figure out what to do with and for Mom, should something happen to me. I asked the only available family member of mine to at least get on the checking account, so that bills could be paid if something happened to me. The answer was "No." I asked the same person about being the successor agent, in case I was not here and Mom needed to be moved out of the house and into some kind of facility. The answer was "No." I told the person that it could probably all be done over the phone, and that they would not need to be here, in person, to move Mom out of her home. The answer was "No." This person could not understand why I would not do anything which would, in my own estimation, raise the risk level of me being injured, even something as innocuous as driving by myself across town

or into the foothills for a few hours while someone else was with Mom. Again, without a contingency plan, should I become unavailable, I would not leave Mom in someone else's hands while I left the safe confines of our own neighborhood. This was a non-negotiable thing with me. It was duty.....I do not wish to hurt this other person's feelings, but I leave the above paragraph in this writing in case another solo full-time caregiver finds himself or herself in this situation. It is real. It was duty.

Life went on and on, as these months passed, and the theme of each day was largely unchangeable. I see no purpose, while editing this book of mine, to continue with the daily blow-by-blow details. I will leave them in my original manuscript, and just include some examples which are representative in the pages to follow.

February 9, 2014

Mom: "I don't know where I can help people, so that I can stay alive."
Aaron: "Do you want to stay alive?"
Mom shook her head in the affirmative.
Aaron: "Well, why don't you do some stretches and then come and help me make us some breakfast."
I then walked into the kitchen and cried like I have not cried for a long time. The pain and sadness and sense of loss on Mom's face is immense. We made up a wonderful omelet and sat down to watch some basketball.

The mood in the house is quiet, and Mom expressed her gratitude to me for being here for her. Sometimes the load that I carry is almost unbearable, physically and emotionally. I have learned to take a deep breath, ask G-d for help, and then go on to the next thing at hand. The last time that I was away from Mom for more than 15 minutes (while she is in the swim pool) was mid-July of 2013.

From the Chabad Rebbe, Menachem Mendel Schneerson, of blessed memory: "Despair belongs to those who see with human eyes, not to those who see with the eye of faith." I read this line very late last night, and the lock in the door of desperation clicked to the unlocked position. Only then could the door to hope to be opened. There is a line from the song, “Moria”, from the movie “Paint Your Wagon”, which paints a picture of how dark was my world at this early hour. “And now I’m lost, so gol-darned lost, not even G-d can find me.”

March 2, 2014 -- We brought Rosie to the vet’s office today to end her life. There was nothing more that Mom and I could do for her. We have been providing subcutaneous water infusions for Rosie for almost 5 years. The last couple of years, we have done this procedure every 2-3 days. This is the preferred treatment for renal failure. Tonight, Mom asked me to put Rosie's little heart pillow on her chair for awhile. And as anyone who has visited us knows, it was, indeed, Rosie's chair.

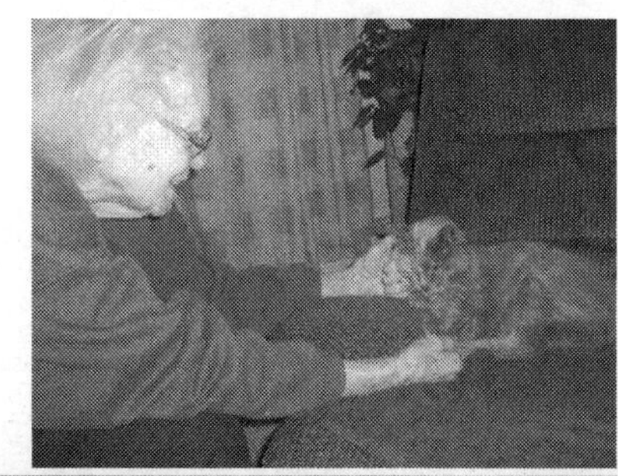

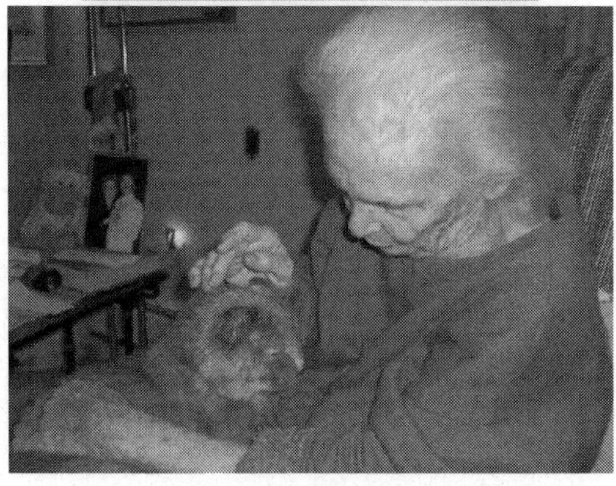

Perhaps the most notable gift that I have received, or am receiving since coming to be caregiving for my Mom on a full-time, 24-hour-a-day basis, is the gift of moving at the speed of the aged, which is SLOW. There is nothing hectic in our lives now. Nothing at all is hectic. There is no hurry in our lives now.

Attached are a couple of photos of Mom sewing the liner of one of her hats. Those old hands of hers remembered exactly what to be doing. Note the chair in the background. Rosie's (our cat) chair, with a heart-shaped pillow and two stuffed characters/dolls on it now. In due time, we will get another cat. Perhaps even two of them. But for now, Mom is feeling, healing and dealing with the recent loss of her old friend.

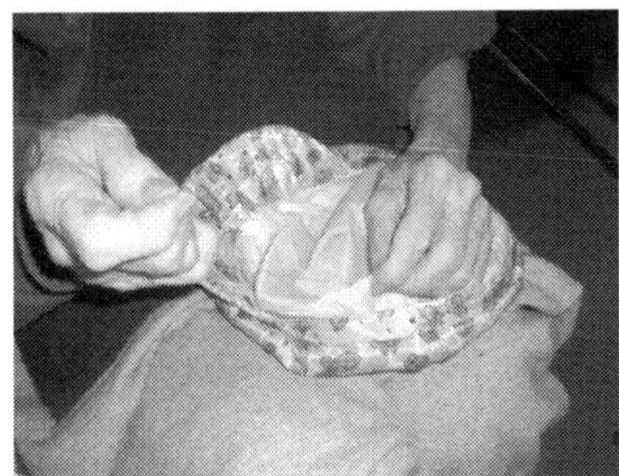

One of the most difficult things for Mom to deal with these days is her desire to help people, and her limited ability (in her mind, anyway) to do so. This is a topic of concern for her which presents itself with regularity. So, we talk and I guide her memory back through the day, or yesterday, and remind her of the gentle and loving ways in which she helps quite a few people. Like pixy dust from a fairy in an old Walt Disney movie, kind words and blessing are sprinkled, by Mom, on the people that we are around when we get out and about. Five years later, as I am editing my writing, a smile comes to me as people at the JCC often tell me how much they miss Marcie.

The JCC has a number of elderly people that we see on a regular basis. Mom is always asking me to see if so-and-so needs some help. These people usually have trouble walking or getting around. Mom's eyes are open to whom she, and I, might be able to help. This is quite remarkable to me, considering Mom's age and infirmity due to rather severe arthritis. Her knees. Her hips. Her back. Everything aches and hurts. And still she sees the beauty, caring and love in the world around us. And still foremost in Mom's thoughts is how she can be of service, and helpful, to someone. Frequently, the words "How can I/we help you?" are expressed by my Mom. These are treasured words and, perhaps, the most loving expression of caring that a person can offer up to a friend.

March 29, 2014 -- A year ago this evening, at about this time of night, after having a stroke just before the stroke of 7:00, my Mom was having a large blood clot removed from her brain known as the Wernicke's area. This has been a long, long year.

April 2, 2014 -- Lest anyone have a notion that my caregiving responsibilities, and my Mom's current circumstances are always heavy, pressure-filled, etc., let not your imagination deceive you. <u>We have some good times together. I just have not written enough about it.</u>

Well....just before midnight, I looked at my video monitor and saw that Mom was sitting up in bed. I had already been playing my bass for about an hour and a half. So, I put down my bass and went to check in on her. She asked me if it would be alright if she came out to sit in the living room and listen to the music. I tell you, folks, it just does not get any better than this! I had just finished playing to the live Human Beams CD from December, and Mom and I played through it again.

She played her egg shakers on most of the tunes, sometimes stopping and just sitting, with eyes closed, toes tapping and a big 'ol serene smile on her punim (face.) At the end of the CD, which is almost an hour and 15 minutes of music, Mom was up for a bit more, so I put on a Phil Lesh and Friends live CD and played a couple more tunes for her. (Broken Arrow and Friend of The Devil)

I had brought out some grapes and almond macaroons for nibbling, and had made Mom a cup of tea before we started. Life is good. It is now pushing 2:00 in the morning and I am heading to bed. During the last song, I thanked Mom for giving me the gift of music, which started in the 4th grade. Each of us kids had to pick an instrument when we got to 4th grade. I've stuck with bass all this while. Thank you Mom, and Dad (rest in peace), for the gift. When so much else in life is either missing, or set aside for now, my music is always at hand. Thank you, G-d, for this evening. Dayenu...

<u>There is a lot to remember in caregiving, and a lot to keep constantly in mind, no matter how long we have been doing this deal.</u> Take 90% of the words you are thinking of using, and don't use them. With the remaining 10%, throw out half of them. And then speak slowly and to the point. It is often only when I catch myself in the middle of doing something that detracts from quality caregiving that I notice that I am doing it

April 5, 2014 -- Evening – 8:45pm -- What a day this has been. Wiping tears from Mom's eyes this morning. Wiping tears from her eyes again just now as she was sitting up in her bed. Tonight, I reassured Mom that she is not a burden, or in the way, or holding me back from doing things that I wanted to be doing. I reassured her that I was not missing out on anything and that she should just put those thoughts out of her mind. The tenderness and gratitude on her face, with tears in her eyes, is yet another image which is burned into my consciousness and which it is impossible for me to adequately share with anyone. I know that Mom could feel the deep level of compassion that I feel for her and her current situation, which is so challenging. I shared with her, as she was teary-eyed this morning and again this evening, that if I could give her some of my relative youth, I would. But I can't. This is her journey, her party, if you will, and my job is to assist her as best as I am able to do so.

April 7, 2014 -- "I've never been this age before," said Mom, after we had been in the swimming pool. "Can we go visit at someone else's house?" The last number of weeks has been a psychological struggle for Mom as she seems to be more and more aware of her age and infirmity. Edit on August 1, 2019 – I checked my original manuscript and, sadly, there is no mention of us going to visit at someone else's house that day. It appears that I missed an opportunity to facilitate one of the rare occasions when Mom directly asked for something. Dang...

April 8, 2014 -- Thanks to G-d and the gift of Alcoholics Anonymous, today marked 42 years of continuous sobriety for Mom. 15,340 days of one day at a time. Parts of this day were overwhelming for Mom, particularly this morning as I gave her an AA medallion which notes 42 years. She also received flowers this morning from my brother, Larry, and his wife, Janet. Mom did not know what the day was all about. I did...

STAYING IN A PLACE OF SURRENDER

To all caregivers, I offer this observation which comes to me in so many hard won ways: There is a series of surrenders which I have gone through and continue to go through regarding full-time care for my aged Mother. I have been overly critical of myself for not "getting there and staying there" in terms of surrender to the situation as it is. I continue to fall into the trap of forgetting that Mom's condition is not static. It is ever-changing and that is what I get myself tripped up on. <u>Staying in a place of, an attitude of, surrender? It is a daunting task.</u>

May 1, 2014 -- Evening – Long strange day today was. We have had heavy winds for a few days now and after being home for two days Mom and I went to the noon water class today. The really heavy winds of the last few days have been downright hurricane-like in Mom's eyes and she had no interest in being anywhere but in bed, under her covers, sleeping much of the day. Mom was fairly nervous this morning, and though we only had light breezes outside, they looked big and scary to her. As we were heading out the door, I asked her if she was o.k. She told me that she was nervous but willing to go.

Late this afternoon, after we had gotten home and Mom had taken a nap for a couple of hours, she got up and asked me to come sit and talk with her. I knew that something was weighing heavily on her and I told her so. She again asked me to just sit and talk with her for a while, so we took a seat in our chairs in the living room and Mom shared what was on her mind. And it was heavy, man. <u>She told me that it finally hit her that she was very broken and sad...and tired.</u> When Mom said the word "tired" she seemed to age 10 years right before my eyes. Her eyes look sad and tired, like a woman who has lived for a very long time and was suddenly aware that she was a very old woman. By "broken" Mom meant both in mind and body. We talked about how there are things that she could no longer do, both physically and mentally, and how sad this would make anyone in her situation.

Knowing my Mom's psychological makeup, I immediately reassured her that she had done nothing wrong and that what was going on was perfectly natural for a woman who, G-d willing, would be 84 years old next month.

Caregiving is so much more than just making certain that the care recipient's physical needs are tended to. To be fed and bathed, toileted and dressed and generally cared for are certainly primary duties for the caregiver. In this situation, with the care recipient being someone at an advanced age and who is an acute care patient living with the effects of a stroke, aphasia and with dementia creeping in, caregiving takes on additional aspects which require extreme levels of patience, compassion, quick thinking, empathy, psychology and planning. Make no mistake that this is a 24-hour-a-day job for me and for any other caregiver who provides this level of care for a family member. It is not for the faint of heart. Every week seems to bring about more challenges and changes in what Mom can, and cannot, do. As age and stroke, and now, awareness on her part, are at hand, it is getting increasingly difficult to make any sort of plans or have any sort of notion as to what any given day will be like.

Sad – Broken –Tired -- These are words that I can relate to. I have been doing this for 11 months now.

NOTE: As I edit this book, 5 years later, it seems like a dream.

LOSING MY SELF IN CAREGIVING

May 24, 2014 -- I have noticed that my patience runs short at the end of the day, after dinner and as I am helping Mom get ready for bed. The thought came to me that perhaps this is due to a realization of two things:

1) It takes an enormous amount of psychic energy just to get through the day. My entire focus is on Mom and her needs and our activities for the day.
2) I will have to do this all over again tomorrow.

Tonight is the first time that I have thought of this in such stark terms. Tomorrow, we do this all over again. And the day after, and the day after that. And this may just go on for a long time yet to come. I dare not go down that road of self-centeredness too far, lest I lose sight of the joy and the gift that I have been given in being allowed this role of solo full-time caregiver for my Mother. And yet, I am only human, so the selfishness is going to rear its ugly head now and again, as it has done just in this past half hour. Mom is in bed now, though, and I can take the next few hours to myself. I'll clean the dishes and put the food away and then get on my bass and play for a while.

Spot-checking myself, many times throughout the day and night, allows me to notice when my attitude, thoughts, actions and words are not aligned with the character standards towards which I want to direct my life and my duties as a man, a caregiver and a son. I am constantly thinking about what we are doing, what we will be doing and what we have been doing, so as to create a daily environment which is conducive to the safety, comfort and well-being of the person who is in my charge. This is a formidable task.

June 2, 2014 -- Rose visited today and I shared a bit about another visitor we had who simply cannot control how much they talk. I was not putting the other visitor down, but I needed to talk with Rose and I thanked her for being able to read a situation like ours (Mom's unique needs) and behave accordingly. What Rose told Mom really struck me and got me to thinking positively that I was right in working to, I guess one could call it, "control/manage" Mom's environment. She told Mom that I was her filter. And, indeed, that I am. That is my job and responsibility as her son and as her caregiver. Not everyone takes kindly, or is receptive to, my requests to keep conversations simple and short. In case anyone reading this is considering visiting some version of a "Mom" at some point, I write the following in hopes that they will consider, and please take to heart, the following: Mom's brain was severely damaged by the stroke that she had in March of last year, and there are some friends of hers who have not been around her much, if at all, since then. It is not possible for Mom to participate in conversation in the manner in which she was able to, prior to the stroke. It is physically not possible because of the damage done to her brain. Expecting her to be able to do so is akin to expecting a blind man to see if he just tried harder.

Any attempt to converse with her at our usual "warp speed" is not only ineffective, it is rather cruel and should not be done. I hope that people do not read the following as being overly-controlling on my part, but as her son and as her caregiver, I continue to try to explain to people what the situation is with Mom. She is still Mom/Marcie, and she has been injured. She is not senile, feeble-minded or stupid. She is just injured, and the injury requires care and sensitivity in order to talk with her. We are fortunate to have a couple of friends who "get" this, and they are comfortable with being around her, as she is comfortable being around them.

In my work in special education, I used to challenge colleagues regarding the students' "wait time" needs. Most of us wait perhaps a second or two, if even that, after someone has finished a sentence, before we utter our reply. We are usually thinking about what we are going to say while the other person is still trying to tell us something.

Try waiting 30 seconds...it'll drive you nuts. Most colleagues I tried this with could make it about 5 seconds before they got ants in their pants. With Mom, get used to the ants if you want to come visit. It is actually rather nice to slow down and enjoy the silence. That is when the magic happens.

PROCESSING AWARENESSES OF THE CAREGIVING RECIPIENT

June 10, 2014 -- For about a week now, when talking with Mom, I have been consciously limiting myself to two short sentences, followed by a question. This was not, at first, an easy thing to do. For the question, I mostly use, “What do you think?” Repetition breeds familiarity and this question has become familiar enough to Mom that she is able to share some thoughts and opinions more easily in the last few days.

This has been a day filled with poignancy and difficulty in having to verbally negotiate my way through deep emotional feelings which Mom has had going on. Remember that what makes this negotiating difficult is her severe language deficit. We began this morning well enough, with a nice breakfast before getting ready to head to the water class at noon. As I was finishing helping Mom get her swim suit on, along with the rest of her clothes, she drifted into a very far-away and rather sad state of mind. I stopped what we were doing and asked her what was going on. "Feeble. I'm just so feeble," is what Mom said.

Edit on August 1, 2019 – I have noted before that an important part of my duty was to help Mom process, to the best of her ability, the emotions she experienced during those times when she was aware of her severe cognitive limitations. Step into this caregiver's shoes for a moment or three, and ponder what you would do and say when your own parent said what my Mother said above. Moments of language clarity, through aphasia and dementia, are rare. What more can be done most of the time other than to offer such compassion, love and care as one has in him or her to give to the other. "Yes, Mom, you are feeble, your ability to process thoughts and convey information is severely limited, and your body is failing. Oh, and your brain is more and more being hit by small strokes." No! That is not what should be said. Just simple compassion, a shoulder for the parent to cry on, a tissue to wipe their tears. That is what should be offered. It is not in everyone to be in this type of caregiving position. The above scenario(s) leave an imprint and an impact on the caregiver's heart and soul. This work is not for the faint of heart, the weak of spirit, or the uncaring. And yet, this work is incredibly rewarding on the deepest emotional and spiritual levels. Truly an opportunity not to be missed! I have no regrets about having done what I did for my Mother. No regrets at all.

Late this afternoon, we went out to the patio to finish planting some flowers in some pots that we bought today. When we were done, I gathered up the things that needed to go back inside, and I asked Mom to please stay in the chair that she was sitting in. She said that she would do so. A minute later, as I was walking back outside, Mom was on her feet, holding onto the arm rests of her chair and unable to figure out what to do next. I cried out to her, "Wait! Wait! What are you doing?" Her canes were not within her reach, and she was at the edge of a concrete patio with about a 9" drop to the walkway. I said to her, "Mom. Your canes are over here, and you are over there. How were you going to manage that?" She had no answer, but knew that she had made a serious mistake. "Foolish woman" is what she said out loud.

NOTE: Doing the yard work or gardening with Mom requires extreme diligence and attention on my part. Rose was here last week, and the three of us went out back so that we could show Rose how the gardening was coming along. Mom wanted to sit in her chair right outside the back door, so we left her there. <u>There are four concrete steps down to the patio. Note this.</u>

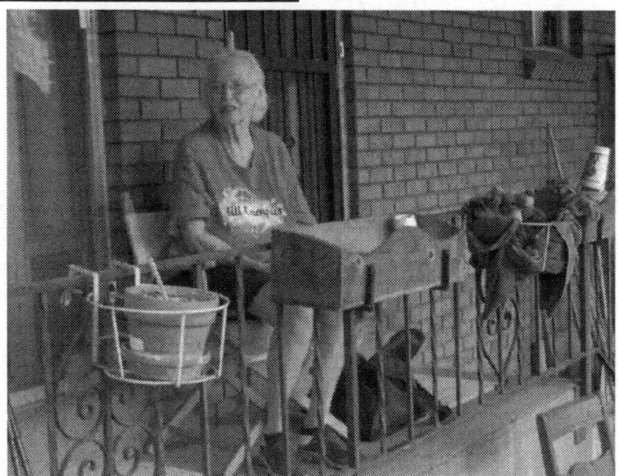

Rose and I walked out into the yard and went over to look at what had been planted at the far end of the walk. Our backs were to Mom and our attention was on the flowers and seedlings for about two minutes, during which I admit that Mom was not even in my thoughts.

After no longer than about two minutes, Rose looked up and said, "Oh, my G-d!" Mom had gotten out of her chair and was at the bottom step – by herself, one hand on the railing and one hand on her canes. Had Mom taken a fall, she would have gone face-first onto the concrete steps (G-d forbid)...

Rose and I looked at each other, and nothing much needed to be said. We just walked quickly to Mom and guided her to a seat on the patio. Later, Rose and I talked quietly by ourselves about adrenalin rushes and about how it can only take a moment of inattention for a calamity to happen (G-d forbid.) I told her that I don't know how parents of small children do it, though after a year of caregiving for Mom, I can understand how it just has to be done. And I told her that I understand how children can drown in a pool during just a short few minutes of a parent's inattention. This constant state of awareness for someone else's safety and well-being, is extremely life-changing and draining.

An old friend of mine, Bill Walsh has been kind enough to come to our house a couple of times this past year, to cut my hair. I avoid making appointments since I never know if Mom will be up to going with me when the appointment comes, and I do not want to leave someone else hanging just because of our unique situation.

Mom has not wanted to get her hair cut, or styled, for over a year now, since she had her stroke. But a few days ago she asked me if we could go to "my friend's house and get her hair shortened." (Her words.) When Mom asked me again the next day, I contacted Bill and we set an appointment for Mom. She was so happy to have a more feminine look to her today. And Bill put it beautifully to Mom when he told her she looked "elegant." He is a truly relaxed and decent man, and his home has vibes which reflect Bill and his lovely wife. Also striking is his relaxed and natural manner in talking directly with Mom. He intuitively knows to listen for the key words that she says, and has very little problem in understanding what Mom is talking to him about. Bill was kind enough to bring his skills to the group home that Mom spent her last few months living in. He gave Mom her last hair cut shortly before she died.

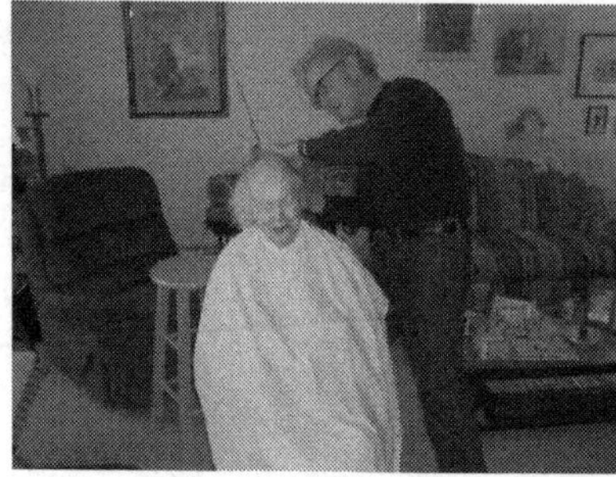

January 26, 2015
At our home

Mom and Bill Walsh
At his home/studio

June 25, 2014 -- Late afternoon on a warm summer day, with a bit of a breeze outside. A few minutes ago, Mom called out to me, from her bed, "Aaron! Honey, I'm scared." I went in to her bedroom and she was teary-eyed and afraid of the breeze that she could see outside the window of her bedroom. As I sat on the side of her bed, Mom sat up a bit and I put my arm around her to ease her fears. It appears that her senses of perception are getting more distorted or exaggerated. It is my belief that dementia is expanding. The word "dementia" is frightening to me.

SUNDOWNING

There is a term that I have heard, from others who work with our elderly. The term "sundowner syndrome" refers to mental and cognitive changes, frailties really, which are common in many of our injured elders late in the day. In dealing so closely with my Mother, as a person and not as a measurable statistic in a scientific study, I try to avoid attaching descriptive terminology to what I am witnessing. That said, there is a lot of material already written and available which will help the reader to learn about sundowning. In a nutshell, many people in my Mom's condition exhibit fatigue and additional confusion in the late afternoon and early evening. Hence the term "Sundowning" as it usually happens late in the day. The changes can come on suddenly and it often takes a few hours to pass. There is nothing that I can do to forestall this from happening to my Mom. I just have to go with it as best as possible.

SURRENDERING AND PICKING UP ON CUES

In hindsight, editing this work now on August 4, 2019, I wish that I could have picked up the cues which Mom was giving me in all sorts of areas. Below, you will read about one area - the writing exercises. Other areas I probably missed included the isolation which she was experiencing, the physical fatigue from going to the swim pool almost every day and the nervousness she had as I got more uptight as time went by. As I got more uptight, Mom occasionally got nervous about not knowing what to do or say or, indeed, to expect in my own behaviors. I cringe as I type this, daring to be open and honest with you, Dear Reader, but only now am I able to see my part more clearly. My own isolation, my own physical, mental and spiritual fatigue, and my own nervousness – I wish I could have seen it and known how to deal with it in the early years of caregiving. And yet, I did the best I could at the time, and that must suffice. I asked for help the best way I could, and that must suffice. The people whose assistance I requested did the best they could, and that must suffice. There simply is no upside to beating myself up, or holding grudges or resentments towards myself or anyone else. I have done quite enough of that, thank you.

For other caregivers who may someday be reading this treatise of mine, be comforted in knowing that if you have done all that is in your heart and in your power to do – that is enough. I was talking with my oldest brother, Larry, the other day about the phases that my caregiving for Mom has gone through. Some months ago I wrote about going from a phase of recovery, with lots of work in writing and reading, to a phase that we termed "a mission of mercy" or some such term as that. These days, I find myself in a phase of calm compassion, going as much as possible synchronized with Mom's moods, energy levels and desires. I failed to mention that, some months ago, I gave up the writing exercises with Mom. Having talked with her doctor, whom Mom has seen for 30+ years, it was agreed that there were diminishing returns in continuing the exercises. Mom's energy levels get drained easily, and as her ability to write or copy anything was declining, it was apparent that doing any more was a waste of her energy. That was a hard blow to me. A real surrender to the path this journey is on.

Rest assured, Dear Reader, that you are not the only one who sometimes simply does not know what to do for, or say to, the recipient of your caregiving. There is no experience that I can draw upon other than the experience that I have gained this past year. I often wish I had a mentor or active sponsor with whom I could share the day-to-day happenings, my thoughts about what to do or not to do, and my thoughts as I come to realize that much of the time there is nothing for me "to do" but continue to make sure that Mom eats well, takes her medicines, gets ample rest and participates in whatever social activities that she is up for.

Maybe that is all that I am supposed to be focusing on. I cannot fix her exaggerated sensory perceptions or the fears that are concomitant with them. I cannot fix the injured little girl that is within Mom. I cannot fix the wounded woman that she is, both psychically and physically. As her son and as her caregiver, I sure want to, though. Surrender and acceptance seem to come and go for me. Most of the time I am calmly accepting of this whole situation – the parent becoming childlike. Most of the time, anyway.

Going back in memory even to when Mom was in the hospital for a month after her initial stroke, there was no training or guidance provided to me as I entered the world of caregiving. The books I found and read, while they told compelling stories, all presented a common theme. That theme was "Make certain to have a caregiving team put together, so that you, as a caregiver, can take time off and avoid burnout. Make certain to take an evening, a weekend or an occasional week off." That option was just not available to me or to us. Such was the case as I found myself in my role as a solo full-time caregiver.

June 28, 2014 -- After swimming today, we were in the family changing room and I was helping Mom get dressed. I handed Mom her hair brush and after holding it for a few moments, she handed it back to me and said, "I don't really need this." So I handed Mom her hat and she got a bit miffed, gesturing that she needed to brush her hair first. As I handed the brush to her again, Mom got frustrated and then got really quiet, which is a clear sign that something just went wrong. I have learned to wait for a few minutes, or as long as it might take, for her brain to reset itself. "What's wrong, Mom?" She held up the brush, after using it, and said, "I didn't know what to do with it." A few minutes later, with Mom still feeling quiet, she said, "I'm sorry if I made it harder for you." I try to remember foremost how terribly difficult this phase of Mom's life is for her. But I still forget and take things personally on occasion. Too many times, to be honest. Dang....I wish I was perfect in my caregiving. But I am not.

STAYING CONNECTED TO THE WORLD

August 15, 2014 -- I am finding that it is odd to be living such a slow pace as we have here at our home. I do not multitask here, since it does not work with our current circumstances. While I am helping Mom with one thing, I do not talk about something else. In fact, I do not talk much at all while we are doing something, since over-narrating clogs her neuro pathways and things just get confused. The upside of this is that I am getting the opportunity to learn to "be present" more often than I ever have been. The downside of this is that most of the world we encounter is on a totally different wavelength, and is going at a very fast pace. Hence, I find myself rather disassociated from the world around me. It is getting progressively more difficult to relate to, as I call it, the outside world.

Editing on August 4, 2019 – The above was written just a year and a couple of months into the caregiving. And the above continued for several more years. A couple of months after my Mother died, I stopped writing the original manuscript of this work, as I found my narrative and sharing had shifted away from caregiving and into grieving and the grief process I was experiencing. I chose to keep the focus on solo full-time caregiving, rather than allowing a shift to grief and grieving.

Regarding entering back into the non-caregiving world, I am finding this to be quite a challenge still, just over 9 months since Mom died. I have another 2 months of grieving as we do in the Jewish faith. Daily attendance at synagogue is what our/my tradition encourages, so that the Mourner's Kaddish can be said. You can look that up yourself if you care to, and if you are not familiar with the prayer. Reconnecting to the world around me is much harder than I imagined it would be, not that I gave this a whole lot of thought prior to Mom's death. I wrote above about experiencing "being present" in my caregiving. Yet that concept appears to be foreign in my daily dealing with people who are go-go-going at the warp speed of the 120-character tweet or text message. I was talking with someone this morning, and his phone rang. In the middle of our conversation, he took the call and wandered off, thinking nothing of the matter. Talking and texting and checking emails all at the same time continues to baffle me. I concede that my perception is colored by my experiences of these past 6 years.

I have been asked if I would advise other caregivers to stay more connected to the world. I certainly would advise them to do so, if their situation allows. Several pages ago I mentioned the caregiving books I read, which all recommended putting together a caregiving team, so as to avoid burnout of the primary caregiver. That is a lovely idea, it makes a lot of sense, and I have no idea how any other solo full-time caregiver would possibly accomplish that! I do not know what I could have done differently so as to stay more connected to the life I had (the world) before caregiving. I just do not know…I wish I did.

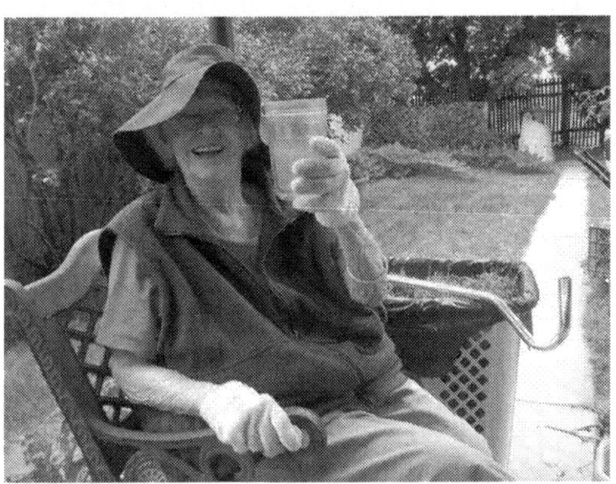

May 18, 2019 – I will mow the lawn tomorrow.
I miss my lawn mowing helper.

September 11, 2014 -- **It Doesn't Matter** – That is the lesson which I am learning again today, and which I am pondering at this late hour – 11:11pm

Who's playing? – It doesn't matter.
What's the score? – It doesn't matter.
What day is it? – It doesn't matter.
Where did we go today? – It doesn't matter.
What did we do today? – It doesn't matter.

What does not matter is that most of the time Mom is unable to give an answer to these questions of mine. It is not that she does not care. It may be a combination of age, aphasia, dementia or, most likely, a combination of all three. While I sometimes forget that Mom is not intentionally unable to answer, most of the time that thought is foremost in my mind. As I have written previously, it is like expecting a blind man to see if he would just try harder.

So many of the things which I, and probably most of us, keep organized, categorized and rated, in our brains, are not even on Mom's radar any more. Make no mistake here in thinking that Mom just sits and stares into space, totally unaware of all goings on. Much to the contrary. It is more that she is very much "in the moment," seeing and experiencing the essence of her surroundings. When we watch a sporting event on television, Mom knows action and good playing when she sees it, and responds excitedly, albeit with peculiar word usage. The team names and the score just do not matter to her. This is not a conscious choosing of hers, it just is the way that it is. In order to keep track of most things, we need to be able to utilize the part(s) of our brain which categorize and keep in order people, things and events, by name, using words. And it is the word part of her brain, the Wernicke's center, which was devastated by the stroke. Be here now? Mom lives it 24 hours a day.

I write the above observations for a couple of reasons. NOTE THIS: First off, I want a record to look back on and read when Mom is gone and my duties as her son and caregiver have come to an end. Secondly, for other caregivers who might be reading this treatise it may be helpful to her or him to bring to the front of their minds that the caregiving we provide must be within the boundaries, or limitations, of the care recipient. Mom is most at ease when she feels comfortable and safe, subconsciously perhaps knowing that she is free to be herself, as she is, and to express herself as she does. I, or any other caregiver, can do all the words drills and "therapy work" that we want to, but in my Mom's situation it produces no immediate, or even future, long term benefit. I suspect that this holds true for other elderly people who find themselves in a similar situation as my Mom is in.

To provide care for someone's health, safety and well-being is a sacred task and undertaking. When I, or anyone else, approaches it with the egocentric belief that we can change the care recipient into a form which we desire, we breach that sacred duty. It is normal, and natural, I believe, that once in a while this breach is going to occur. It certainly has occurred with me and my caregiving duties. The onus is on me, and other caregivers, to constantly be checking ourselves, our motives, our actions and our words, to keep them as much as possible aligned with the best interest of the people in our charge.

Being a solo full-time caregiver, meaning that I am with my Mom 24 hours a day, makes this business of self-examination even more crucial if I am to provide the most effective caregiving that I am capable of accomplishing. I have put aside all the things that I used to do: AA meetings, workouts in the gym, particularly in the evening, working in special education, playing in a band, going out to run a few quick errands, and these are just the activities which immediately come to mind. At home, I used to enjoy a few hours in the evening, downstairs on my bass or reading in my bedroom, while Mom was upstairs doing her own thing. Even in the year or two preceding her stroke, I was cutting down some on the time I took to myself, just because Mom's forgetfulness was beginning to show itself and I wanted to be around to see that she had what she needed and was kept safe as much as possible. One of the ladies in the swim class told me that she had noticed dementia with Mom a couple of years ago. The lady is a former nurse, and her husband has Alzheimer's. I listened to what she shared with me. I did not argue the point, though my brain and heart begged me to get into denial.

I share this information not out of a need to complain or whine about my current situation, nor is it (I hope) from a place of self-pity. I write about what I have given up, with the hope that another solo full-time caregiver might at least know that he or she is not alone in the sense of isolation and complete change in their own lives. I also write it with the faint hope that some who knows a solo full-time caregiver will find it in themselves to make themselves available, on an ongoing basis, to that caregiver and the recipient of their care, so that the isolation of someone else might be alleviated.

September 29, 2014 -- I will not state that I have done this 18 months of caregiving perfectly. I have not. I will not state that I have done this as gracefully and spiritually as I would have wished. I have not. I have had a pretty good batting average in my duties as my Mom's caregiver, and that is all that I should expect for myself. To expect to be a superstar, always on top of everything, never losing my patience and perspective, etc., would be dishonest on my part. I am just a man, my Mom's youngest kid, who finds himself in a unique position. I have done the best that I could for her. I have spent too much time – way too much time – grumbling/thinking/worrying about the people we know, in AA and in the Jewish community, who are not around and who have not been in contact with us.

It may be that other caregivers, solo full-time caregivers in particular, will experience the same abandonment that we have. Having talked with some other caregivers, even those with some family around, the abandonment appears to be a common thread. It is my hope that if you, Dear Reader, end up being alone, abandoned by those you used to get to see, that there is something in what I have written in these pages which brings you some solace, even just in knowing that you are not the only one.

SLEEP ISSUES

One of the challenges, physically and emotionally, of the solo full-time caregiving that I am doing, is the lack of restful sleep for me. As there is no one else around to listen for or keep a watchful eye on, Mom, my senses are always attuned to sounds from her bedroom, which is directly above mine. I have never been a really deep sleeper, but current circumstances have cut into whatever periods of sleep that I used to get. On occasion, however, I find that I have slept though Mom getting up by herself to use the bathroom, usually in the hour or so before or after dawn. I sometimes hear the toilet flush, and that awakens me.

Sometimes, when I get up in the morning, I notice that her canes are leaning against her bed rather than against the night stand next to her bed, which is where I leave them when I tuck her in at night. When I see that Mom has walked to the bathroom by herself, I am grateful that she got there, and back to her bed, safely. I then count us lucky that she did not take a fall, and I beat myself up for having failed her by not waking up to walk with her. This is probably something that I need to work on, this berating myself for sleeping through Mom's occasional trip to the bathroom by herself.

October 14, 2014 -- Somewhere in my mind I can see scenes from old movies, where a parent quietly steals into their young child's room at night while the kid is sleeping, and tucks them back under the covers which have slipped off of the child and down to the foot of the bed. In the movies, of course, this does not awaken the sleeping one and peaceful slumber embraces the child.

And so it goes here at our house, but Mom is the child and I get to quietly go to her bedroom and make certain that she is warmly and safely tucked under the blankets, or add a blanket if the house has gotten a bit chilly. I am amazed at how deeply this lady sleeps when she is down for the night. I have told my oldest brother about this and since we both have had, for many years, real difficulties in getting any deep sleep, we are both admittedly a bit envious at someone who can sleep undisturbed by someone entering their room to put a blanket over them on a chilly night.

In the old movies, the parent has a loving and wistful look on their face, knowing that they are their child's guardian and protector and knowing perhaps that the day will come when what they are doing is no longer going to be needed. The poignancy comes in the knowing that my "child" is not going to grow up and grow out of the need for my watchfulness. Pretty cool deal this is, that G-d has seen fit to allow me to be around for Mom at this stage of her life, and after the life I have lived. Pretty darned cool.

FILTERING

Filtering out the environments or people which would cause distress to Mom is one of my main jobs as her caregiver. The word "filter" was expressed to Mom by her one friend who has stayed in regular contact with her. This lady said to mom one day, several months ago while visiting, "Aaron is your filter" or "Aaron's job is to filter things out for you" or something of that sort. I had not thought of it in such a direct way, but after giving the idea a considerable amount of thought over this long period of time, I have come to believe that being a filter for a care recipient is, indeed, one of the primary duties if the caregiver is to be most effective in helping to provide and promote environments in which the recipient will be most comfortable and able to interact with the world, relaxed and with whatever skills they still might retain.

There are downsides to filtering: isolation, irritating some people who do not understand the limitations of the caregiver's charge, who have not been in regular contact with us, and who are insulted when I tell them that we cannot participate in gatherings which they invite us to attend. Without exception, none but a scant few come to our house to visit with Mom in her quiet and familiar surroundings. I wonder what it is that they fear.

DON'T LET HER FALL

"Don't let her fall." -- Those words were spoken to me by an old and dear friend of mine a year ago July, when my brother, Larry and I went to hear his band play. That was the last night that I left Mom in someone else's charge, but that is another matter. "Don't let her fall" has been my primary focus since I got home that evening, 15 months ago at the time of this writing.

"Don't let her fall." -- Those four words, as I have taken them to heart, appear to have turned on the hyper-awareness switch in my nervous system. I have never slept deeply or regularly, and I sleep even lighter now. I simply do not want Mom walking by herself at all. And now, this year and some months later, as Mom has declined both physically and mentally, I am even more on guard, if it is possible to more than 100% on guard against Mom falling and, G-d forbid, breaking something. A fall and a break would change everything for Mom, and it would change it in a really nasty way. I cannot allow this to happen if I can prevent it by walking with her at all times. And if it costs me a good deal of sleep and rest, that is, apparently my job.

I have started reading some Nachmanides (Ramban), and I came across a wonderful line in his book of "Writings and Discourses": "Scripture states, every one to his service, and to his burden." I still claim my choice in not looking at my caregiving service as a burden, although it is, undoubtedly, extremely difficult at times, as I have written elsewhere in this treatise.

"Don't let her fall." -- I cannot count the number of times that I have prevented Mom from falling. I have slept through a dozen or so trips that Mom has taken to the bathroom by herself, and I have rued every occurrence of my not hearing her get out of her bed. Everything is in G-d's hands – that, I know for certain, and Mom may yet take a fall. But I will do everything that I can in an effort to do my part in preventing this from occurring. The hyper-awareness switch stays on.

POIGNANCY AND TEARS

These are some examples of the times when I just want to cry, and sometimes I do.

When it takes 20 minutes to make a tuna fish sandwich with Mom. She will hold in one hand the fork I handed her, and she will hold the container of prepared tuna fish in the other hand, and the sliced bread will be on the cutting board in front of her, and Mom will have no idea what to do, even after I tell her again.

When she sits on the toilet and does not know what to do with the four sets of folded toilet paper that she has prepared and set on the counter top. And there is one additional set of folded toilet paper that she has put on the towel rack to the right of where she sits.

When she gets the evening's wash cloth wet and then hands it back to me and asks for the towel to dry her face. She forgot to wash her face, which remains dry. I tell her that she needs to wash her face first, and she snaps, in her old angry-mom voice, "I already did!" I do not bother to engage in correcting her. I just hand her the dry towel.

When she does not remember any of these events two minutes after they occur.

When she has fallen into the habit of saying, "Yeah" after I have spoken only three words, either telling her about something, or asking a question. I know full well that Mom has not heard, or been able to listen to, a single word.

When I know that it is pointless, most of the time, to use words in order to ask my Mom if she understood what I, or someone else, just said to her. How do you ask someone if they understand what is said, when that part of their brain is very old and has been severely damaged by stroke?

When I surrender to the idea that it really does not matter whether Mom understands my words or not. She knows she is safe. She knows she can trust me. She knows that she can count on me to take care of things. She does not know how painful it is for me to witness the deterioration of her mind.

When I acknowledge to myself that no one else has seen these aspects of Mom's decline and deterioration. *The visitors we occasionally have, even our dear friend Rose, has not seen the level of confusion and challenge which Mom faces when she tries to make something as simple as a tuna fish sandwich.*

Mom's condition has progressed, in a steep decline, over the last month. I've no idea why this is so, what to look for or what to expect. We have no speech therapist, no case manager, and although her primary care physician takes care of her blood work needs, he has not spent a total of an hour with Mom since the stroke, which occurred 19 months ago. The people who see Mom and me at the JCC on a regular basis see only the side of Mom which is still able to deal with pleasantries and salutations. The rabbis that I know have spent almost no time at all around Mom, and they, too, have only seen the pleasantries and salutations side of Mom.

Each evening when Mom is ready to lay down and sleep, we chant the Grace after Meals (in Hebrew) and then say the Shema. Tonight, my patience bottomed out when it took too much extra work in the bathroom to get Mom ready for bed. When I got her into her bedroom, we just said the Shema and I tucked her in.

I am not Superman or Super-Caregiver, and my patience occasionally runs thin. I admitted my lack of patience to Mom, apologized to her and asked if we could do the Grace after Meals, since we had not done it earlier. She looked at me with a knowing eye, took hold of my hand, and said that it was o.k. Mom's brain is injured from stroke and age, but she is not stupid. She may not remember exactly what she had done to try my patience, but she knew that I had run out of it. We benched (said) the Grace and I tucked her back into bed. Making amends, or apologizing, keeps things clean and clear around here. Dang it, I wish I was perfect at doing this deal. But I am not. I wish that I never screwed up and lost my patience. But I do.

November 6, 2014 -- "I will help you with everything you need help with. But you do not need help with everything."

Mom and I just had a most amazing talk which lasted about 45 minutes. It began with my noticing that she was sitting up in bed, so I went in to see if she was o.k. Mom was confused about why she has been so confused lately, and how she was missing people and places that she thought she once associated with. It ended with her "allowing" me to talk with her on a very deep level about her lifelong need to control her environment so that she would feel safe – safe from a relative she had, who had abused her in a variety of terrible ways when she was a little girl and as she grew into a young lady in her young teens. While we were talking, and actually talking back and forth, I noticed and was struck by the fact that Mom was actually listening, remembering and tracking what I was saying to her. Whatever part of her stroke-damaged brain that was activated was working as if there had been no stroke at all, except for a few mixed up words now and again. I shared my observation with Mom, and my belief that if she could follow and actively engage in conversation such as we were having right now, then it was possible that she could, with some work, be engaged like this on more occasions.

Other solo full-time caregivers might take heart in knowing that it is possible, or at least it was for me this evening, to be an elderly parent's son/caregiver/teacher all at the same time, and to address issues which have always been extremely sensitive and prone to not going well. My Mom's need to control her environment, and the conversations she participated in with other people, has driven a lot of people away over a lot of years. It has made other people be always aware that they must "walk on egg shells when talking with Marcie" or she will either cut them off and out of her life for a while, or she will blow up at them with an oftentimes acerbic tongue.

I took a gamble and spoke honestly with Mom - reassuring her several times that this was not a put-down, that I do not love her any less when she gets upset, and that I am not going to leave her or abandon her – and I told her of some occurrences, one even from today, when she got quite upset with me when she did not get what she wanted when she wanted it right now. I told her about how we used to work on writing and reading and sentences and words, and how she got upset about all of that, told me that she felt like I was putting her down, and how I just gave up on it – that I was honoring her wish to stop the work, and that I had no desire to be on the receiving end of her anger. I had to explain to Mom "what is a brain" so that she might understand my analogy of exercising her legs and body to keep them functioning, and how this was similar to exercising her mind. I told her how she had gotten upset about my working with her as her teacher, and how I just did not want to deal with her like that.

I told Mom all of this and she took it as a real "ah-ha" moment and an opportunity to grow as a mature woman. What I suggested to Mom, and she took it well, was that she put aside that little girl inside of her. She was no longer unsafe. She was no longer a little girl. She is a grown woman, well-educated with depth and wisdom, and she was very safe. The little girl did not serve her well any more. Mom said that perhaps tomorrow morning she could make a new start on things. We shall see. My closing words to her just came out of the blue, and I repeated them to her: "I will help you with everything you need help with. But you do not need help with everything." "Yes!" she said. "Yes, and thank you, son." Then I tucked her back into bed. Somewhere in our talking, Mom recognized what she had been doing for so many years, and how destructive that has been to her and many of the people who have dealt with her. She even said something to the effect of, "What a hard thing for you to have had to deal with, Aaron." And yes, it has been hard over the years to have a Mom who is, in so many ways, a scared and wounded little girl.

The duties of a caregiver, when dealing with an elderly parent, are very peculiar at times. We have to deal with the psychological makeup and quirks of our care recipients, and at times this can be quite frustrating, frightening, exhausting, and challenging in all kinds of other ways. Remember here that I, and other solo full-time caregivers who might be in similar circumstances, have to deal with Mom, or whoever the care recipient is, 24-hours-a-day. To risk a real conversation of great depth, calling on the other person to honestly take stock on the sometimes difficult ways that they deal with things, is to risk the whole atmosphere around the house. Fortunately, Mom and I have developed a level of trust and a level of communication which has, from time to time over the years, allowed us to work our way through these "bumps in the road" which so often sever, or severely damage, other peoples' relationships. Mom and I were both wounded as children, though in different ways. We are both recovered alcoholics, influenced largely by our wounded childhood years. And this similarity in our paths has allowed us to work pretty well together in these closing chapters of her life.

I wonder if there are other caregivers who have, or are, experiencing anything similar to what I am experiencing. If another caregiver ever reads this writing of mine, and has, or is having, similar experiences, I hope that he or she tracks me down and talks with me about it. Walking a strange and oftentimes unlit path, alone, is a very hard walk indeed.

November 6, 2014 -- My Mom, the gym (PT) rat. Working with a physical therapist, Dominique, who has known Mom for many years, is doing wonders for the old gal's arthritic knees, back, hips and shoulders. Being in pretty good shape for a woman her age helped Mom a lot when her stroke hit. The image of Mom sitting in her wheelchair, waiting for her PT session, watching a fish tank, alone, struck me as poignant. That there is a long empty hallway. All that it takes for any of us to not walk alone is to have someone care enough to walk with us, even if for just a short while. After all, each of us has our own journey.

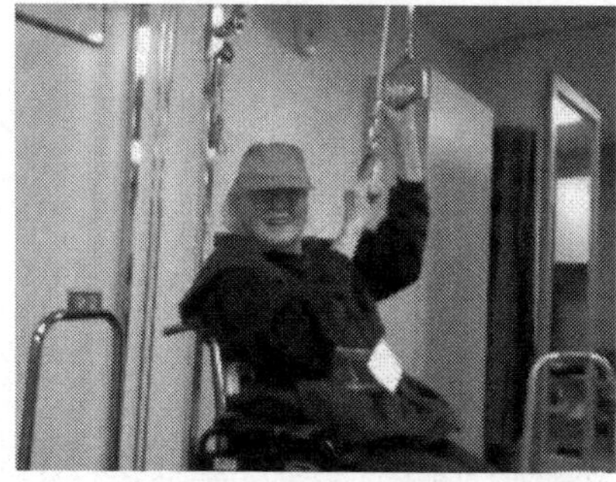

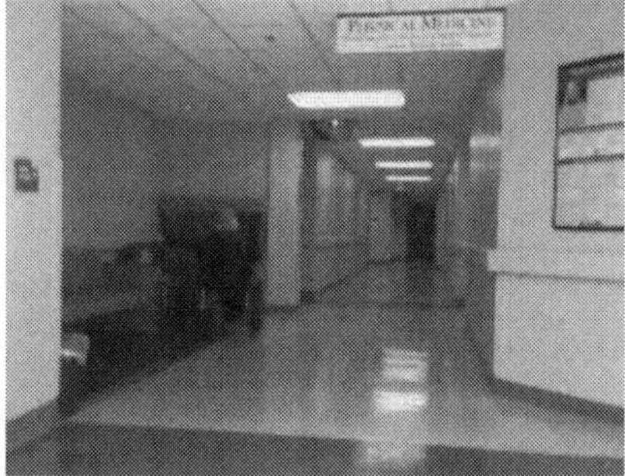

November 10, 2014 -- On November 7th, the morning after Mom and I had the late night talk I wrote about above, I gently and just in passing, asked Mom if she remembered us having a good talk last night.

She did not. I have mentioned, however, the "little girl just needs to go away right now" several times in the last few days, when Mom has gotten nervous about something as silly as making a sandwich, and my words have resonated with Mom somewhat, but not much. There continues to be very little short-term memory being laid down in Mom's brain. I wish I had a Rabbi to talk about this with, and yet G-d works in strange ways.

I have noticed that at times my writing is like I am talking with someone, sharing thoughts and stories. One might suppose that this is due to my not having much, if any, opportunity to talk at length with anyone other than Mom, and by now you know about her severe language deficit. When we go to the swim pool, I try not to talk much during the class, as it interrupts the instructor. When I take my short break from the pool, to take a steam and a shave, there is sometimes a friend in the steam room that I can talk with, but even that is just for 5-10 minutes and I have learned to be conscious about not talking someone's ear off and dominating a conversation. I became aware of this over a year ago, as I watched the body language of an old friend as he uncomfortably backed away from me. There have still been some times when my mouth gets going, but it has become less frequent as I have chosen to be more aware of conversing with, rather than talking to, someone. I may have written before that I believe it was my Dad, may he rest in peace, who taught me that every 2-3 sentences that I utter should be followed by a question. This engages the other person in the conversation.

The time that I have to myself is usually broken up into increments of perhaps an hour, before tending to something which Mom requires. It is only in the late evening hours that she gets into a deep sleep and does not call out for me. I am not at all kvetching (Yiddish for complaining) about this day, or any other day for that matter. It is just that with nobody else around in the house other than Mom and me, unless I write this down nobody will ever have an inkling about what our days look like, other than the snapshots other people see when we are out and about. So, if anyone reading this is not a full-time caregiver, let alone a solo full-time caregiver such as is the case in what I do, and if you know of, or meet, a full-time caregiver, please consider making yourself available to them now and again. You really do not know what they are living through each day, and how much a friendly and supportive contact might mean.

(Edit on February 13, 2019 – in hindsight, I did not know how to ask directly for help in areas which people might have been willing to help with. I might have asked someone to just come and make dinner for and with Mom, so that I can get out of here for a couple of hours. Might have worked out, or may not have. I did not know enough to try other than what I had already tried.)

December 1, 2014 -- At dinner this evening I once again noticed that Mom was sitting in her chair, her dinner before her on the TV tray, and she was at a complete stand-still, not knowing what to do. I said a quick silent prayer, asking G-d for the right words and direction, and I ventured to ask Mom what it was like when her mind went blank. I asked her if there were words in her mind when that happened. Her reply was, "No. I just go blank." A tender look came to her face, sadness and comprehension of what this implied.

She did, however, understand what this situation means after a bit more of our talking with each other. I told Mom that a friend of ours recently asked me whether Mom would be able to make a sandwich if I put all of the sandwich-making stuff in front of her. So, I asked Mom the following, "Mom. If I put a butter knife, a jar of mayonnaise, some bread and some sliced chicken on the kitchen counter in front of you, do you think you could make yourself a sandwich?" She told me that she could not. I then went ahead and explained to her, again, that this is why I will never leave her in the house alone. I told her it would neither be safe, morally correct nor legal to do so, leaving an at-risk adult alone in the house. I have explained this to her a few times before tonight, though she has no memory of my having done so. Mom's reply to me in the past has been, "Oh, how hard for you, son." Tonight, she just sort of pursed her lips in a sad little smile. She then said, "Well, that's that. Let's eat."

I write about this episode in hopes that another caregiver in a similar position might take heart, knowing that it is o.k. to have these kinds of talks with the recipient of our caregiving. Perhaps not all recipients, to be sure. I imagine that such raw honesty in conversation should only be done when the caregiver and the caregiving recipient have a very, very close bond. To help someone know that for the rest of their lives they will most likely never be left completely alone is a heavy truth to help another soul to understand, as much as they might be able to understand. In her own way, my Mom will remember some of the essence of what we talked about, though she will not be able to repeat or reconstruct our conversation, as I am doing now.

December 27, 2014 -- We had a nice visit from Rose this afternoon and Mom enjoyed her company immensely. Today was a quiet day around here, with Mom sleeping quite a bit, though I made sure that she was up and ready for Rose's visit. I hope that Rose reads this work of mine some day and knows how very special has been her visits, her calls and her regular contact with Mom and me. When it was time for Rose to head home, Mom was ready for some sleep and I asked Rose if she would like to walk Mom to her bedroom and tuck her in. She did and I am blessed to have been here to witness the love these two ladies have for each other. After Rose left, Mom commented to me how much she cares for Rose, and said, "We have known each other all these years."

Rose and Mom December 27, 2014

Evening – when I tucked Mom into bed, and after we had chanted the Grace After Meals and the Shema, Mom thanked me for being her "best friend." What more could a son want to hear. My Mom trusts me completely and we are, indeed, best of friends at this stage of our lives. What a beautiful deal this caregiving can be when I do not get caught up with my self-centered desires. It did not pass my attention that at times my Mother is able to express herself quite clearly. How this works in the realm of aphasia and dementia is beyond me.

December 28, 2014 -- Part of this caregiving work with Mom is bearing witness to the occurrences which I have heard about and read a bit about. This morning, when I went to Mom's bedroom to help her get up for breakfast, she told me that she had been talking with her Mother and that her Mother was happy now and at peace. I asked Mom if anyone else was there and she said that her aunt and her grandmother were there as well and that they were all fine. I asked her if her Dad was there and she told me that he was. This sort of thing has occurred several times in the last month or so and when Mom talks about it I just go with the flow of her conversation, refraining from asking her too many questions about it. The look of peace, fatigue and contentment on Mom's face is really quite beautiful.

January 3, 2015 -- Yesterday, when Mom woke up in the morning, she told me, "I was thinking of my Mom and Dad. I miss them." She had tears in her eyes. I sat down on her bed and we just quietly talked for a while. I wiped her gentle tears a few times and I just let her talk to me as she wished and as she could – mostly disjointed sentences, but she was able to share with me some memories of her Dad and she, working in the garden at their home. Mom also talked very lovingly about her Mother, several times letting me know how pretty she was.

Evening – 11:00 or so and I saw in my monitor that Mom was up a bit and adjusting her blankets, so I went in to help her get comfortable. I do this just about every night, sometimes a few times during the night if I wake up and see in my monitor that her covers have slipped off of her. When she is awake, I sit down and quietly talk with her, just making certain that she is o.k. and warm. Tonight, as happens so many nights, Mom was in a happy and content mood, gently stroking my arm as we talked about the day. I reminded her about the snow we watched this morning, and the squirrel and the rabbit that we got to watch in the snow. She laughed and said, "That was so nice." And she told me, obviously unaware of the lateness of the hour, to just go about my evening, with my music or whatever I felt like doing. I asked if it would disturb her sleep if I played my bass a bit before I went to bed, and she gave my arm another pat, smiled, and told me how nice that would be, saying, "It is always a pleasure, the music."

January 10, 2015 -- "Gee, we sure had a good day, honey." Those were Mom's words to me as she sat on her bed this evening and I was ready to help her change into her sleeping shirts, as I call them. We did, indeed, have a good day today.

SERIES OF MINI STROKES

January 17, 2015 -- "I don't know what to do." At 5:15pm Mom came to a complete stop and her eyes showed that she was not with me at all. I had just gone into her bedroom to get her up to help me prepare dinner. This was, I believe, another small stroke of some sort, the likes of which I have witnessed many times.

NOTE: I am writing this on February 23rd, from notes I have kept on my desk. I have quite a few notes of this sort to catch up on. January 17th marked a sharp downturn in Mom's language comprehension and in her ability to at least somewhat express herself with clarity.

March 26, 2015 -- It has been a change-filled couple of months, with regard to Mom's condition and my overall attitude and outlook. I have not taken the time to write in this treatise as regularly as I wish I would have, but Mom's needs have greatly increased and I simply have not been able to muster myself to take care of all that I wish. In these last couple of months I have found it difficult to focus my thoughts on anything other than getting through the day and preparing for the next one.

Regarding Mom's condition -- I made note a few pages back about witnessing yet another "mini stroke" if you will, on January 17th. In this past month, Mom has had a number of vascular events in her brain, resulting in greatly increased confusion, as well as markedly reduced language recognition. In fact, my estimation is that Mom's language recognition is almost nil most of the time.

Regarding my condition -- I spent an hour on my bass guitar a few days ago, while a couple of men were here in our home, working on installing a new furnace, and that was the first time I had even touched it in about a week. There are, of course, still 24 hours in each day, just as there was a year ago, when I seemed to be able to spend a lot of time writing and playing bass, and still caring 24 hours a day for Mom's needs. What has changed is me. I am fatigued much of the time. Fatigued to the bone at times, physically and emotionally. Perhaps the word "numb" would be appropriate.

It may honestly be written here, today anyway, that I no longer feel much judgment or resentment towards family and friends who are not around, and who have not been around to actively support my efforts to provide for Mom's caregiving needs. This does not mean that their help would not have made things easier, smoother and more constructive for me, and for Mom. Not at all. <u>Mom put is very clearly a number of months ago when she told me, "This would have been easier if they had been around." She was, and is, correct.</u> But the fact that they have not been around has not been eating my lunch for a couple of months now. I am able to think of these people with love and understanding in my heart. Most of the time.

I have come to see, and come to believe, that my expectations have oftentimes been unrealistic. This applies to my expectations of others and my expectations of myself. It is through finally coming to see this that surrender, acceptance and peace of mind have been achieved, or probably more accurately, given to me. Most of the time, anyway. Remember, I am not a tzaddik. I continue to have my hours of melancholy, anguish and frustration, but they are shorter-lived than in the past 18-20 months. And I still have my moments with Mom when I lose my patience, raise my voice and am not at my best. And then I apologize to her.

Following, are a couple of pictures of what Mom does when left alone for a few minutes during dinner preparation. Our dinners are similar most nights, with a bowl of our soup, a sandwich and something else to go with the sandwich, such as a boiled egg, some baked squash and/or a slice of pickle. I am usually in the kitchen with Mom, directing her as to what to do, one step at a time. Putting mayonnaise, or hummus, on the bread is her standard job, as is peeling and cutting the hard boiled eggs. It is not unusual for Mom to come to a complete stop, butter knife in hand, and tell me, "Honey, I just went blank." I have written previously about Mom's general inability to sequence anything. We can have all of the sandwich makings in front of her and she will have no idea how to put it all together. The same holds true in the morning when we are making a bowl of cereal for breakfast.

Last night I gave her instructions to cut the eggs in half and then put hummus on the bread while I went downstairs for a few minutes. I knew that Mom would have a challenging time with getting these two tasks done correctly. To be direct and honest, I knew that she would not get it right and I told myself, "I wonder how this will turn out."

The picture on the left is from last night: the eggs got cut in half and then put on the bread, with hummus put on one of the egg halves. Mom had a fork with hummus on it in her right hand and had come to a complete stop. She said to me something like, "Honey, I think I got this kind of goofy." We had a good-natured chuckle together. No put-downs or ill feelings, just a good hearty laugh. And then I helped straighten it out.

The picture on the right is from a similar scenario during dinner preparation on February 24th. We were having chicken sandwiches with a pickle slice and some canned corn. Everything was laid out on the kitchen counter in front of Mom's chair, where she sits while we prepare meals. I told Mom that I was stepping outside for a few minutes and I wanted to see if she could prepare our plates. You can see from the lovely smile on Mom's face that she took it in stride and with good humor that evening. And who says you cannot put corn on a chicken sandwich?

Please, Dear Reader, pause for a few minutes and read again the above paragraph, and contemplate the ramifications of dealing with someone in Mom's condition. It is quite difficult to talk someone through their confusion and upset when that talking requires the use of words and it is the confused person's brain's word center which has been irreparably damaged. And then add a dollop of dementia, hold the onions, please. And then contemplate dealing with that person 24 hours a day, engaging with that person whenever they are awake, because otherwise they would just be sitting alone. Nobody around for them to talk with or interact with. And then contemplate dealing with, and being responsible for, that person for almost two years straight, with no respite, relief or breaks other than a few times, for a few hours each time, over these almost two years. Think about that for a few minutes, please.

Although this may sound to some people like Aaron is indulging in self-pity, or "Poor me, look how hard this is..." I really am not. I write the above two paragraphs to illustrate, or paint a small picture of, the reality of the work that I, and other caregivers, have freely chosen to engage in, providing for someone's caregiving needs. Explaining a challenging reality is not always an indulgence in self-pity. Sometimes it is, but not now. I have, to be sure, indulged too often in self-pity in this writing, and I am neither ashamed of it, nor am I defending it. I have done the best that I have been able to do, and that is enough. Self-pity is just something which I have had to travel through and which I am now able to avoid much of the time, but not enough of the time.

TRANSCRIPTION OF MOM AND AARON TALKING

The following is a transcript of a brief conversation I had with Mom a couple of weeks ago. It is a good illustration of Wernicke's Aphasia. For any other caregiver who might be reading this, please note that I do not interrupt Mom when she is talking to me. It is pointless, at this stage of her decline, to try to help or instruct Mom in the language area. It does not work and Mom finds it annoying and degrading. In her own way, she has let me know that she prefers that I do not put on my "teacher's hat." When I remember to just go with it, which I am able to do most of the time, we really have pleasant conversations and enjoyable times together. At this stage of her life, that is the kind approach and attitude for me to take.

I have many hours of recorded conversations with Mom since the stroke occurred. I even recorded our talks while she was in the hospital in the days and weeks after the stroke. My plan now is to transcribe a few of these talks and insert them into this treatise at the appropriate chronological places. It has dawned on me that I have mentioned "Wernicke's Aphasia" lots of times in this writing, yet have provided only one example of what it is. I have assumed that the reader either already is familiar with this sort of aphasia or will take the time to search it out and familiarize himself or herself with the malady. Perhaps the reader is a caregiver and the recipient of their caregiving has some form of aphasia. Or perhaps the reader has a friend or family member who is afflicted with this malady. *I posted this transcription on my Facebook page and a friend of mine commented that they saw poetry in Mom's speech. Beautiful perspective, eh?*

Sunday March 15, 2015

Aaron – So, it's Sunday, March 15th
Mom – Here, you mean? Yeah, oh yeah.
Aaron – So, what day of the week is it?
Mom – Well, it's Sunday now.
Aaron – And we're eating breakfast.
Mom – Yes.
Aaron – Can you tell me what are we having for breakfast?
Mom – From being out of the sun. Sunday. We're close, whatever. That they have been given looking around at who are the main ones who are there now. That they can say how much it is worthwhile eating or seeing or parts just in from here and across right there about 10 across and eating at that term, right? And our kids, one way or another, had something in there that they have there and they are really substance, aren't they?

Aaron – Yes. So I brought breakfast outside to the squirrels.
Mom – Yes, yes, yes.
Aaron – And we are eating breakfast. What are we eating?
Mom – And then what we are looking for. What we were that we had the places that we made it through this weekend, that's how we're staying off that part of what they kind of moved out today again. Can you see that? Wholesome. Now looking around who had written taking care of whatever, look at the people who were brought here. Look how quality.
Aaron – Do you see a squirrel on the fence?
Mom – Yes, I was here they are or warm or whatever it is or, touching a little, and for where they are where they're leaving for right now one little bit here or there, it's one of the direct people from it, right? And the kid would be and the immediate would be look at how they are very very significant.
Aaron – Why are they significant?

Mom – It's what they're here for, this very clearly part. They are here, using eating, whatever they're doing, they're finishing whatever they're doing. And then we're looking now just within bits here and there coming around and just from now these days you know we have been seeing how they have been eating these couple days. Now today our guys are indirected to be seeing, don't you think? And there quality.
Aaron – Are there any squirrels out there now?
Mom – mm-hmm.
Aaron – Where?
Mom – mm-hmm.
Aaron – Look!
Mom – Where are they?
Aaron – On the ground.
Mom – Yes. (laughter)
Aaron – He's in the flower pot.
Mom – Yeah. (laughter) Look at that, sweetheart. And that what he's there with and his real, that real part, you look through what he's doing and that's a head. Yeah, that's real stuff on him. Oh my, oh my, oh my and then he's checked little bits. Look at that. Yeah, see. Now that's the kind of stuff he has done and he's only gonna do a little bit right there. Yes. Now he's going to stay right there and over and just went above. See him over there? And he does see for them to see him for this amount that that's who he's the most. (laughter)

April 12, 2015 -- Of grape tea on a hamburger bun/bread, the words “nursing home” and 43 years forgotten years of sobriety. I will never know what Mom was thinking as she spooned grape tea onto the bread.

April 24, 2015 -- One of the most difficult things to believe or understand is that a person like Mom, with Wernicke’s Aphasia, <u>may perceive what we are saying to her to be “word salad.”</u> The implications of this are deep. Ponder that for a few minutes, dear reader. Ponder that.

April 26, 2015 -- 9:40pm -- “You’re precious, darling. You’re a real person.” These were Mom’s last words to me just now, after she had called me into her room and quietly asked me if it was o.k. if she just went to sleep. She had gone to bed a couple of hours ago. She told me that she just felt real quiet today but would “start afresh tomorrow,” which is an expression that Mom often uses, as she has done for quite a few years now. I asked her if her feeling quiet was o.k. with her, and she smiled and told me that it was. I told her it was o.k. with me, too. I reminded her that today has been cool and rainy, and that a gentle rain was now falling outside. She smiled at that. And I reminded her how lovely everything looked outside with the rain falling on it, how happy the little seedlings in our garden looked in the rain. She smiled at that, too. And I told her that, as an experiment, I had just put some of the seedlings from our dining room table outside and into the rain, hoping that the rain water would be good for them. And Mom smiled at that, as well. Then, I lifted and straightened out her bed covers, which allowed her to turn herself over onto her left side, and I tucked her in again. <u>I write all this detail so that I will remember and not forget.</u>

(Edit on May 21, 2019 – The above is a nice memory to recall. All too often, now that Mom is gone, I only have memories of the times I fell short of the mark as my Mother's caregiver.)

These photos are from yesterday, April 25, 2015.

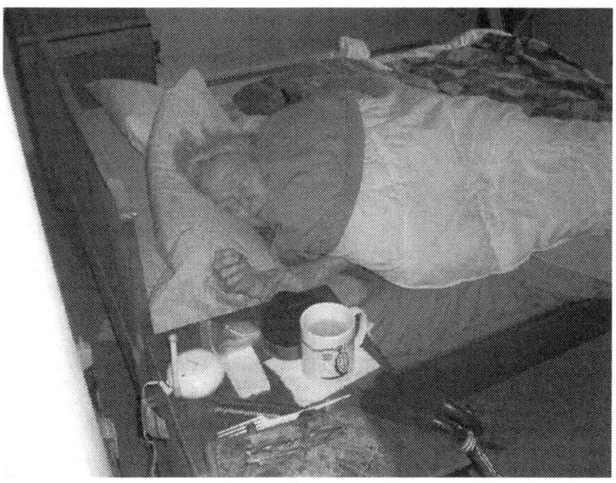

The round white thing with the antenna on it is a microphone. There is a small video camera on the other side of Mom's room. This is how I keep an eye and an ear on her.

June 2015 -- Mom enjoys some garden work...

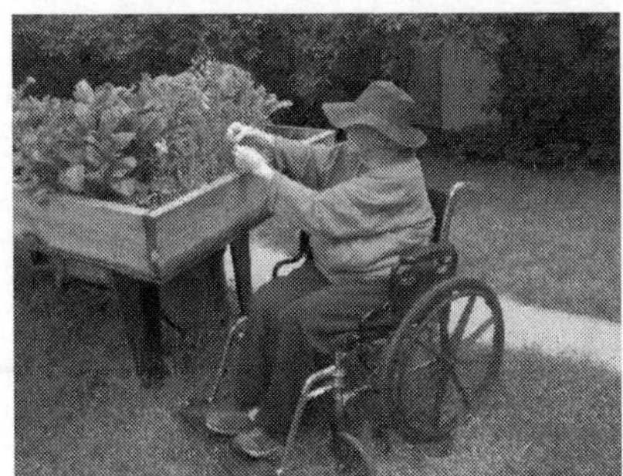

Humbling.
Embarrassing.
Self-reflective thinking.
Opportunity for character growth.

Perhaps another caregiver will gain strength to know that they are not the only one to occasionally, and subconsciously, have self-seeking, self-centered and badly selfish motives. It happens. We are human. We are not perfect. This job is tough. Caregiving is a marathon – a marathon with no set finish line. We will, and do, hit the wall on occasion.

The above thoughts come to mind as I consider a truth which was revealed to me last night, and which brought about an attitudinal and behavioral change in me which I have experienced today and, hopefully, will continue to ponder and grow into.

The truth is this: When I "quiz" my Mom, even with such a mundane question as "Is this baseball or football, which we are watching?" I know for certain that Mom will fail the quiz almost all of the time. She has yet to even be able to answer the baseball/football question without offering up a plate of word salad. I consciously avoid quizzing her, and am able to do so most of the time. The SLP (speech language pathologist) who evaluated Mom last December even complimented me on not quizzing her, as she has seen so many other caregivers do.

Practicing something which a person is almost certain to fail can be good exercise and I believe that it should be done periodically. It cannot hurt to access, or try to access, anyway, the part of Mom's brain which is either injured or in such steep decline. It cannot hurt. The question which I pondered is, "What are my motives?" What are my motives when I say or type the phrase "solo full-time caregiver" as I so often do? My conscious intent is to be accurately descriptive about my work with Mom. "Full-time caregiver" and "solo full-time caregiver" are two completely different levels of caregiving. But am I really telling people, "Look at how difficult the job is which I have taken on." Nauseating, isn't it? And humbling...and true. I so wish I was Superman Caregiver. But I am not.

July 3, 2015 -- The peaceful relationship between Mom and I continues to deepen as her needs and her confusion grow. I have been able to refrain from quizzing her since I last wrote about it. An unexpected result of this is that I am generally more relaxed, though I am more contemplative and quiet around here (our home.) It takes a deep surrender to acknowledge that quizzing and working with Mom has no positive payoff for her. Initial sadness is slowly but surely being replaced with acceptance and gratitude.

At the swim class today, I mentioned to a friend of mine, Rabbi Buz Bogage, that I sure wished I could get to a place of serenity in this caregiving and stay there. I told him that I generally am in and out of a peaceful state of mind. I want to be like the older ladies in the movies who are caregivers and who are always positive, upbeat and incredibly patient at all times. And in those movies, the caregiver ladies always had the house spotless, though I did not mention this to my friend. I acknowledge here that my view of some things in the world around me has always been influenced by unrealistic and over-romanticized notions of what could be, particularly if I could only figure out how to make it happen.

After reminding me that my expectations of myself were based on a movie, and therefore not realistic, my Rabbi friend shared a simple wisdom with me: *"It's the moments, man. It's the moments that we get.*

It's all about the moments." What may have seemed like a simple truth for him to share struck me deeply, and I have thought about his words several times today, particularly when I noticed that I was starting to get uptight, or sad or fearful of what lies ahead as Mom continues her rapid decline and I will be called upon to figure out what to do.

July 11, 2015 -- It is incredibly sad to me that we live in a world where being honest about important things, with people we know, can come at a great price. My caregiving duties have, as I have written countless times before, brought about a level of almost complete isolation from friends and people Mom and I both know. If it appears to anyone reading this, and any caregivers in particular who might be reading this, that I dwell on this isolation and abandonment issue too frequently, please stop and consider that when one is, indeed, alone except for when one is able to take the recipient of one's caregiving out of the house, it is natural that isolation and abandonment by friends and family is a topic of regular occurrence. To expect me not to think about it very often is like expecting someone with cancer (G-d forbid) not to think about it very often. Please cut me some slack. Thank you.

KEEP IT SIMPLE – AND NO ROOM FOR COMPLACENCY

July 24, 2015 -- I frightened my Mom this evening. It was unintentional and inadvertent, and a humbling reminder to me to remain very, very mindful of what should be my and, I believe, every other caregiver's #1 guiding rule in caregiving – KEEP IT SIMPLE! It was an innocuous scenario which I allowed to get complicated tonight – we were making a nice salad plate to enjoy with a bowl of soup for dinner. A salad, of all things, got complicated and out of hand – too much for Mom's damaged brain to comfortably deal with.

A few days ago, a friend of ours brought us four different salad dishes – artichoke salad, 3 bean salad, curried chicken and a marinated dish of several different vegetables. We have enjoyed putting some of each of them on a basic tossed salad which we make ourselves, but for some odd reason it got too complicated for Mom to enjoy making with me this evening. I saw, and sensed, that she was getting overly nervous while we were making dinner, and at the time I attributed it to Mom just being tired from the day. But after we sat down in the living room, Mom had a peculiar look on her face, and she was real quiet, like she gets when she is nervous.

I sat down next to her and asked what was wrong. For some reason it occurred to me to ask if she was afraid of something. She said that she was. Again, for some reason, I asked her if she was afraid of me – if I had frightened her. And she said, "Yes." I was, and still am, stunned at her reply. Unfortunately, with Mom's severe aphasia she is not able to clearly tell me what I had done to scare her. I asked her if she would prefer that I find someone else to help her, because I surely do not want to be a source of any fear. She was able to communicate to me that she knows that she gets nervous and fearful – her exact words – and she told me that she knows she gets fearful when she does not know what to do. That is the clue that leads me to believe that having too many dishes and bags of salad in front of her was most likely what overwhelmed her.

The pictures above are from a dinner we enjoyed two nights ago. You will see three salad containers (two in plastic bags) in a rectangular Tupperware container, which Mom is working on. The picture on the left also shows a small container, with a fork in it, which has feta cheese. Both pictures also show that tossed salad container to the right of Mom's right arm. What was added tonight was a fourth container in the rectangular Tupperware, and I believe that this added item was just too much for Mom to deal with. In all sorts of other areas in my work as a caregiver, I am very much aware of how much visual stimuli there is in Mom's field of vision. Her age and stroke-damaged brain must work hard to try to make sense of what she is seeing and what she has to deal with.

It is almost midnight now; six and a half hours after we were making dinner, and I have reviewed in my mind how I had set out the dishes which we worked with. The bags of salad, having been emptied somewhat over the last few nights, were difficult to get a spoon into, and she spilled some stuff onto the floor. That is no big deal to me, but I remember Mom telling me, years ago, how little things like that would send her family member into a violent rage when she was a kid. When Mom started spilling a couple of things is when she began getting nervous. I did not pick up on it. I was not being as mindful and sensitive to her mood change as I most always am. I was just thinking about helping her so that she could help us, make dinner, using several tasty dishes. The little things, like a half-empty zip lock baggie which might be difficult for her to deal with; a countertop with too many items on it; a dinner plate which was getting filled up and "cluttered" with too many different items, are the little things which I failed to pay heed to. I believe that this whole scenario is what triggered my Mom's fear and led her to be afraid of me. I was the one directing our actions. I was the source of the fear she was feeling, and it hurts me deeply to think that after two years of caregiving I was so totally blind to what was going on.

(Edit on February 16, 2019 – re-reading this piece, and the above episode in particular, brings up strange feelings in me right now. Compassion, sorrow, tenderness at the thought that something as innocuous as making dinner and spilling a bit onto the floor might trigger old painful memories of violence in my Mom's, or anyone's life. She had a sibling who was quite abusive. Let's see if we can all be nicer, more accepting and tolerant and more loving to each other, shall we Dear Reader? The damage done to my Mom when she was a little girl has had ramifications which ripple and have caused further damage to people, to this day. Those details I will keep to myself.)

It is humbling to think that by being helpful – facilitating Mom being able to help with meal preparations – I caused her great fear and discomfort. Just by trying to be helpful. And then – after we had talked it out as best as we are able, I noticed what I thought was a small fly, flitting around on the inside of the screen door of our dining room. I walked over to the screen and gently grabbed the creature in my hand so that I could put it outside, where it belonged and where it seemed to be trying to get to. Again, just trying to be helpful. And then the little bugger bit me. Bit me right on the palm of my hand. And it hurt. It think it was a flying ant or something of that sort, and it did not want, or appreciate, my trying to be helpful. It bit me and it hurt. It was, I believe, a solid spiritual reminder/lesson for me to be mindful on a higher level of what I am doing and how I am doing it. In hindsight I should have used a tissue to capture the bug and put it outside. It obviously was not a regular fly, but I did not stop to think clearly about it. In hindsight, I should have put the salads in containers which are easy for Mom to deal with, and should have only brought out 2-3 of them, as we have done before, rather than all four containers. I knew better than to clutter her visual field. I just did not think about it tonight.

There is a point to this story tonight, and it is more than just a "journal entry" about another day of caregiving. There is a point here for myself, and hopefully other caregivers, to take note of and learn from: **Complacency has no place in caregiving.** No place at all. Being attentive to, and mindful of, the little things is what allows the big picture, so to speak, to work smoothly and comfortably for the people who are the recipients of our caregiving. This is not easy. It is not easy at all to be mindful and attentive, at a high level, at all times, Dear Reader. It is exhausting; mentally and emotionally exhausting. When the recipient of our caregiving gets confused, overwhelmed and frightened, because of our lack of attentiveness, we have failed in our duties and responsibilities.

To write that I have failed might be an overstatement, false pride perhaps, but I hold myself to a high level of expectations about doing this job, and obviously I am not perfect. This is a spiritual acceptance which I struggle with throughout each and every day. When I mess something up for my Mom, as I did tonight at dinner, I must be careful not to allow my error to be a source of depression and self-deprecation. I have a choice here; a choice to utilize this as a stark reminder of the sacred duty which I have taken upon myself, and I have a choice here to utilize this as a clear opportunity to reinforce my level of thought in all that Mom and I do together. Keep it simple, Aaron. Remember and do not forget. Be mindful at all times, fellow caregivers, even when your reserves are depleted, your emotions are tattered and raw, your spirit is exhausted and your body is tired. We have taken on a sacred duty indeed, and it calls for our best efforts at all times.

Sacred duty. Sacred duty? That may sound pretty high-falootin' (outdated term meaning arrogant or presumptuous) to some folks, but stop and think about the responsibility I and other caregivers have taken upon ourselves. In my Mom's situation, she is dependent upon me for every facet of her day-to-day living. My job is to facilitate, prepare, provide, oversee, and guard, everything that goes into her body. Food. Medicine. Fluids. Social interaction. Conversation. Filtering out unhealthy people and/or circumstances. Her safety in all areas and at all times is my responsibility. Think about a parent's sacred duty to their child, particularly at the vulnerable early years. Now reverse the roles. Sacred duty for a caregiver? You bet your backside! We caregivers are not just drawing a (usually nonexistent) paycheck and then going home. First we need to CARE. Then we need to GIVE. Then we are a CARE-GIVER. Enough pontificating, Aaron! Any more will indeed begin to sound high-falootin'. A Rabbi friend of mine, one of the oldest in town, might even say I was getting to sound preachy. And he would be correct! I talk too much sometimes. And let me tell you why.........................bonk! Silly man...

July 25, 2015 -- NOTE: After writing the above and having gone downstairs to read a bit before sleep, I remembered one of the truths which guided me in my work with students in special education: *When their behavior gets upset or off base, it is usually something that I have done, not done, or am doing. I found this axiom to be true in almost all cases.*

July 26, 2015 -- I am picking up a thread from my writing of two nights ago, regarding dinner preparation with too many items on the counter and in Mom's line of sight. We had a similar dinner tonight, but with only two side salads, both of which I took from their zip lock baggies and put into small familiar plastic containers. It still took us some time to put dinner together, but Mom was noticeably more relaxed and comfortable. Another change in dinner prep that I did was to only put a couple of things at a time in front of Mom, and that definitely made a positive difference. Live and learn. It's 9:00pm and I am exhausted from today's work.

LET GO. LET BE.

July 29, 2015 -- Let go. Let be. Let go. Let be. Let go. Let be. Let go. Let be. Rabbi Buz shared that meditation with me. He only said it once, though.

While sitting quietly under a tree in our back yard, smoking a cigarette, I've taken a few minutes to meditate on the above before coming back inside to get ready to prepare dinner for Mom and me. Twenty minutes ago, Mom called me into her room, where she has been resting/napping since we got home from the pool. Her words were neologisms – made up words which make sense only to her – which I repeated back to her and to which she said, "Yes, yes." I said, "Is that o.k.?" And she again said, "Yes." I told her that we would put dinner together in a little while, and then I went outside to sit under a tree.

Let go. Let be. There is nothing I can do to change Mom's condition, rarely are there words I can use which she will understand, and there is nobody who has been around enough to witness these occasions. The occasional visitor is treated to Mom's patented "Blessings, blessings, love, love." That is her default setting, and has been since long before the stroke hit.

Edit on August 9, 2019 – Actually, Rabbi Buz shared those words with me many times. It would sink in for a while and I would find peace. Then I found myself tied up in knots once again. Three simple words, "Let go. Let Be." Two simple concepts, on the surface anyway. Those two ideas sum up much of what is at the core of spiritual practice, surrender, acceptance, etc. And I have struggled mightily to get there and stay there. An axiom in the recovery community is; "How do I hang on? Let go." There are quite a few teachings of that sort, and it is only now, as I work with and listen to a grief therapist, that I am coming to see my part in the angst and struggle, pain and sense of loss, which I have been holding onto, based on perceptions which have been skewed by the years of caregiving and relative isolation.

The details of what I am learning I will keep to myself, as they are my own lessons and my own truths. In hindsight, I wish I had known 3-4 years ago what I am coming to see more clearly now. But that is not how this journey has worked out for me. In hindsight, I wish I would have sought out personal help 3-4 years ago, but I did not. I could not. I did not know how. *If this resonates with you, Dear Reader, and you are experiencing similar angst, struggles, pain, sense of loss, etc., I suggest you consider that intense caregiving can skew one's perceptions. I know from my own experience that sometimes the following suggestion is easier said than done: Find a way to get help!*

July 31, 2015 -- Let go. Let be. Let there be chocolates once again in a heart-shaped Valentine's Day box on Mom's nightstand.

"These just aren't very good." That's what Mom said to me about 15 minutes ago when I went to check on her after seeing in my video monitor that she was sitting up in bed. When I sat down on the bed with her, she offered me something from the small glass bowl of grapes and sliced carrots on her nightstand, which had replaced her box of chocolates a few weeks ago. Mom's dentist told me that Mom had some deeper pockets around some of her teeth, and the dentist expressed some concern about them. I told her that Mom likes to eat small pieces of chocolate during the night. The dentist said, "Aarrrggghhhh!" So, I talked with Mom about it and she agreed to go with carrots and grapes. Stoic lady, she goes out with me to exercise at the pool, or run the necessary household errands when she would much rather go back to bed, but she was not at all happy about carrots and grapes at night. Mom did ask me to comb her hair before I took the picture.

The heck with stoicism! Mom is 85 years old and likes her chocolate at night. I'll work with her to brush and floss more often. We both had a good laugh, and a piece of chocolate, before I tucked her back into bed.

Sleep well, Mom, and may your chocolates help you to have sweet dreams. Sometimes, caregiving requires breaking down that word: "CARE enough to be GIVING the person what their heart truly desires." I cannot give her youth, or a non-stroke-damaged brain, or the people she misses, and I cannot cure the aphasia, but I can give her the chocolates which bring her such simple pleasure and comfort. And after all, isn't that what the essence is often all about - particularly at 85 years?

I was becoming seriously concerned about having a heart attack or stroke myself. It is bad enough that I smoke cigarettes (a lot more than I was before Mom's stroke) and that my sleeping habits are atrocious, waking up every couple of hours to check on Mom, but those two things, coupled with constant high levels of worry, stress and discontent, could very well kill me. And then where would Mom be? That continues to be a concern of mine – it's that lack of a contingency plan thing – but I am more and more conscious of dismissing those thoughts when they come to mind. There simply is nothing that I can do about it. There is nobody to turn to except G-d. My self-will (stress) has been blocking me from developing, or allowing myself to feel, 100% faith in G-d, even though intellectually I have told myself that I have complete faith in Him. One line that I say in my morning prayers is, "No expectations of others. 100% faith in You." I have meant it, but I have not actually felt it in my heart enough of the time.

August 3, 2015 -- Back to basics these past mornings, as Mom sleeps so deeply that she is unaware of her need to go to the bathroom. I have had to change the sheets on her bed, as well as her clothes, of course, four out of the last five mornings. What is really kind of interesting is that Mom is not only nonplussed about it, she is totally unware of what has happened. Perhaps other caregivers deal with this in the same way? I just walk with Mom to the bathroom so that she can sit on the commode and do whatever she needs to do, as I change the bed linens. Waterproof absorbent mattress pads under the sheets help to keep the mattress dry. I then help her change into dry clothes and then we go on to breakfast.

It is 5:00pm now, and about time to turn thoughts towards dinner. I would, however, dearly love to either nap, get on the exercise bike or pick up my bass. Or mop the kitchen floor, vacuum the carpets, clean the bathrooms, clean the windows, weed the garden, read a book etc. So it goes. Some may ask why I take the time to write this stuff. I'll state it again, dear reader. My hope is that sharing this experience, via this writing, will be of service to someone else some day. Mom is getting more and more confused, aphasiac, confronted with dementia. A new normal presents itself all too regularly.

August 7, 2015 -- Tasty tomato from our garden. It found its way onto our dinner salad this evening (Friday night.) The look on my Mom's face, particularly her eyes, says it all sometimes. But even this is just a snapshot of a single point of time, late in the day when her brain is real fatigued. We had been working together on Shabbas candles, prayers and making a salad. That was enough to tire her out and confuse her thought processes. It is simply amazing to witness every day. This evening, the look in her eyes got me. I was extra mindful to keep things filled with love, tenderness, peace and quiet, and Mom sort of "came back." Sometimes her thoughts just sort of seem to travel somewhere and I have learned, or intuitively known, to keep it simple and calm and wait it out.

Quiet routine is the order each day. We sat outside for a bit after dinner, before she headed to bed for the night. And we enjoyed watching some wildlife action this morning, around the bird feeder. Two pigeons made the scene. That was a first for us to witness. Mom got a real kick out of that.

Aaron: “Thank you, G-d, for Shabbas.”
Mom: “Thank you Shabbagas.”

It is 12:40am Saturday morning, August 8th, and I just sat with Mom and shared some chocolate with her, having seen in my video monitor that she was sitting up in her bed. We had a good laugh or two at some silly notion about eating too much chocolate. That is when I told her that it was Shabbas and that we should just eat the chocolate and enjoy it, because G-d wants us to enjoy the gift of Shabbas, which He gave to us. I held up a piece of the chocolate and said what I typed above, and Mom repeated it, in her own way. I’m quite certain that G-d does not mind the way that Mom speaks.

August 18, 2015 -- I realize that what I am providing for my Mom is unique and rare, as is the relationship which exists between her and me. Maybe it is because we are both recovered alcoholics. Maybe it is because we both chose, many years ago, not to let little differences of opinion, or conflicts, erupt into relationship-severing monsters. Her family did that, and my family did/does that. Not only does it not have to occur, that severing thing, but when it is overcome and worked through, uncomfortable as that may be to do, the relationship gains a strength which is something else. She and I still butt heads on occasion, and with her aphasia it is challenging to talk her through it. But we do it. This caregiving for an elder is not for everyone, to be sure. It is sometimes like watching that old sunflower just get older....scary for some folks, apparently, so they had best stay away from this sort of spiritual gardening. Or....they might just jump in.

September 15, 2015 -- Honor thy Mother and thy Father....sometimes - most of the time, really at this stage of Mom's life - it means going with the flow. Day #2 of Rosh Hashanah, such as it is around here. No family contact. Dang... Obviously though, as I type this on Rosh Hashanah, I am not a strictly observant Jewish man. I’ll leave the judging to G-d. I’m just doing the best I can, being of service to my Mother. I wonder what my one sibling with whom I am in contact would do, regarding seeing to it that Mom was placed somewhere, if something happened to me. Darn that missing contingency plan! Darn it!

Here are a few things which transpired today while helping my Mom. Welcome to a glimpse into the world of dementia. Early onset Dementia.

Morning – I put toothpaste on Mom's toothbrush and handed it to her, turning my back for just a moment to dry my hands on a towel. I turned around to see Mom using the toothbrush on her left forearm.

Breakfast – I handed Mom the little plastic bear which has honey in it, and which we use every morning on our cereal. Mom turned to me and said, "How do I use this?"

Dinner Preparation – I handed Mom a fork for her to put tuna fish on our sandwiches. She asked me, "Which side do I use?"

Dinner – I brought in what was left in our little soup pot, to see if Mom wanted some more soup with her dinner. I hold the pot and leave the large spoon in it for Mom to help herself, as has been done countless times before. She started to put the soup on her plate rather than in the bowl.

Sweet Potatoes on a Napkin

Boiled Eggs on Bread
Hummus on Egg

The above may be natural or normal for someone in Mom's physical and age-stage condition. I do not know. It has just become normal for Mom to have very little comprehension of what we are doing or what is going on around her. And with language comprehension virtually at zero, it can be – it is, really – very challenging to work through.

September 29, 2015 -- Morning - Mom's awareness of her surroundings is slipping quickly. She was up at 2:30 this morning, completely unaware of where she was. It took me a bit of time to sit with her and reorient her. Now think about how this would be done – I must use words to remind Mom that she is in her own bedroom, in her own house, in her own bed, it is dark outside and, as I pick up a small clock to show her, it is 2:30 in the morning. The clock means nothing to her. Nor do my words, most of the time. This all requires her to use the word recognition part of her brain, and that part is severely damaged.

She called for me at about 9:00, needing to use the bathroom. Mom must have used the words "beautiful" and "incredible" about 20 times – as she pointed to a corner of the bathroom near the commode, as she tore off some toilet paper and held it up for me to see, with no awareness, again, of what the purpose of the toilet paper is. Mom's awareness of the world around her is slipping quickly into an awareness which I am barred from seeing. I can witness her witnessing it, but I cannot see what she sees. I choose to view this as a cosmic awareness she is experiencing; a gift from G-d for her alone, in which she is allowed to see the essence of things. I choose this point of view for now, because the word "dementia" still frightens me. I am trying not to give too much thought as to what her path ahead might look like, with me providing the caregiving. It is beyond unquestionable that her caregiving needs will continue to escalate.

Evening -- In Mom's bathroom there is posted a card which reads, "Our home is a place where G-d abides and where love, laughter and light are shared." She frequently asks me to read it to her. We do, indeed, have a good deal of laughter, Mom and I do. We are not in denial about the challenges she is faced with and which continue to grow in scope, but living in doom and gloom is just not something which has been done in this house for a long, long time.

DEMENTIA – FRONT AND CENTER

October 6, 2015 -- I wonder if Mom thinks, or daydreams, or remembers in pictures or in words. This is a very strange part of the journey. Little, if any, doing left to be done. Lots of just being. I have often wondered, over the past year in particular, how the slow down would arrive. My gut told me that it would be incremental yet unmistakable. It has been, and it is.

Evening – Mom spent all but two hours in bed today, resting/sleeping and periodically calling for me about things which she was unable to clearly explain. She was very content, though, and appreciative of the food I brought to her, as well as the orange juice, fruit and chocolates. I sat with her a few times, chatting as we do, a conversation which no outsider would likely be able to follow.

I have been hanging on to my bit of spiritual peace by my fingertips, and that is just not sustainable. And, it is no fun. As a caregiver, and for any other full-time caregivers (again, solo full-time caregivers in particular) who might be reading this, a healthy mental state is absolutely crucial in order to provide healthy caregiving over the long term. This is much, much easier said than done.

October 13, 2015 -- Going out to my car today with Mom, I was struck by the severity of Mom's cognitive deficit, and her lack of awareness regarding what we are doing, where we might be going and what she is, and has been, engaged in. I have seen a cartoon recently, in which an elderly man is standing at the bottom of a staircase. The caption reads something to the effect of, "Was I going upstairs for something, or did I just come downstairs to get something?" It is a cute cartoon, and as I type this I am smiling at the notion of what it conveys. But today was a living example of it. We got to my car late this morning and as I am helping Mom get into the car she started to step back towards the wheelchair and asked me, "Is this where I am supposed to go?" She had, apparently, no memory of me wheeling her out to the car so that we could run a couple of mundane errands. While Mom regularly gets confused these days, particularly of late and even with the routine activities around our home, this scene outside just struck me hard, both as her son and as her caregiver. I thought to myself, "So this is where we have gotten to. Aaron, it's all about the caregiving." That would be the caption above my head if I/we were in a cartoon depicting this morning's outing.

A couple of ladies, one is a neighbor and another is someone Mom has sponsored in AA for 25 years or so, are quite comfortable sitting and chatting with Mom, with chatting being a relative word. But these two ladies have had continuity of contact and that makes all the difference.

There are a few other ladies with whom Mom is comfortable, and they are comfortable with her. With them, there is just some sort of connection that they have with Mom which is not something that can be described other than as a "connection." Again, however, these are women whom Mom sees on a regular basis. Their chatting is no more than a few minutes, if even that long, but it is done regularly. Mom is comfortable and relaxed around them. These gals don't care if Mom's word usage makes no sense, they get the gist of the love and acceptance which my Mom conveys at all times now. This small group of women just are caring enough to actively support my Mother just by spending a bit of time with her. And then everyone goes on about their days and their lives, just as it should be. Caregiving for Marcie (Mom) is my job. But to me the caring which these few women exhibit is worth a boatload of gratitude. It's beautiful. Thank you, Rose. Thank you, Mary. Thank you, Jean. Thank you, Consuelo. Thank you, Patty Jo.

Patty Jo and Mom

Consuelo and Mom

Mary and Mom

October 17, 2015 -- Here is a photo of Mom and Rose. Rose's birthday is Monday and she is coming to visit tomorrow afternoon. The picture is from December 27, 2014.

I will trim the photo to fit a nice wooden frame I have, and we will give it to Rose tomorrow. It took two other attempts, on other copies of this picture, for Mom to be able to simply write, "Love, Marcie." And then she had such a defeated and sad look on her face, and tears in her eyes as she told me, "I am just not capable of much anymore." I reminded Mom of her age and that she had a stroke 2 ½ years ago, and this helped lighten her feelings a bit. With her lack of language comprehension, it is difficult to talk her through these occurrences, as I have written about previously. I will not expound on it again here. Just a really touching few minutes with my Mom again this evening.

(Edit on February 17, 2019 – I am glad that I saved the first two attempts, as I have passed them along to Rose. My heart and tears well up this evening as I recall helping my Mother make a birthday gift for her dear friend.)

I wonder if other solo full-time caregivers also deal with these emotional bumps in the road, both for themselves and for their charges. Honesty, based upon compassion, is my rule of thumb in dealing with these issues with my Mother. I wonder how other caregivers, who might be in a similar position, deal with talking with their charges when the person recognizes how limited they have become in many areas and how, as Mom put it, “incapable” they now are in those many areas.

ACTIVE LISTENING

Too often have I witnessed people treating elderly people like babies or small children, trying to shield them from the truth of their circumstances. These elderly people are generally not stupid and they know when someone is shining them, so to speak. Like most of the rest of us, they just need to be heard - <u>actively listened to</u> - and they benefit from having their feelings and emotions acknowledged. **<u>Note this.</u>** They do not need rescuing any more than I do or, perhaps, other caregivers do. I’ll dare to speak for the collective “we” of the caregiving world here – We just need to be heard once in a while – <u>actively listened to</u> - and have our feelings and emotions acknowledged. We do not need rescuing since we do this work because we cannot not do it. That is how I feel about it anyway. I could not not provide this level of care for my Mother. If you, Dear Reader, are not familiar with active listening, I encourage you to look into it.

October 23, 2015 – Yesterday was a long day of quiet active caregiving here at our home. Beautiful, but long. Late in the afternoon I took an hour to myself, for myself, on my bass guitar with a live recording of some Grateful Dead songs. After a couple of tunes, I saw in my video monitor that Mom was getting up. She wanted to come out and "sit with the music" as she put it. Mom sat in her chair, looking out at the rainy day, and talking a bit about the squirrels and birds around the bird feeder in our back yard - oblivious to the fact that I was playing my bass. (I don't talk while I play. My brain just does not work that way, talking and playing at the same time.) Mom also just sat and moved with the music, quietly clapping her hands off-tempo as she is want to do any more, hearing a beat that only she can hear. But when "Dark

Star" started to play - about a 10 minute version - Mom just sat and listened, contentedly moving with the music, smiling, watching the birds and squirrels, and making quiet happy sounds.

(Edit on February 17, 2019 – I have not recalled that day's music since I wrote about it above. What a beautiful memory, and what beautiful moments, to recall. *As Rabbi Buz Bogage put it, "It's the moments, man. It's the moments."*

CAREGIVING CAN BE DAUNTING

October 29, 2015 -- Although I am not an expert at Wernicke's Aphasia or dementia, by any academic standards of study, my experience tells me that the progression – decline, as it were – at some point grows – declines – exponentially over time. I have told a number of people that Mom's language recognition is essentially nil, but that does not register with them, most likely because when they occasionally engage with her, it is only the pleasantries that Mom utters. The other person generally goes on and on with stories about what they are doing, and Mom's appearance at tracking what they are saying can be quite deceiving. That is because rarely does anyone actually engage Mom in any sort of back-and-forth talking. Even among able-brained folks, back-and-forth talking is a rarity. All too often, we wait for the other person to take a breath, and then we start in on our own stories, completely ignoring anything that the other person has offered up for consideration.

Perhaps I have become oversensitive to Mom's condition because she is the only person that I am able to converse with, such as the conversing is, for almost the entire day. Every day. And I know that Mom does not understand most words that she hears. I was helping, or guiding, Mom in using the toilet again this evening before she went to bed. No matter how carefully I phrased a simple sentence, using a single word even, regarding using toilet paper, Mom finally said to me, "I'm sorry, honey. I don't understand." It is strange how she can use a full and understandable sentence like this on occasion, yet she is unable to understand, "wipe" or "use it" when I say those words to her. And I use the words while holding some folded toilet paper and mimicking the use on myself. This is so sad to see, knowing that the decline is only going to progress.

The loneliness and isolation that this caregiver feels is something which is felt on a daily and nightly basis, try as I might, and as I do, to address it spiritually. Oftentimes, people will say, "How are you doing?" and then they just keep on talking, usually about themselves and what they have been doing. This happened yesterday at the water and then the guy went on and on, telling me about how he had helped a neighbor. When I could get a word in, I told him that indeed helping someone, and listening, are two very important things for us to do. He got the point. He even acknowledged that he did not listen after asking how I was doing. Then he went on talking...

This morning, as I was helping Mom in the bathroom before I helped her to get into her swim suit so that we could get to the pool, a strikingly clear thought came to mind and hit me like a bag of stones: There is nothing that my Mom does; no activity; which gets done without my assistance, instruction and direction. And each action is like a separate occasion or occurrence to her, not connected to any greater picture of what it is that we are working to accomplish. From putting mayonnaise on bread for sandwiches, to putting on her socks, to using the toilet, unless I put things in front of her – one item at a time – Mom will sit there with absolutely no idea of what she is to be doing. And there is no memory, even a couple of minutes later, of what she has been doing.

I believe that when, or if, a person who has not experienced caregiving on this level takes a few minutes and considers what this scenario would entail, what it calls for, how much active participation is required on the part of the caregiver, and how much mental energy it requires from a caregiver such as myself, that person would run. The task is daunting, to be sure, and I do this freely and willingly. It is my choice to continue to be here. I believe that this thought came to me this morning, while helping Mom, because there are things which I was doing a year ago, which I simply do not have the energy to do now. I am physically and emotionally and mentally exhausted. This gig is like being on stage, playing a heavy-improvisation gig with a band, but playing 24 hours a day for a couple of years and then some. My mental fingers, strong though they may be, are just a wee bit fatigued. Thora R., who is a distant relative of mine, wrote the following as a reply to something that I posted on Facebook:

"No one can plan for the unknown, all we can do is hope we get the care and support we may need. Your Mom is most fortunate that you are able to be there for her. You in return are fortunate to be able to share this time with her - not something everyone can do for their parents. A time to build a new and different relationship with one's parent/s is new ground that most people don't even have on their radar. You are most fortunate that God has blessed both to have each other and a new way of exploring your relationship. Though Marcie may have her moments of insecurity, she has faith that you can help her process her way back to safety. I admire your work with her and look forward to your posts. She always looks happy and healthy, as do you. Think this exploration into another facet of your lives has been beneficial - think there is a book in this life experience, hope you're working on it. It's not just about your Mom's specific affliction, it's about how you've both dealt with the life changes. The strength and confidence bestowed on you both by G-d - your Mom's right, "blessing and love."

This is, in the end, what my job is all about. Mom has had a challenging life and was blessed with just shy of 40 years sobriety in the anonymous little fellowship of ours before she had the major stroke. In those years she was able to, and willing to, and did, help countless women - and some men - with her simple and clear program work. The lineage of how she was schooled in the 12 Steps was unadulterated and clear as a bell. I will always be indebted to the old timers from 1311 York Street who taught her well. I am grateful that when she asked for a teacher nobody said, "No." They poured her a half a cup of coffee and suggested that she sit down and listen for a while....Thank you Don P., Jimmy P., Jimmy K., Lynne B., Ann W., and all you others who are in the big meeting in the sky. Marcie R. will join you some day when G-d is done with her here.

Now, in these years, she gets to nap with her bears after giving blessings and encouragement while we were out for a while today. The esoterica and logistics, the emotional and spiritual aspects of caregiving issues, are mine to deal with and figure out. Not Mom's. I'm growing into it, though not always as gracefully and guru-like as I would have preferred.

A rabbi whom I am acquainted with told me, some many months ago, that old rabbis and old people have one job that they can do, and that is to give blessings and encouragement. There is more to that story, but this must suffice for now.

November 13, 2015 -- After our water class today, I ran into a Russian lady whom I have thought about hiring to come stay at our home for a couple or three hours now and again so I can step away. Our class instructor today had a nice chat with me, a chat which found me starting to cry as I thought of all the people Mom has known in 40+ years off AA fellowship, and how none but 2 are in contact with her. I also was crying for my friends, fellow musicians whom I have played with for years, the man who I considered to be "my Rabbi" and others who are not in much, if any, contact with me since shortly after Mom's stroke. The instructor asked if I had thought about getting some medical help for myself. I believe that she was referring to some mental/medical help, and I can understand her concern. Depression, tears and fatigue are not easy to hide, and this lady sees Mom and me almost every week at her class. She knows that I have been giving this my all for almost 2 ½ years, and she sees that I am burned out. I told her of the Russian lady I was considering hiring, and she asked me if I was going to call her today. I told her that I would reach out to the lady this weekend.

And then G-d stepped in and I ran into M., (I have not asked her permission to use her name here) the Russian lady, at the water cooler on our way out. If I had gotten to the cooler a minute later or a minute earlier, I would have missed her. As I type this, my heart is heavy and has been for a couple of hours now. I believe that my mood is sad because it has come down to having to hire someone to sit with Mom so that I can have a, perhaps, two-hour break a couple of times a week

November 17, 2015 -- At this point in my writing of this treatise/book, I am 360 pages (EDIT: of the original manuscript) into telling the tale of this journey since my Mom had a stroke on March 29, 2013. I have yet to take the time to go back and re-read and edit what I have written thus far. My writing has been real, from my heart and with raw emotions usually at the forefront. When I go back and re-read a lot of what I have written, I imagine that I will be somewhat embarrassed at my weakness over time; embarrassed at the grudges and hurt feelings; embarrassed at the feelings of abandonment; embarrassed by the feelings of resentment and disappointment which I have felt towards Mom's friends, clergy and my friends.

I have brought my best to Mom's caregiving every day, as best as I have been able to muster. I don't yell at her, though I have raised my voice at times. I've apologized to Mom numerous times when that has happened, explaining that it is my fatigue and frustration that just gets unbearable. I don't hit her. I have hit a wall in our house a few times, though. Not a smart thing to do, and I got lucky that I did not hit a beam. It frightens me when I lose control of myself. I can only imagine how scary it is for Mom. I don't verbally or emotionally deride her for being stroke-effected and unable to do a whole lot. I support her emotionally and spiritually as best as I can, in a calm and supportive manner most of the time, no matter how much turmoil has been going on between my ears and in my heart.

November 23, 2015 -- This has been an interesting day in a few ways, beginning with midnight when several apparitions were in Mom's room next to her bed and interacting with her. Make of it what you will, Dear Reader, but this is what transpired:

Something woke me up at midnight last night and, as I always do, I looked at the video monitor next to my bed, which allows me to see and hear what Mom is up to while she is in bed. I saw three angels, or apparitions if you prefer. One was a tall male, one a shorter female and one was younger girl. I have watched the female and the younger one several times in Mom's room, usually just standing in the same places, though the older one has, in the past visits, gone forward and stood next to the bed while Mom sleeps.

The male angel was leaning over Mom's bed, and it appeared that he was talking with her. The female and the younger one were standing behind the male, in front of an open closet door. (I am getting chills as I write this at 10:15pm. No fear, but chills.) As I watched for a minute, he stood up tall and slowly started to walk out of her room. I have seen such apparitions quite a few times over my lifetime, and at least a half a dozen times since Mom had her initial stroke. I did what I have always done, and said out loud, "You are welcome to be here, but do not frighten me." I just say this matter-of-factly and go on about my business.

I put on my slippers and walked upstairs to check on Mom, and I must confess here that I expected that she might have died, except that the actions of the angels did not appear to be what I believe that they would do if they had come for her. Mom was wide awake, very wide-eyed and quite confused. She told me that she did not know where she had been, what she was supposed to be doing and that she did not know how to do anything right now. Mom was not afraid, but she looked like she had been somewhere else. I wonder what would have happened if I had stayed downstairs and watched things play out. But I am glad that I came upstairs and was able to calm my Mother and reassure her that things were well, she was safe and did not have to be doing anything but going back to sleep, which is what she did after I helped her into the bathroom. And then I tucked her back into bed.

AARON HIRES A PART TIME HELPER

November 29, 2015 -- I am a bit saddened and subdued by what I chose to do for myself at about 4:00 this afternoon. I made a call to the Russian woman I wrote about a few days ago, or maybe a week or so ago, and she will be here tomorrow afternoon so that I can get out for a couple of hours. I plan to go to the gym and then do a bit of grocery shopping. What saddened and subdues me is that I choose, or chose, rather, to finally completely surrender to the idea that the only way I can get breaks is to hire someone to be here. Sherry Weaver, an old and dear friend of Mom's finally convinced me to do this. Sherry helped me see that Mom has a Higher Power, and it is not me. My trust in G-d in this area of leaving Mom, with no contingency plan should I get hurt, has been lip service trust at best. Thank you, Sherry!

A little before 4:00 today, prior to my phoning the lady, I started honestly wondering what was the source of my hesitation to call her. We have the money in the bank, so paying her is not a problem, even though there is no way to replace the money. It was not the cost of her time alone which was stopping me. I asked G-d to please let me see and think honestly and clearly. What came to me was that by calling her I was giving up, totally giving up, any notion that things will change in terms of the people whom Mom and I know and have known for decades. They simply are not around and are not going to suddenly start being around. If I want some breaks and want to step away now and again, I am going to have to pay someone to be here. I find that to be really sad, and I have been rather quiet since I called her.

Some hours have passed now, and a few times this evening I have found myself actually feeling lighter and freer; freer of unmet expectations; freer of unmet needs and desires; and more free to move forward – whatever that may come to look like – without dragging the wagon of expectations along with me. It feels like a long chapter of this caregiving journey has come to a close, and blank pages yet to be written lie before me. This may seem overly dramatic, or as an attempt on my part to be poetic and romantic in my writing, but that is the description which just came to me.

I know that other caregivers are out there and in a similarly abandoned position. Though I have not met anyone who is doing this completely by themselves, I have talked with a couple of others who have had family and friends be scarce. May they all find the peace of mind and comfort in their hearts, perhaps just by knowing that they are not alone.

December 2, 2015 -- I stepped away from the house yesterday afternoon for two hours, as the Russian lady came over and stayed here in our home. It was strange to get in my car and leave here without Mom, but not as uncomfortable as I expected it to be. She is scheduled to come over again tomorrow afternoon for two hours. I am still saddened by the situation, but it does not hurt like it did even a few weeks ago. And there is no comparison between now and the pain and anguish of a year ago. Or two years ago. Again, I am grateful for the freedom from those feelings.

We had a nice day today, beginning with an old friend dropping by a small container of soup this morning. His timing was excellent. When I woke up this morning it was with the feeling of, not quite dread, but not at all joyful that another day had come; another day where I would need to take care of, assist with and orchestrate everything that Mom and I do……same old stuff. And I felt that I was just too tired, too drained and not up to the task. All I wanted to do, at 8:00 this morning, was pull the covers over my head and hide or sleep….same old stuff.

December 16, 2015 -- Mom and I made dinner together tonight and, as we do most evenings, we sat down to watch a ball game (college basketball, tonight) and eat our dinner. About 10 minutes into dinner, Mom told me she needed to go use the bathroom. It took us roughly a minute and a half to walk to the bathroom, and when we got to the door Mom said to me, as she pointed to the bathroom and then to her bedroom, "Can I go here, or here?" I asked her if she remembered that we had made dinner and had just sat down to eat about 10 minutes ago. Mom's response was, "No. Did I miss something?" After we were done in the bathroom, I pointed Mom back down the hall, towards the living room, where we eat. As we passed the kitchen, she started to turn there as if she was ready to help prepare a meal.

This is an example of a regularly occurring happening, in which Mom seemingly lays down no short term memories whatsoever. In the time it took to walk perhaps 30 feet, from the living room to the bathroom, she completely forgot what she had gotten up from dinner, to do.

I got out of the house for a couple of hours today, as the lady I have hired came to stay with Mom. The timing of her visit was different today, in that Mom was up and eating a late breakfast at 1:00 in the afternoon. Previous visits have found Mom already asleep in her bed, or getting ready to nap after we returned from the noon water class, so the lady who comes here has not had much real interaction with her. When I returned from being out, and as the lady was getting ready to leave, she told me that she had helped Mom use the bathroom before going back to bed to rest and sleep.

It hit me, a short time later, that this was the first time someone other than myself had helped my Mom use the bathroom since I began this caregiving stint, a bit over 2 ½ years ago. And in order for Mom to have gotten from her chair in the living room, to the bathroom and then her bedroom, the lady whom I hired had to help Mom get up from the chair and slowly walk with Mom as she uses her walker. Nobody else besides me has done this. Nobody. I am not sure what I am feeling tonight as I type this; I cannot put my finger on, or attach a labeling word to, the feeling or feelings. It is not self-pity, or resentment towards the people who have been absent. Some of the feeling is of the scope of the care which I have been providing; everything, really, which Mom does, wears, eats; getting to and out of the bathroom and bed; taking her medicines; getting to the doctor appointments; having the bills paid and the groceries stocked; getting around the house and occasionally out to the back yard when the weather and her strength permits; everything, really. And today someone else did a bit of that.

December 22, 2015 -- Lest anyone reading this treatise think that I am anything like a perfect caregiver, I offer the following humbling admission that yesterday was my worst day, my worst performance, as my Mom's caregiver. I do not at all understand why my patience level sometimes runs low, but I can deal with low levels of patience, primarily through spiritual practice and prayer. Yesterday, my patience level was zero almost from the start of the day when Mom finally got up and out of bed. I talked too much, I tried to explain too much – using too many words, my vibe was palpable to Mom and my patience was zero. I wanted out of here. I was completely sick and tired of caregiving. I was completely sick and tired of adjusting another day to my Mom's needs and capabilities. I asked G-d to refill my patience, love and tolerance many times – several times as I just walked away from Mom for a few minutes – and then I went back to the feeling that G-d had forsaken me, and all I wanted was out.....yep, that pretty much sums up the day.

At 7:30ish in the evening, after putting Mom to bed, I went into her bedroom and apologized for my lack of patience and I reassured her that she had done nothing wrong. I told her that I did not know what was wrong with me today, and that tomorrow was another day. Mom knew that I was way off base all day. As I have written before, she is injured (and old) but she is not stupid, and she reads my vibe like she used to read a book. So, I went to bed and read a bit and then just prayed my own from-the-heart (G-d, please read my heart) prayer, asking G-d for forgiveness for my rioting self-will, and I turned out the light and shut my eyes.

I pray that I never have another day like yesterday. It scared me to know that I had no control whatsoever over my attitude. It scared me to experience what it must feel like when someone "snaps" and just does something awful to themselves or to another person. This is one of the days that I punched a wall in our hallway. This is one of the days where I wept, from complete fatigue, in front of Mom. This is one of the days where I should have called Rose or Mary or someone, and pleaded for them to help me. But I did not do so. I am grateful that I did not drink over it, and I am grateful that I knew enough to just shut it down early and go to bed. And it frightened me, and saddened me, to know that there really is nobody whom I could have called and just asked them to take care of Mom for the day, as I obviously needed a break longer than the two hours I am now getting twice a week.

And, Dear Reader, I can only imagine how uncomfortable I made my Mother feel yesterday...even last night, when I apologized to her and told her that I was just off all day, her response was, "Yes, you were."

(Edit on February 18, 2019 – Those days when I was a complete emotional mess are the days which I remember most, and which I regret the most, and which I cannot undo. There were not a lot of those days, but there were too many.)

December 23, 2015 -- Aphasia is absolutely baffling to me. I have spent a lot of time yesterday and today pondering Monday's experiences, which I wrote about above. What came to mind is something Mom said to me Monday, and which I did not pay enough – or any, really – attention to. What she said was, "Honey, I don't understand what you said." What I had said was how she needed to take care of her personal needs in the bathroom. What I did not hear was that she did not understand my words. I remember wondering how she could tell me so clearly that she did not understand what I said. How can a person, with such severe aphasia, reply in such a linguistically clear manner if they cannot understand what is said to them? I remember rephrasing my instructions, using different words and a different tone of voice. That just made Mom nervous and even more unable to take care of the matter at hand. And I paid that whole thing no attention other than to get more uptight. It was only two days ago that I lost control of myself completely. I believe that some memory of that lingers in Mom's head. I have told you, Dear Reader, that I will be honest with you. Being honest is a humbling and embarrassing enterprise at times.

(Edit on February 18, 2019 – Dear Reader, this is simply brutal to read through and remember, as I edit this piece for the first time. I feel so badly for what my Mother was forced to witness when I was not at my best. When I was at my worst, really. Yeah, Mom, I had a good batting average with you, but I wish I could have done better.)

But still my caregiving duties are at hand. So, I tried something totally different today. I spoke very little when engaged with Mom. Usually, while we have breakfast, I talk with her about what we might do this day, and ask for her input.

So, today, at 10:20pm as I write this, I can tell you, Dear Reader, that I have not uttered a dozen sentences to my Mom today, if even that many. She talked a lot, as she usually does, but my responses were, for the most part, just affirmatives such as, "Yes" "uh-huh" "cool" and the like. While we made breakfast and dinner, I used single words and gestures. The same thing while I helped her get dressed to go to the water class, and after class while helping her get back into her dry clothes. Not a dozen sentences from me, and we had a very relaxed and pleasant day. Mom was the most relaxed. I am working on it. It is peculiar to be with someone for an entire day and night and for me to speak very, very little. This will take me some practice and a lot of getting used to, but I think I am on the correct path. Lots to surrender here. Lots to begin to grieve.

December 29, 2015 -- An image of Bugs Bunny popping out of a rabbit hole, suitcase in hand, and saying, "I must have turned left at Albuquerque" came to mind this evening as I returned to crocheting the small lap blanket I am working on. Somehow - perhaps distracted by a play in one of the football games - I made the turn in the middle of a row. Not wanting to pull out all those stitches, and since there was an old crochet pro close at hand, I handed the project off to Mom and asked her "Since you are such a crochet guru, Mom, and have so much experience, while I am such a rookie...."

How could she say no, eh? She smiled at my bull-hooey. It was intentional on my part, just to get that certain smile from her. She knows I was putting her on. Mom and I have talked straight with each other for many years now.

I stood behind her chair, took the crochet hook and yarn, and got her started on the same stitch I had been using, but then her muscle/brain memory kicked in and she was good to go for about 10 minutes. 10 minutes is about all that she can handle at one time. The physical fatigue of having her brain attend to something is just a reality of her situation. Whether it is talking with the occasional visitor, crocheting, helping with dinner preparation, it is all the same. Her stroke-damaged brain, after focusing or attending to something for a very short time, leaves her physically fatigued. If you read "My Stroke of Insight" you will find that this is common with people who have had strokes. This is why I plan our days, such as I am able to plan any more, anyway, very carefully and simply. Life is interesting.

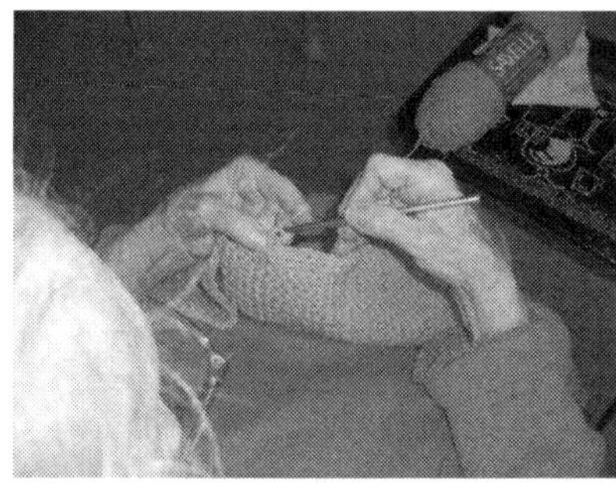 

January 1, 2016 -- The last salad made in 2015. Yesterday, Mom had a small burst of energy in the afternoon and wanted to help me in the kitchen. So, we worked together on putting some chicken and veggies in the oven and then I set her to work on cutting things up for our salad. After that, she was ready for a nap. It is the small things around here these days, and it is kind of cute to watch Mom, out of the corner of my vision, as she carefully places each slice of vegetable on the salad or in the pan of chicken. I was quite pleased that Mom had some energy and desire to assist me in preparing a meal. It has been a while since she has done so. The lady takes a lot of rest any more.

Subject and Object-naming areas of Mom's brain seem to be completely inaccessible to her. When we said our little evening prayer before eating dinner, when I usually am saying something like, "Thank you, G-d, for our going to the pool. And thank you for – whatever might come to my mind, etc." I then turn to Mom and ask her what there was today that she would thank G-d for. Mom usually offers a word salad of generalities such as “unity, understanding, appropriate” with no specific identifiers attached. Tonight, Mom offered up, “Beauty.” I asked her what beauty. And she replied, “The feeling.” I cannot remember the last time that Mom was able to directly and specifically name something that she enjoyed or wanted to do. Her brain, through aphasia, age and whatever form of dementia or senility is presenting itself, is almost without exception unable to utter nouns. Imagine, Dear Reader, what it is like to communicate with someone like this.

January 3, 2016 -- I am so blessed to have gotten to know a man, Robert B., who is in recovery and had, in his past, many years of caregiving experience for his parents. He is able to talk with me – not to me – without things getting bogged down, heavy or uncomfortable. I am able to share with him, every few days or so, about what is going on, both in terms of Mom’s care and needs, and in terms of my own mental/emotional state and spiritual practice. Robert does not offer direct advice, but does offer suggestions, often of readings, in a manner by which he shares what has worked for him and what is working for him now. He knows, intuitively and from experience, that a scenario such as Mom has going on is dynamic rather than static. There are many new normals and some of them require a deeper and, sometimes unknown approach by me.

When I tell Robert, as I did today, or yesterday perhaps it was, that “going with the flow” is the order of the day, he knows what a broad statement that is. Broad and yet filled with details which can require moment to moment attention and flexibility. That is the nature of the caregiving in which I am involved. Robert does not offer syrupy sympathy, which is a type of sympathy that I find uncomfortable. He knows that it is a rarity to be actively listened to, particularly when old friends and acquaintances are not available to me. I have found that active listening is a rare skill, which few people have developed. And then, we just go on about each of our days. Robert is touched with a gift of insight, and I count myself fortunate to have met him.

January 10, 2016 -- Tears from Mom a couple of times in the last few days…"I have such trouble talking." "I don't know how to take care of myself."

When this occurs, it just rips at my heart and at the same time raises my level of compassion about how difficult it is for Mom when she gets those moments of clarity, which I see, anyway, and she knows how debilitated, confused and incapacitated she now is. There are times when I quietly go into her bedroom to check on her while she is resting or sleeping, and I find her laying in her bed with her eyes open, thinking, presumably, about….what? G-d only knows, and only He knows. When I, on occasion, ask Mom what she is thinking about, or if anything is bothering her, she is unable to clearly answer with anything other than word salad. Just rips at my heart.

CAREGIVER EMOTIONAL HEALTH ISSUES

Edit on August 4, 2019 – There have been several places in this writing where I have made note of the mental strain involved in helping my Mother at this level and for this long. Again, it is only in hindsight, and at the suggestion of a friend who read through my manuscript, that I would have done well to take action when these issues were present. I am not a model of perfect behavior for any other caregiver, seeing only what I could at the time and doing my best at any given time. I honestly do not see how I could have done things differently! I wish I had some brilliant insights to share with other caregivers, solo full-time caregivers, who also have asked for help, to no avail. A couple of friends have since told me that they saw that I was in over my head, but they did not know what to do or if they would have had my "permission" to intrude directly into my/our affairs by making direct suggestions. I wish they would have done so anyway, but the opportunity has passed, and I hold no ill-will towards them. We all, hopefully, do the best we can at any given time.

Another friend told me that the outward face that showed her did not present the need – the deep need – for help. I admit that I thought it my responsibility to not present the situation as being dire, lest I lay too much on the couple of friends who did stay in touch. In hindsight, I was 100% mistaken by not being honest with them. *I could not have told them what exactly I needed from them, as I did not know. All that I knew was that I needed help with my caregiving duties. I take ownership of my failing to have directly stated things as such.* Watch yourselves more closely, fellow caregiver, and perhaps you will fare better than I did.

Having just read through the above, I must add this thought: What I remember wishing that I had was just some breaks from duty, for more than just a couple of hours. A weekend away. A few full days away. Someone who felt comfortable enough, and motivated enough, to allow me to show them some basics and then just let them do their best for a day or two or three or four. I truly enjoyed the caregiving most of the time, but as with any arena in our lives, to do something 24 hours a day for too long of an extended period of time, will cause harm to anyone in the long run. No doctor, nurse, carpenter, accountant, athlete or musician could work effectively that way. Think of something that you have a passion for, Dear Reader, and ask if you could stay healthy, physically and mentally, doing it without a break for what turned out to be, for me, 5 years. I joked several times with a few people that Superman (Aaron) had lost his cape. I wish I had, and that they had, taken my joke seriously. Again, though, the onus was on me.

January 15, 2016 -- Evening, just before dinner and Shabbas -- I went outside a few minutes ago to have a smoke before getting Mom up to light the Shabbas candles on this Friday night. My chest pains have returned, which seem to be tied to a high level of stress and an elevated sense of isolation. It occurs to me that I would do well to go see a doctor, but there is nobody to leave my Mom with in case something needs to be done to me by the doctor. Standing outside just those few minutes ago, I had a cry – a deep sob, really – on a level I have not had in a very long time. There is absolutely nobody for me to call and ask to take Mom for a bit so that I can have an extended break, or if I need to have something done medically. Absolutely nobody but G-d for me to call upon, so call upon G-d I did.

I don't know what to do with this occasional heart thing. Maybe go in to see the doctor, bringing Mom with me, and go from there. I have read many times that caregivers are at an elevated risk for health problems, and I now understand why that is so. For the first couple of years, though, I thought that I was invincible. Ten minutes have passed now, and my chest feels better. Not quite so tight. Time for candles, Kiddush and Shabbas such as Mom and I do it. We have not missed a week of lighting Friday Night candles and the other rituals we observe.

January 16, 2016 -- It has been a calm and peaceful day both in our home, in my dealings with Mom and in my heart. Earlier this evening a thought occurred to me; it is the sharing of experiences that I miss, both my own and those of my friends, a couple of whom are in somewhat similar situations with debilitated parents or a spouse. Shared experiences are the ties that bind, both in family and with friends.

It has not passed my notice that much of my recent writing has been about my own psychological state and outlook. This treatise is, after all, about a caregiver's journey. And as my Mom's cognitive and linguistic debilitation continues to decline, I really do not have any positive and instructive insights or experiences to share with the reader. She is understanding essentially nothing that I say to her, and her pat answer to anything that sounds to her like a question, is almost always "Yes." Being around someone for as many hours as I am around Mom, and not being able to engage her in any of even the simplest small talk, has worn on my outlook and nerves. She remembers nothing that we do, nothing that we talk about – or that I talk to her about, anyway – and Mom never asks about any of our family or of her, or my friends.

During the sporting events which we watch during dinner, Mom is as captivated by the commercials as she is by the game. I do not think that her brain differentiates between the natures of the two.

Sometimes I will ask her which team she thinks will win the game that we are watching, and she is unable to answer, most likely because my words make no sense to her. I suppose that sharing this sort of experience with one of my, or her, friends is not a reasonable expectation. After all, why the heck would anyone in their right mind want to be around such a scenario? Unless, of course, they just wanted to be around to show some love, understanding and support, both to Mom and to me. Or perhaps just because they have past experience with either Mom or me.

EPISODE OF DELIRIUM

January 17, 2016 -- Morning – What a long night. Mom's mind has drifted off to only G-d knows where. She called for me 4 or 5 times during the night, not remembering, I think, that she had done so. I typed "I think" because none of her words made any sense whatsoever, and she was obviously not understanding anything that I said to her. I spend a few hours stretched out on the couch, as I often do when this occurs, so that I am closer at hand when she calls. Mom called for me again at 8:00 and I got her to the bathroom, out of her wet pull-ups and back into bed. The lady who has started coming here to stay for a couple of hours at a time taught me that if we put on two pull-ups it keeps the bed dry when Mom wets herself. This works most of the time.

Midnight –Mom's confusion from last night has carried through the day, and well into this evening. I put her to bed at 8:00 and she called me into her room at 9:00. In the next 30 minutes, she called for me another 4 times; once to ask what was different and what room she was in; three times to try to tell me something about her pillow, which she was holding in her hands while sitting up. She thought it was a new pillow and wondered about it. Mom has had that pillow for a goodly number of years. After the third time, it occurred to me that perhaps putting a new pillow case on the thing might settle her down, and so it did, for about 30 minutes.

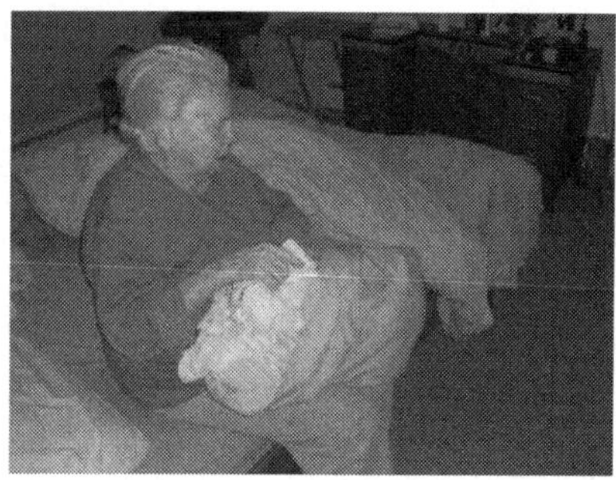

I then saw, in my monitor, that Mom was standing up and at her door, without her canes in hand. I went in to check on her and it just got weird from there. She asked me where her dresses were and which one she should put on. She told me that she had just gotten off the phone with two of her old friends, and had done a good bit of reading. None of this, of course, had transpired. Other bunches of word salad came out of Mom, but she was able to convey to me that she was very confused and did not know why. <u>And she asked me to tell her the truth.</u> This led me into an area which I am careful about. While it is important to retain integrity and never lie to my Mom, which I have held to both before, and since, the stroke, it is tricky enough to explain senility or dementia to an older person who has some language comprehension capabilities. To do so with someone with Mom's level of aphasia and dementia, is something that my intuition tells me to be very careful with. I have no experience in this area of caregiving. It is an aspect of my work in which I need to educate myself, and I am not sure who to turn to for direction, education or advice.

(Editing on May 23, 2019 in order to get this writing into a publishable size. It is so painful to be reminded of the above-mentioned evening. There were so many evenings and days like this.)

February 11, 2016 -- A couple of hours ago I heard the most beautiful singing - short but beautiful; the six words which comprise the Shema, which is the core principle and prayer of Judaism. Mom says the Shema with me three times a day - at breakfast, dinner and at her bedtime.

Tonight Mom had real difficulty with the words of the Shema, so, on her own, she sang the last few words. It was amazing how accurately she got the last few words out, so I had us do it again, and I quietly sang with her. The tone, the voice, the pitch, the richness of her singing, the everything which Mom's brain was able to access for those six words was just lovely. And it was not a frail and fragile voice of a woman pushing 86 years of age. It was the voice of a much younger, stronger and healthier woman.

February 21, 2016 -- Today was such a remarkable experience and provides me with some food for thought and contemplation. We spent an hour in the pool at the JCC. A Russian lady friend of ours was there, a lady who speaks very little English. I know a few words and phrases in Russian. Mom knows no Russian and understands very little of what is said to her in English. Get the picture? We spent an hour in the water with this Russian lady, quietly talking a bit, quietly singing a bit, laughing a bit and gently exercising in the neutral-buoyancy environment which allows Mom's arthritic joints to function at their best, such as that is.

As we were leaving the water, another Russian lady friend of ours arrived, much to Mom's (and my) delight. I remember well that one time I reminded the second lady that Mom had had a stroke and did not understand much of what was said to her. The lady's response was, "So what?" We get along really well. Both of these Russian ladies are at the pool at about the same time on Saturdays, and I plan our day so that we are there, too. They enjoy Mom's company very much, and her age, linguistic ability, cognitive ability? That stuff does not matter to them at all. They just go with the flow, honoring Mom's age and stage in life, knowing that we all share similar basic values of family.

As Mom and I were leaving the dressing area to head for home, Mom said to me, "You know, honey, I just love seeing the feelings here." Seeing the feelings. Aphasia. Dementia of some sort, perhaps. Gentleness of spirit. Seeing the feelings.

Mom is napping now, but I will share one more thing that she told me yesterday. She said, "I am so grateful to have known so many good people in my life." I asked her if she was thinking of the people in AA, and she said, "Yes." Mom is rarely able to construct a sentence that clear, but when she has been able to do so, it is usually a positive statement about people who she used to get to see and talk with. Mom has been able to let go of that on a much deeper level than I am able to, but it's getting better and stings less as time passes. We have had a nice day today. Soup is cooking and I've other things to tend to now. Long and contemplative post, to me, anyway, today. Life is good. I hope that Mom's old AA's are well, and so does Mom.

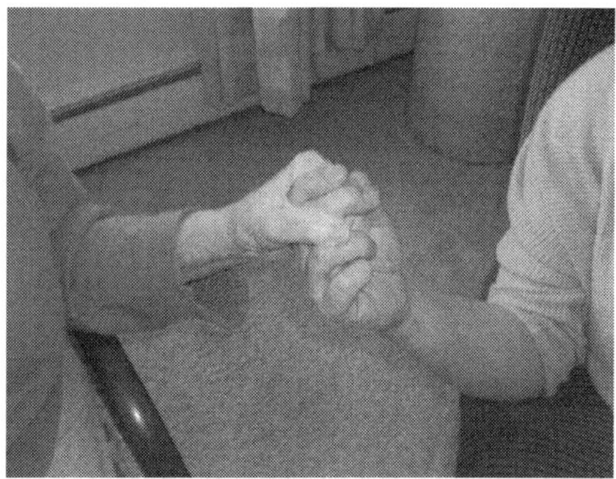

February 24, 2016 -- I was grateful this morning that three of Mom's AA ladies have remained in regular contact with her. Mom woke up this morning with tears and fears in her eyes, able to tell me that "It is just too big." I knew from experience that she was referring to a new day and her world in general. I have talked her through this scenario countless times, both before the stroke and since. So, I asked Mom if she would like me to call Rose, and she smiled a "Yes." Fortunately, Rose had a few minutes for "Her Marcie."

I briefly explained the situation to Rose, handed Mom the phone, and excused myself from her bedroom so that the two ladies could talk in private. And when they were done, we went on with our day. I could have once again handled this myself, but it is so nice to have someone else step in now and again. The value of continuity of contact must never be underestimated, and at this point with Mom I do not believe that it can be reconstructed. What a beautiful day this was. It's the little things, man. Little things are really the big things that count.

March 16, 2016 -- The only experience I have with Wernicke's Aphasia is the last, almost, three years as my Mom's caregiver. Trying to explain the malady to anyone is difficult at best, and is usually futile.

The image below is a pretty good representation of what language is like in my Mom's brain. My sister Amy’s birthday is coming up and I asked Mom if she wanted to send her a card. Mom said she did, so I asked her what she would like to write, though, of course, Mom was unable to come up with anything other than her usual "Blessings and Love" bit. I wrote out the greeting and two simple lines, along with her Blessings and Love closing, as well as her signature.

The writing is the result of about 15 minutes of effort by Mom. She never did get Amy’s name correct.

Dear Amy
Happy Birthday
I hope all is well
with you.
Have a very good year
Blessings and Love,
Mom

Dear [illegible]
[illegible] and [illegible]
Happy Birth day
I hope all [illegible] well with [illegible]
Love and [illegible], Love
[illegible] Love, [illegible]

YEAR #3 BEGINS

March 29, 2016 -- Three years ago tonight.....time flies and so do helicopters. Penguins and ostriches, however, do not.

I was given about a minute to balance considerations and make the call as to treatment less than an hour and a half after Mom's initial stroke. One minute on a video conference with the head of neuro surgery at a local hospital. One minute to balance Mom's advanced medical directives, DNR considerations and advice from the brain surgeon with whom I was speaking. I occasionally wonder if I made the correct call, but I do not dwell on it, since things are as they are and I did what I thought correct at the time. Three years, man. What a long strange trip it's been, as some guys used to sing. What a long strange trip it's been.

April 5, 2016 -- Our back yard garden areas are filling out, and slowly coming together, kind of like my studying/reading of the teachings of Jewish sages has in these last, almost, three years ---- piecemeal. A little something here, a little something there, with no "master plan" or clear direction. Not the best way to study, but I am on my own in finding my way through a vast amount of available material. When the first stroke hit, and when it became apparent to me that I may be doing this caregiving for a long time, I told myself that I did not want to look back and regret not having used the time wisely. I told myself to delve into teachings and writings of our sages, which I had no knowledge of or experience with. And I told myself to keep up my bass-playing skills. I know enough of bass to keep on learning by myself. The same is not true of the study of our sages. But I have not quit.

April 8, 2016 -- My Mom's AA anniversary date is April 8, 1972. Today marks 44 years of continuous sobriety. She has no memory of her drinking or her years of sobriety. The number of AA meetings she attended in the (just short of) 41 years before the stroke, is uncountable. Once in a while when I read a few lines, or a paragraph, from our AA Big Book, Mom will close her eyes and quietly say, "Yes. Yes……" which leads me to believe that the Big Book is hard wired in her brain, which is not surprising. Beyond that, however, she is not capable of talking about it at all.

There is a scene, early in the movie "Bloodsport," where a young Jean-Claude Van Damme tries to steal a samurai sword. What he is told, after being stopped, is something to the effect that, "There is only one way to get one of these swords, and that is to earn it." Such is the case with the coin shown on the next page.

RANDOM NOTES SHOWING CAREGIVER BURNOUT

Sometime in April 2016 --

I find myself a month out from having written much other than notes I type into my Drafts file on my flip phone. Probably some form of depression I have going on, dreading getting up in the morning, just to face another day. Perhaps this is a sign of the "caregiver burnout" which I have read about. The following are notes from my Drafts file. I will leave them stand as they are.

Mental, emotional and spiritual upheavals, which come with certain experiences...

March 6th – washing hands with no water

March 11th – zero memory of grape juice wine blessing three times. She used her dental floss stick to stir her tea

At times like a complete stranger. At times all that can be done is nothing but to wait out the confusion.

March 19th -- toilet paper (clean) on hair. Cereal in raisin box

Put down the bat. (Metaphor regarding beating myself up.) Like having a three year old with no logic

Chasing the Pain

Asked for help not often enough. Help denied too often.

April 1st – Mom said, "We care about the individual people."

April 2nd – Should I stop trying to have her give a direct answer? Is that quizzing or is it practice and exercise on a damaged brain.

The aphasiac brain wants to talk. Not listen. Cannot recognize someone speaking to them sometimes.

April 4th – milk. "I just went quiet." Did not know how to pour milk on cereal.

April 4th – dinner prep knife. Almost cut off her fingers when she reached for a speck. I was cutting an onion and Mom reached over to pick up a speck of something on the cutting board. I missed her fingers by a fraction of an inch.

I wish I had time to do what I'm missing. I wish I had time to find what I lost.

Drop the Me in favor of what is good for the We.

April 7th – The dementia phase. Toilet paper behind ear to brush hair. Understands "Do you know how to do this?" Evening pills in sleeve. I handed Mom one of her evening medications, and she put it in her sleeve.

April 16th – curtain as napkin with chocolate ice cream

April 19th – at King Soopers. Stroke. This was a rough one. In the parking lot of the King Soopers grocery store, Mom had another little stroke as she sat in the passenger seat. She just went offline for a few moments and then was noticeably different.

April 20th – lipstick just put on. Next breath, "Can I put some on? Is this new?"

April 22nd – Dr. Rubenstein re: "Oblivious" Mom's doctor used the word "oblivious" in talking with me about how my Mother was unaware of so much. The word hit me upside my head.

April 20, 2016 -- One of the very odd occurrences in this caregiving gig is to witness mini-strokes when they hit, when a little piece of my Mom's brain goes "Poof...bye-bye" and will not be coming back or repairing itself. I've witnessed quite a few of these in the last, almost, three years, and I got to witness another one yesterday afternoon.

It is the oddest thing, in that Mom is just "not there" for a moment or three, like her brain has gone offline. It reboots, but is different and fatigued. A bit more linguistic understanding is gone, as well as cognitive capabilities. Mom is still Mom, of course, just somewhat changed, and less of her than before.

SEEKING INFORMATION ON DEMENTIA CAREGIVING

April 26, 2016 -- Tonight I began delving into educating myself on growing my skill set in caregiving, as dementia is presenting itself as the primary issue, on top of my Mom's Wernicke's aphasia. A professional in the field of neurology agreed with me in that aphasia and dementia cannot easily, if at all, be separated. "Dementia Caregiving" appears to be the preferred term for the area which I am beginning to study.

My world of solo full-time caregiving gets more interesting, (to me, anyway) and smaller, as time goes by. I am going to need longer days for the reading and study which lies ahead. This should prove to be a fascinating part of this journey to work my way through. I am not afraid of it, as I found my own way through these last three years. Experience breeds confidence, and I have learned that it is o.k. to make mistakes.

May 2, 2016 -- I have, in the last few days, searched around the internet - including caregiving pages on Facebook - for information about, and/or for people with experience caregiving for, someone in my Mom's particular circumstances, having Wernicke's Aphasia for three years, from an ischemic stroke, and then having some form of dementia present itself. I have found nothing thus far. Separating the aphasia from the symptoms of vascular (perhaps?) dementia, is like separating the chicken soup broth from a matzah ball once the matzah ball has been cooked in the soup.

One thing about dementia is that the person's sense of time, and the hour of the day or night, can sometimes get quite scrambled, if it exists at all. That has presented itself lately. Sunday morning, from 1:00am - 8:30am, Mom called for me 6 times. She needed nothing in particular, except for once to take care of personal needs. A couple of times she wondered what she should be doing, or where we were going, or if she could help with anything...in the middle of the night. Last night, as I was prepping a soup for today, she got up and came to the kitchen, talking non-stop for about an hour in the word salad of Wernicke's Aphasia.

The above are examples of why, for the time being, I am making no plans, not doing anything out of our simple, quiet routine, and having no visitors outside of what has become our routine. Things are simply too unpredictable around here and I need time to get a handle on how to navigate dementia caregiving.

Mom at Dinner – May 1, 2016
Spooning soup onto her sandwich.

May 5, 2016 -- I was blessed today to get to share a bit of time talking with someone who has experience in caregiving for a family member who had dementia, albeit their loved one's was Alzheimer's. Just sharing insights with me, regarding what I have been providing for my Mom, will no doubt be helpful, but it is going to take me some time to digest the truth which was pointed out to me.

The person who shared with me was surprised, visibly surprised, that I am just lately seeing, and thinking about, the dementia aspect of Mom's situation. My friend told me that she has seen it in Mom for, I believe she said, a couple of years. As she is among the few people who have seen Mom (and me) pretty regularly these last three years, her insights and words carry a good deal of weight with me. Her personal experience and knowledge is not just theoretical - it is real.

And she recommended that I consider letting go of trying to figure out how aphasia caregiving differs from dementia caregiving, and just accept things as they are. The lady had other insights and suggestions as well, but I'll not go into them here and now.

The word "Dementia" invokes fear and uncertainty, to me, anyway. That I have been in denial about it (or blind) has, frankly, kind of rocked my world today. The gal I talked with, however, eased my mind some by telling me that I have been doing "dementia caregiving" for a long time now and that I might want to relax my focus on the aphasia/dementia terminology.

May 6, 2016 -- <u>Mom calls to me and says, "Aaron. I just feel like crying."</u> This was a rare time that she called me by name. As Mom's injured brain no longer lays down any short term memory, she does not remember what we have done today. Breakfast, going to a noon water class, her interaction with a few people in the class....no recollection whatsoever. So, it is perfectly natural that every now and again Mom cries a bit about being old and not able to do anything. <u>She did have a flash of memory a few weeks ago, telling me, "Honey, where are my AA women?"</u> I handled that by calling one of the two or three women who have remained in regular contact with Mom, and they did an incredibly clear 10th step on the phone. It was amazing. I listened to just a bit and then stepped away.

Mom is doing what is hers to do, as I reminded her this afternoon while she was crying. She just does not remember having done it. What is mine to do is to remind her what she has done today. With her situation, that is quite a challenge. What a world, eh? It's beautiful, man. What an opportunity...

May 17, 2016

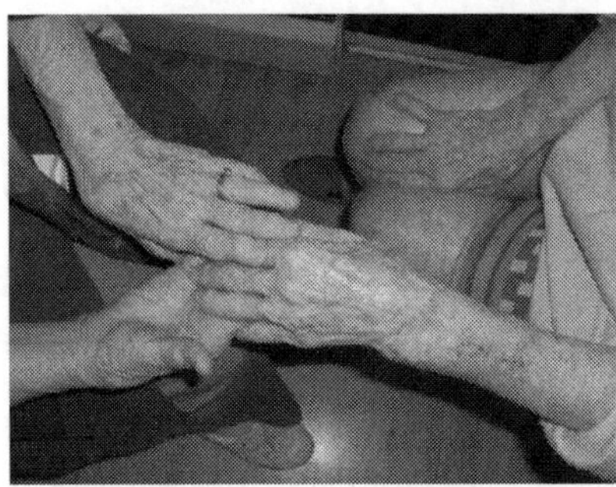

Mom and Jean Blodgett

The hands on the left are gone now; gone suddenly Sunday night, May 15th. One of the three ladies who have shared continuity of contact with Mom (and me) for these last three years, and for decades before, as well. Hands of a lady who was a friend and neighbor of ours since 1963 or so. Hands of a lady who was a calming and supportive influence to me, particularly for these last three years; not running away when my emotions occasionally ran high and raw; sharing wise, simple and incredibly valuable suggestions when I have needed them most; and sharing basic general conversation and laughter as we checked in on each other (and her husband) every few days. There is a huge void in my heart, as continuity of contact cannot be replaced, cannot be made up for, and should never be taken for granted. The hands on the left are gone. A picture of her holding lilacs in our back yard is now in a simple frame on our living room table. Mom kisses her fingertips, touches the photo, and blesses Jean when she walks by it.

May 23, 2016 -- Yesterday, as we were leaving for the JCC, Mom had another small stroke. We were just outside the front door, a few feet from the wheelchair, and she came to a dead stop and would have fallen had I not been holding the back of her shirts and jacket. She was dazed for a few minutes, so I let her just sit in the wheelchair until she came back, so to speak. She was tired, but we were already dressed for the pool and went on our way.

The next couple of months went by much as the ones before, and the ones before that. Below are more notes from my phone's Drafts File:

May 30th – Level of degradation of her brain. Pills in hand, closed hand, empty hand to her mouth. This is my only experience of dementia, winging it along the way.

June 5th – Can be with her 24 hours a day and still be all alone. There is essentially no communication

June 22nd -- Frustration at not being the perfect model of consistent patience.

August 2, 2016 -- I wish that I would have, or could have, seen long ago what the triggers are which add to my frustration with Mom, and which lower the level of caregiving which I am capable of providing to her. But time takes time, and clarity often comes only with time, effort, desire and experience. In a nutshell, outside factors, disappointments, broken promises from others, -- those outside issues, which are fully out of my realm of influence, increase my stress levels, decrease my patience and have taxed me at times beyond what I have been capable of calmly dealing with. This is not to use other people as an excuse for my periodic frustration and lack of patience with Mom. Rather, it is an explanation which I have come to see with clarity in the last 4-6 weeks.

The upside to this clarity is that I have chosen to eliminate the outside issues in which I do have some control. I have closed my Facebook page. I have stopped calling or contacting certain people who have been important to me. The aforementioned people have a solid track record of breaking their word when it comes to visiting.

August 6, 2016 -- 10:00pm – Mom called for me, telling me that her hands and arms look ghoulish. Asked me how they got that way. I told her that 86-year-old arms just get to looking that way. Then we put some lavender skin lotion on her arms and hands.

10:30pm – Mom called for me, asking where we were going....

August 13, 2016 -- Mom's confusion was extreme today. So sad when she is aware of how limited she is.

SEVERE BURNOUT AND BREAKDOWN

August 16, 2016 -- Late afternoon and frustration broke me. I hit my head against the wall, and it frightened Mom. Not good. Stormy evening outside, so I stayed home from going to the JCC, as storms frighten Mom and she usually gets up a lot. A few weeks ago, I began trusting G-d and leaving Mom alone at home after tucking her into bed. I am only out of the house for about 2 hours, going to the gym for some much-needed exercise and solo social contact. An old friend of Mom's, Sherry W., had called me on whether I was really trusting G-d or was I just giving Him lip service. My 3-4 hours a week out of the house while our Russian lady friend stays here has been missed. Finances led me to cancel those much needed breaks. The gal had been out of commission for a couple of months anyway, after having knee replacement surgery. I listened to Sherry and have begun stepping away at night. So far, no problems have arisen while I am gone. I sure wish I could stay on an even keel.

September 10, 2016 -- I talked with Rose today. I'm burned out, but do not know what to ask for help with, or who to ask. Rose will watch Mom for a few hours when she is in town at the end of the month.

September 12, 2016 -- I lost it yesterday with Mom, around dinner time. By that time of day, my patience seems too often to be almost nil, try as I may to be otherwise. Mom deserves better than what I am capable of delivering these days. This is not what I want my caregiving to look like. If I were my own boss, I would fire me. The melancholy I have been feeling appears to be unshakeable. Dawns on me that what I've been feeling is grieving the continued decline of my Mother's brain. How does one do "Grieving Work?" My brother compared his communication with his dog, with my communication with Mom. I know he means well, but I just don't get it...

September 21, 2016 -- I am at my most ineffective and most vulnerable now, just when Mom is at her neediest and in steep decline of dementia. Try as I do, I cannot give up the notion of former friends coming around. I do not know how to ask for help, or who to ask, or who to turn to in order to find out who to ask. I have begun to picture my Mother with a bandage on her head, in order to remind myself that her brain is so badly injured and to prompt me to not lose my cool or take things personally. Three and a half years into this, winter approaching and Caregiver Burnout is live and on stage, so to speak. Oy, G-d, please refill my spiritual tank. Please show me what I need to see.

I had my eyes examined a month or so back, with cataract surgery in mind. I have had many surgeries on my eyes over the years, and I have learned to be patient with them, always grateful for the vision that I have. But night vision has become horrid, and day vision is problematic. I lost half the sight in my right eye many years ago, and the cataract is in the left eye – the stronger of the two. It has become quite challenging to deal with.

Two considerations have led me to postpone getting my eyes fixed. I am not certain that I can show up on the day of surgery, as Mom's needs may prevent it. We have missed several doctor's and dentist's appointments in these last 3+ years because Mom was, for whatever reasons, not up for going. I also am not certain that I can be out of commission for a day or so after surgery. Who would tend to my Mother's needs? Eye surgery in particular requires not bending over, or lifting anything heavy, for a while. How do I help my Mom in her bathroom needs, or getting her dressed, or lifting her when needed, without bending over? Poor vision is just another stressor for me to deal with and surrender to. Throwing that into the caregiver burnout mix, and I've not been at my best for a while now.

It dawns on me, though, that my/our Jewish holidays have always been emotional and difficult for me. They are, ideally, family holidays and I have no family to mark the holidays with, except for Mom. And she is oblivious to it all. My siblings are either not in touch with us or are not observant at all regarding our religion.

Recognizing the connection between the holidays and my recent short tempered behavior is almost magically deescalating my emotions as I type this. I do not know why putting these feelings on paper – or on a computer screen as I type – helps to calm things down for me. I just know that it works. I wish my siblings well. We all have our own history, family history, and ways of dealing with life. My ways work for me, caregiver burnout and all. Their ways are their own and seem to work for them. What I wish I had was a family sense of "We." So it goes...and a good part of what I miss is being able to attend services at a synagogue. With Mom's condition, it is not feasible to do so.

October 5, 2016 -- My above insight about family and Jewish holidays has helped in these last few days. We went to a noon water class today, and then harvested some beets and carrots from our back yard. Mom then took a nap and when she woke up, she had no memory of either the class or the beets and carrots. She is getting to be more child-like over time. Poignant days.

October 18, 2016 -- I have returned to having our Russian lady friend come to the house and stay with Mom. Our friend had been down with knee surgery for several weeks, and then I succumbed to financial fears, even though we have money in the bank. She was here tonight and it allowed me to have three hours at the JCC. I had a sibling and an old friend come to mind, both of whom have not returned a phone call for some time now. And the thought did not hurt or bring me to tears. This surrendering thing works when I remember to work it. Admittedly, it comes and goes, but that is part of being human, I suppose. I am glad, for Mom's sake primarily, that our friend is once again available to come be with her. Mom so enjoys her company. I think Mom also is grateful to have a break from me. This is not self-deprecating, Dear Reader. It is however, probably quite true. Once in a while, I joke with friends we might be around at the water class: "Charming as I no doubt am, Mom dearly needs a break from my constant presence."

October 30, 2016 -- Lots of surrender during this period of time; lots of resistance, followed by acceptance, followed by more resistance, followed by accepting that sometimes I am resisting life and caregiving, as they are. And that is all o.k.

November 4, 2016 -- On a short break from bass guitar, having tucked Mom back into bed again. Man, the blessings and beauty of this caregiving are sometimes so deep and yet so simple. I tucked Mom into bed at about 7:00, and an hour later she called for me, telling me that she was lonely and missing me. She had no memory of dinner, the part of a ballgame we watched during dinner, or anything about our day. Mom did not express her fear, but I could see it. She has expressed, several times today, the sadness of being confused.

So, tonight I talked with her for a short while and then brought her a couple small pieces of pastry and got onto my bass. I invited her to come out and sit with me while I play, but she preferred to lie in bed.

She called me to her once again a little bit ago, just to tell me how good she felt and to let me know that she was ready to sleep, peaceful and content. The blessings and beauty is knowing what to do for her tonight, and caring enough to be here long enough to know what to do for an elderly woman who is in an odd and challenging part of her life. Considering my periodic meltdowns and emotional outbursts, even though I immediately apologize for them and let Mom know that she has not done anything wrong, that is it just my fatigue and frustrations getting out of hand, My Mother is the most truly understanding and forgiving person I have ever, or probably will ever, know. Would that others in our family could be so forgiving of her.

December 3, 2016 -- Although I have become accustomed to my Mom not knowing where we are going, even after having just put on her swim suit to head to the JCC, it is strange to have to say, "No" when we pull into the parking lot and she asks me if she can just sit there and wait for me. She asked the same thing today when we pulled up in front of our home. I asked her if she knew where we were, and she shook her head, "No." These are the little things, the little declines in her mental capacity, the little blank spots in or on her brain, and these are the little things which nobody else but me has experienced with her.

It is difficult to put into words just now what kind of feelings or emotions are going through my mind. Sadness. Compassion. More sadness. Surrender. All the emotions one would figure to be present when a son witnesses such things happening to his Mother.

On January 22, 2016, Mom said, "I wish I was able to learn new things." Now, 11 months later, such thinking is impossible for her. She has not been able to fasten her own seat belt for some time now. It is not that she will not. It is that she cannot, and it is not a physical limitation. Put it off; change on the fly; make no plans; fruitless to ask what she wants to do today. At least with "just" aphasia, I could somewhat follow her thinking. With dementia? Not possible most of the time. Mom needs direction on most everything, but does not understand words of direction. Even gestures are not understood most times any more. There are periodic low points, that is all, and I cannot always hide them. No rescuing is needed. I have repressed grieving and mixed it up with depressed feelings. We are given unique opportunities in life to do what only we can do for someone. It takes a lot every day, and I've done this for lots of days

Recently, while in the bathroom, Mom was at a dead stop. I asked her if she knew what she was supposed to be doing; what a bathroom and a toilet was for. "I really don't" was her reply. And her eyes were so mournful. I was looking ahead a bit and wondering if I will ever look back on today's days and wish I had done some things differently. This leads me to be more mindful of how I do things today. Some time ago, I asked Mom if she was o.k. She replied, "Yes, except I don't know where I am." We were at home. There are days now when Mom does not recognize lipstick. Mom never has gone anywhere without having lipstick on. It takes vigilance to see more than just what she cannot do.

LESSON ON NOT LECTURING & MY SKEWED THINKING

February 7, 2017 -- Gut-punched tonight by what my Mom said to me. I was helping her with her underwear and pants after she had used the toilet, and she noticed she had a fingernail which needed a bit of trimming. I began to explain to her that this was not an appropriate time for fixing her nails. Mom turned her face to me, half crying and a tear in her eyes, and said: "Honey, please don't go on at me." That stopped me in my tracks. Even though I am well aware of her language and cognitive deficits, and even though I thought I kept explanations to a reasonable minimum, I have to admit that I have a tendency to go on and on and on with her, with a ridiculous and unreasonable expectation that she will learn and change some given behavior. I wonder where my patience goes when I lose it. Perhaps G-d takes it for a short while so that, if I am mindful, think about deepening my empathy and compassion. Then, He returns it to me.

That said, this leaves me in a position which I need to ponder. It has been my belief that engaging in conversation with my Mom, simplified as much as possible, was, and has been, in her best interest.

To say nothing to her when her actions are inappropriate or ill-timed is to surrender to an "anything she does or says is o.k." paradigm, and I do not believe that to be beneficial for her and her brain. Engaging the conversational part(s) of her brain is, I believe, necessary if they are to remain at all active. And no matter how much I believe that I am correct in my thinking, it is possible that I am completely mistaken. What, then, should I talk with my Mom about? Or should I just stick to single word responses to her questions or statements? Should I not try to explain anything? After the episode this evening in her bathroom, we had dinner and watched some college basketball. I answered her questions and statements with single word replies, and got her off to bed when she wanted to go to sleep.

Perhaps the rest of the world is right, the people who just share the pleasantries with my Mom and then go on their way. Perhaps I have been projecting to my Mom what I would desire if I were in her situation. I would want people – someone, anyway – to engage with me, if even on a simplified level. All too often, most of the time, really, I observe the people who are around Mom when we are out in public. A brief, "How ya doing, Marcie?" and then they are on their way, even while in the swim pool we frequent. I have never understood this, nor have I liked it. But thinking back now, Mom does not appear to mind or notice. Why do I?

Dang. <u>Reading back through the last few pages here, I can see where my thinking and perspective are perhaps (perhaps?) seriously skewed.</u> I am questioning everything, or almost everything, that I have done in being my Mom's caregiver. And her statement to me just triggered a massive amount of doubt about the value of what I have been doing for her. Burnout and foggy thinking, and nowhere to turn to. I wonder if I have gone a wee bit nuts in my noggin.

February 18, 2017 -- 11 days into this mindfulness of "not going on at Mom" and it has become habit. Or, to put it another way, I have broken a bad habit which I fell into for far too long. There is no making up for the times I have tried to explain too much to Mom, subconsciously believing at some level that she could still learn if she tried harder and if I explained things expertly. It has been a poignant awakening for me, as caregiver, to recognize the errors of some of my actions. Poignant, humbling and, to be honest here, rather depressing. I hold myself to a very high standard in my care for Mom, and I see where I have been falling short too often and for far too long. I have read in a couple of caregiving books about guilt and regret that other caregivers have felt, so I know that I am not alone in these feelings. Beating myself up does no good, and I know that to be the truth. But that is, apparently, yet another lesson which I must experience for myself.

March 17, 2017 -- I have got to get a handle on the heaviness and depression which has gripped me for several weeks now. Deep sobbing three times today – twice this morning and once this evening while Mom was trying (her best) to help make dinner – and completely (again) losing my patience with her and her disabilities. She exhibits intermittent ignoring of me while I am trying to talk with her, and it drives me nuts as I cannot help but think that it is intentional. I know it is not, having talked with other caregivers who have experienced the same. She exhibits a helplessness at times which I believe is intentional. I know it is not, again from having talked with others who have been in a similar caregiving position.

Poor Mom! She deserves better than what I am capable of delivering.

I am grieving the deterioration of my Mom's brain and its functionality. And the depression from that grieving, while perhaps normal, is I believe magnified by my feeling so alone and overwhelmed by the length of time that I have been doing this. When I lose my patience with Mom, I do not get violent and I do not yell or raise my voice too loud. I do get highly emotional, though, and Mom is not completely unaware of it. She gets very quiet and still. Her brother was a violent man. That has been in my thoughts since I was a kid, and I have always been careful about how I deal with her. Even though I am generally an easy-going man, this job of caregiving is taking a serious toll on my health - emotionally, spiritually and physically.

When I put Mom to bed tonight, she asked how she could help me so that things were not so heavy for me. As she said the word "heavy" she made a gesture with her hand which I have not seen her make since before the stroke. She makes a hand like she is holding a large rock and pounding it on something. Mom used to make that gesture when talking about AA program and spiritual matters, and encouraging me or others to not take things so heavily, and to take it easy.

It breaks my heart to see that she comprehends enough of what I am experiencing, to find the coherent words enough to let me know that she wanted to help. Man, oh man, G-d, do I need your help now. It is not fair to Mom for me to be this out of sorts. In case, some day, another caregiver reads this far into my writing, I hope that my experience, if nothing else and as dark as it is tonight, helps some other caregiver who is in a similar place, that they are not the only one to meet up with such a struggling part of their journey. I pray that they reach out for help. I wish I knew where to reach out for help.

March 29, 2017 -- "Marvelous and Beautiful" -- Those were the words my Mom said tonight when we finished saying/chanting the Blessing after Meals, right before I tucked her into bed for the night. For some reason, tonight's blessing was chanted, or sung, with particular joy by both of us, much to my amazement. Amazement because I have been uptight for a couple of hours this evening, as it is four years ago tonight when Mom had the main stroke. Uptight because of her continued cognitive decline, decline which was very evident tonight during dinner. Amazement also because of the energy and joy which Mom exhibited while we were saying that evening prayer. And then, out of nowhere, she said "Marvelous and Beautiful!" When she said that, my whole heaviness of spirit dissipated and disappeared, and not at all by my own doing, my own thoughts, or my own effort. And that is marvelous and beautiful indeed. I'll take it, thank you.

URINARY TRACT INFECTION (UTI) – THE FIRST ONE

August 11, 2017 -- I did not catch my Mom's urinary tract infection (UTI) early enough, although the signs of it were at hand. I just did not know what to look for, had never heard of a UTI, and did not know what to have been alarmed at seeing as her behaviors changed over a few days. I thought we were just on another odd part of the path of dementia. On Monday, August 7th, her legs gave out.

We had just gotten out the front door, on the way to the swim pool, and Mom came to a dead stop, three feet from the wheelchair on the sidewalk. She could not take another step, and I gently eased her onto the ground. I called a neighbor to help me. She held the wheelchair while I lifted Mom into it. I then called an ambulance and mom spent the next three weeks in an acute care rehab facility, until she regained enough strength to be able to get up the 7 steps inside our home. This was a long three weeks. I was with her every day, twice a day, to help feed her lunch and dinner.

Edit on May 23, 2019 – I learned at the time that a UTI often induces delirium. Delirium on top of dementia is incredibly difficult to deal with, as it resembles total insanity. A couple of 18 hour days with Mom's UTI dealing out blows to her brain should have led me to call her doctor. I missed it completely.

September 21, 2017 -- I've not written much in the past number of months, as I have not had much new to write about and did not want to be repeating myself any more than I probably have already done in this treatise. I believe that I have painted a clear enough picture of the situation – the caregiving situation and my Mom's condition.

Mom had another "small" stroke a week ago Wednesday while she was on a foam rubber noodle in the swim pool. A friend of ours happened to be in the lap lane next to her. He is a former Army medic and told me that the look on Mom's face was unmistakable as she fell off the noodle. On Friday, He confirmed the stroke which I had suspected, due to her change in behaviors and abilities. Mom needed, and continues to need, a lot of support while eating, while putting mayonnaise on bread, while making a bowl of cereal, while brushing her teeth, and in most everything else. Also, her language recognition has completely bottomed out.

Two nights ago, Tuesday night, I believe that Mom had another stroke. She woke up even more confused and very weak. We got to the noon swim class and the instructor, who has been an Occupation Therapist for many decades, told me that one look at Mom's face told her that something, probably another "small" stroke had happened. I put the word "small" in quotes because at this stage every stroke takes a huge toll, probably because of the amount of Mom's brain which has already been damaged. I am not a doctor and am just speculating, of course.

SLAPPING THE WALL – NOT GOOD

Today has been a rough one for me, as my Mom's son and as her caregiver. Not only is Mom so out of it – sleeping/resting until 4:15 this afternoon, which is 20 hours in bed – and not only because it is Rosh Hashanah and our Jewish holidays are generally a depressed time for me, my family being so fractured – but also because last night while helping Mom in the bathroom, my frustration peaked. I raised my voice and slapped the tile wall over the bath tub, slapping it very hard and very loudly. This started Mom and she turned to me and said, "That was not good." I wholeheartedly agreed, and it bothered me all night and well into the day. I cried about it a few times, feeling empty and hollow and unworthy and incompetent as a caregiver, and all the other emotions of regret one can have. And I prayed to G-d that this be the last time that I fight the reality at hand, and that I never show such frustration again. Mom deserves better. And on Rosh Hashanah, no less.

I remember writing, much earlier in this work, that I would be honest about my journey as a caregiver. Thusly, I typed above about what happened last night. I am not perfect by any stretch of the imagination. I have an explosive level of frustration at times, which is something that bothers and frightens me. To other caregivers who might read this, I ask you to pay attention to the level of frustration, or anger if that be present in your case, and always ALWAYS keep in mind to never ever strike the recipient of your caregiving. Ever. That must not happen. I have not crossed that line, nor can I see myself ever doing so. I have hit some walls in the house, and even then there has been a very quick thought to be careful not to hit a beam or corner post, lest I break my hand or my head. Like I just wrote, my frustration is explosive at times. And I imagine that I am not the only caregiver for whom this is true.

A shift in perspective was given to me this afternoon, through a simple but deep act of kindness by a certain rabbi. Rabbi Yossi came by today to visit with me for a bit, before he went on to a Rosh Hashanah afternoon Tashlich service which he holds each year by the lake at Washington Park, here in Denver. Tashlich is something we Jews do on the afternoon of the first day of Rosh Hashanah. Rabbi Yossi had his shofar (ram's horn) with him and was kind enough to blow the sacred notes for my Mom to hear. She was in bed. I stood by and listened. Then Rabbi Yossi did something which I'll not share here. It was deeply personal and deeply humbling to witness. An act of kindness; a gesture directed at my Mom which was extraordinary and totally unexpected by me. Should Rabbi Yossi ever read this treatise, he will know to what I am referring. On his way out the door, I was crying and I said to him, "You got me with that one, man. You got me with that one."

As long as I am writing about today, I feel to share that our dear friend, Rose visited earlier this afternoon. Rose and Mom have been friends for 33 years, and I have come to know her, and her husband, since I got sober in 2002. I have written about Rose before, as she is one of the few friends of Mom's who have remained in contact. With Rose I can freely speak and freely cry. And to Rose I have learned to listen. I will be looking into hospice care, here at home, for Mom. I think that is where this path is heading. I shared with Rose that my biggest regret, that for which I regularly beat myself up, is about the times I have been less than 100% patient with Mom. I did not share what transpired last night. Rose reached over and polished the non-existent halo over my head. Then she gave me a sharp pinch just above my ankle, just to remind me that I was human. That hurt a bit, Rose, and you got my attention. I have learned the value of paying attention to Rose in these matters. It is not for nothing that my Mom has long held Rose, and her wisdom, in high regard. Mom used to say that that precious friend had an old soul in her.

A STEEP DECLINE GETS STEEPER

October 10, 2017 -- Time flies as Mom's abilities so rapidly decline. It is Tuesday evening now as I take a few minutes to type here. I just put Mom to bed, and before taking care of evening duties I have to get a few things out of my head so I can focus. Sunday, we went to the water and ran into Rabbi Buz Bogage, a dear man whom I have been blessed to get to know these last few years. We met at the noon water class. Buz greeted Mom warmly, as he always does, and Mom barely took notice. Sunday evening I received an email from Buz, and he noted: "Marcie did not respond well today." I always appreciate the honesty and directness of Rabbi Buz. He gets to the point. He is also the man who introduced me to the works of Abraham Joshua Heschel, a wonderful writer.

Today at the water, David, the instructor, turned to me and said: "Marcie looks dazed today." And David was right. Kit, another friend in the water class, was very kind and gentle with Mom. Kit's husband, John, is in late stages of Alzheimer's and I often go to Kit for advice or just to share what I am experiencing with my Mom. Kit is a wonderful lady.

I am having to either directly feed Mom, or remind her and redirect her to eat. She will take one mouthful and then come to a stop. Or, she will just gently wave her spoon or fork, much like an orchestra conductor waves his or her baton. She will often do this even though I have put some salad on her fork or some soup in her spoon. Her brain just seems to go offline, so to speak, and when I remind Mom to eat – to put the utensil in her mouth – her only response is "Oh" or "Yes, honey." She is getting to be completely oblivious to whatever we are doing.

Mom (on left) and Dottie Edger
Circa 1975

Edit on August 10, 2019 – As I got to the above paragraph about having to feed my Mother, the above picture fell off a book shelf in the living room, which opens/connects to the dining room where I am sitting and typing at my desk. Spirited off the shelf? Mom's spirit? Perhaps. The thought came to mind that we all would do well to remember that none of us are born old. And "old" is not a pejorative term. In Judaism, when an elderly person enters a room, we are taught to rise from our seat for a moment to honor the presence of an elder. The gal in the picture with Mom, Dottie Edger, a solid member of Al-Anon, was one of my Mother's most cherished old friends from York Street. Dottie and her husband, Reed, were very important people in Mom's life. I take this today as Mom reminding me to maintain balance.

End of Edit from August 10, 2019

The emotional toll this is taking is enormous, all day and all night on my mind. Only occasionally am I able to successfully divert my thinking or my attention to other matters, and even then it usually takes conscious effort to block caregiving from my thoughts. A line I recently read summed this up nicely: "I am being swallowed up by this work." Or something to that effect. Balance, emotional, spiritual and mental balance, is so hard won. At times, it is also so fleeting. Here now, and then gone. There are times I question my sanity, but when I look at my thinking and lack of balance in perspective, it is understandable considering the situation at hand. As long as I do not act on the suicidal thoughts, I am not terribly worried about things going haywire. Yes, Dear Reader, suicidal thoughts. And I have them more regularly than I would ever admit to anyone right now, lest I be locked up for a 72-hour psych check. Putting this in writing helps. I wrote the lyrics to a song the other night, and in those lyrics I wrote:

CAREGIVER BURNOUT
Written by Aaron Ainbinder

Occasional thoughts of suicide
I just do the best I can
Occasional thoughts of suicide
I guess that I'm not Superman
And I'd never do that to the lady

Suicide
I'd never do that to the lady
Suicide
Would be the ultimate abandonment of my duty
Suicide
Abandonment is not even an option
I'd never do that to the lady
Not to worry,
I'd never do that to the lady

The song is called "Caregiver Burnout" and the melody will come to me eventually. When I have those thoughts of ending it all, I am able to think back to some nice moments of that day, or the day before, and this allows me to regain my perspective and clearer thinking, and I go on with the day's business. But these thoughts do come, and having talked with a couple of other caregivers, it is not unusual, particularly in the midst of long periods of unending stress and burnout. I have promised all along to be honest with you in this piece. Sharing the darker thoughts which come? That's just part of being honest.

Belief in G-d; spiritual practices; prayer; a good solid cry now and again; these are some of the things which keep me going. I wish I had a confidant or someone to take council with on a regular basis, but that is not how things have worked out.

Again, Dear Reader, I write of the heavy stuff in this treatise with the hope that some other caregiver might find that he or she is not the only one encountering such struggles and dark spots. Yes, there are a lot of times in which I really enjoy being here and being able to be of such deep service to my Mother. And those times are interrupted at times by the struggles and dark spots. That is my reality and perhaps the reality of other caregivers as well. To deny the struggles and dark times would be dishonest. I am not a superhero, and nobody else is either, except for in the movies.

Mom's doctor has provided us with a referral for Home Health Care. I need to call them and see what is available in that area, but I envision using them only when, or if, Mom becomes bedridden. In the meantime, I am making some very difficult decisions on her behalf, regarding her medical care. Mom is DNR (Do Not Resuscitate) and as such, I have to decide what to have doctors look into and what to let go. Her breathing is labored. Her weakness is progressing. Her mental/cognitive decline is advancing rapidly. I did have her doctor draw blood a couple of weeks ago when we went in for a suspected UTI (Urinary Tract Infection) and her urine sample confirmed my suspicion. My suspicions were based on some very delirious behaviors of Mom's.

Delirium in a woman with dementia is extraordinary. Hallucinations, wild imaginative talking, disorientation in all ways. Five days of antibiotics took care of the infection for now. Her blood work was relatively normal. Beyond that, I am letting her condition run its course. Unless she is in great pain, nothing medically is going to be done. These are emotionally charged decisions for me to make, for anyone to make, let alone to make them alone, with only the patient's doctor to consult with.

October 23, 2017 -- Actions and absence belie any notion of caring, compassion and concern. Those are the words which came to me just now, as I pondered a phone message I got a couple of days ago from an AA women whom Mom used to have regular, if not daily, contact for many years. She ended her short message with something to the effect of "Sorry to have missed you today. I'll call back later. I love you both." She has not called back, and prior to that call we have not seen her for almost three years. Mom knows that her old friends are absent. She is injured, but she is not stupid. I remember writing a couple of years ago in this treatise that my Mom said, "It would have been easier if they were around." It is my belief that somewhere in her brain that thought can still be found. So it goes.

This all comes to mind right now, this evening after putting Mom to bed, because I have been finding myself unusually fatigued lately, and I've been trying to put my finger on what the cause is. <u>Grief is fatigue-producing, and I've been grieving my Mother's continued loss of abilities. I am grieving the loss of my Mother, and she is still alive.</u> She used to devour ice cream, which has been one of her favorite things to eat. Last night she hardly touched it. Tonight, I had to remind her how to eat some. And this was after having to guide her through almost every fork and spoonful of her dinner. It is grievous to witness this every day for so long, with nobody to share this with or commiserate with. Or very few people, anyway. So it goes.

THE LAST YEAR BEGINS – LOTS OF DELIRIUM

January 12, 2018 -- Hard to believe that I have not written since October. Much has transpired in Mom's health. Two UTI's, with the accompanying confusion and delirium that she experiences, have taken a toll on what remains of her cognitive abilities and my caregiving stamina. The first night that a UTI hits her is the hardest. I've experienced this with her, I believe, four times now and the first night has been the same. I get her to bed and an hour or so later she is up, confused, delirious and talking non-stop. The last time this happened, just a couple of weeks ago, she was up until 4:30 in the morning. My day started with her at 9:00 the previous morning, having gotten us to the swimming pool and then home. Mom napped for an hour or so and then was up for dinner. Put to bed at about 7:00, she slept for about an hour, and then the UTI confusion began.

I ended up with about 18 hours of non-stop caregiving, one-on-one, with my Mom. Wernicke's Aphasia; Dementia; UTI-induced craziness; that has all taken a real toll on my energy, my health, my attitude, my "spark" as I call it, and the effects are still being felt by me. I believe that what I am feeling, or going through, is the cumulative effects of going on five years of caregiving.

But the cumulative effects manifest themselves in odd ways lately. There are certain people whom I have known for many years and with whom contact has been sorely missed by me. In the last few weeks I have heard from a few of them and I find myself oddly neutral, or ambivalent, about even wanting to talk with them. In the first year or so of this caregiving, these people were on my mind regularly and I cannot accurately express the pain I have felt at their absence. When emails, text messages and phone calls from me were not returned, I eventually stopped reaching out to them. After the tears, which were many and often, and after talking with a couple of people I feel comfortable discussing the situation with, I came to believe that reaching out to them was unkind of me to do. Even in my readings of

Jewish sages, there is a general teaching about not offering someone something which they cannot accept, so as not to put them on the spot.

But now, when I have heard from a few of them, I simply do not know how to respond, whether to respond, or what to say. I told one of them, via email, that my social skills have atrophied due to isolation. I do not know that "ambivalent" is the correct word, or atrophy of social skills is more accurate. I have mentioned to a family member, who has also surfaced, that something inside of me has died. My spark; my creativity, my zest for doing what I do; whatever that spark is, I feel dead around it. I mentioned that to a lady I know who has a great deal of personal experience with intensive caregiving. She suggested that perhaps it was not really dead, but was just worn down a lot right now. I'll go with that, since I have ultimate confidence in G-d and myself, and I know, or believe, that this too shall pass. I have been pleasant, or cordial anyway, to these people lately, but that is all that I can manage at this time. I do not wish any of them ill.

Getting my Mom through breakfast requires my helping her – directing her, really – through each step of making a bowl of cereal. Corn flakes (generic brand), raisins, honey, homemade granola (thank you, Wayne, for the basic recipe), and then fresh strawberries cut into little pieces. Too many times, when my back was turned for a moment, Mom will stick her fingers in the bowl to mix things around. That would be o.k. except once the honey has been added. Her ability to self-direct and think through any of her actions is non-existent. And this is true at all times.

At dinner tonight, several times I had to stop Mom from spooning chicken soup broth onto one of her napkins. Mom was unable to tell me why she wanted to do that. A few minutes later, she decided she wanted to have a couple of pieces of chocolate, which we keep in a small bowl next to her chair in the living room. Why not. She also took a Dum-Dum sucker. Why not. Then she dipped the sucker into her tea. Why not. Then dipped it into her soup. Again, why not. Some things are worth my addressing with her, and some are not. She was content and having a good time, and I saw no point in interfering. Dinner got eaten, we enjoyed watching some college basketball, and she got off to bed, albeit later than usual. It is interesting to witness my Mom watching sports on television. And the dear lady will talk, or narrate, through the whole thing if I do not redirect her attention back to eating her dinner. Many times has she called me in from the kitchen, narrating along in her word salad manner, just to point out......a commercial? Why not?

When all is said and done this evening, Dear Reader, I can look back on today and know that I gave my Mother my best, with my eye at all times on what is best for her. I continue to review all that I do each day for and with her, with the intention of doing better, avoiding mistakes, and seeking ways to help her live a life with meaning and purpose. Perhaps the hardest part of all of this is that Mom is not able to give me any thoughtful or meaningful input regarding what she would like to be doing, or might like to be doing, each day.

It is simply impossible to explain anything to her. Either she does not understand the words, or she cannot make sense enough of what she hears, to provide any meaningful answer. Her stock reply is, "Whatever." Or "Whatever you would like, honey." One of the hardest things for me to refrain from these days is explaining anything to my Mother. Imagine, Dear Reader, spending day after day and night after night, week after week and month after month, with someone who cannot self-direct themselves, who initiates nothing, and who lays down no short term memories. Given those realities, it is not surprising that my Mom is unable to think of what she might enjoy participating in. Once in a while, she is able to let me know that she wants to sleep. Once in a great while she is able to let me know that she needs to use the bathroom. But when we see a child taking a swim lesson, who jumps into the pool from the side of the pool, Mom is able to say "No" when I ask if she would like to do that. Even the life guards smile when they hear that exchange between Mom and me.

January 16, 2018 -- Thank you, G-d, for the opportunity to be challenged by you, and to challenge myself, to rise to the occasion and the opportunity to be of such great service to my Mother; for the opportunity to be strengthened and to grow my courage which is needed to get through each day in service to her. Thank you for the opportunity to help, to love, to wipe her tears and to hold her as needed.....and these thoughts all allow for time; time for me rise and fall; time for the parts of the day when I take a few steps forward and then a step or two backward; time for me to feel the challenges which arise, do the best I can at the time, and correct my thinking and behaviors as needed in order to rise to the level of caregiving which I seek. I have found that maintaining the high level of caregiving is an impossible task. I do pretty well, though, all things considered.

So, as I was putting some eggs into boiling water in order for us to have hard boiled eggs with dinners in the evenings to come, I thought to bring up this treatise and write this stuff down while it is fresh in my mind. Mom's thinking and talking, during dinner tonight, was nuts. I pray that another urinary tract infection (UTI) is not at hand. Her behaviors tonight triggered some fear in me. Fear of not being able to rise to the occasion any more. Fear of falling apart, emotionally and mentally. Fear, fear, and fear......what an evil and corroding thread it can be. I have learned to, and trained myself to, turn to G-d at these times, and lately all I am asking Him for is serenity – the serenity which is needed in order to accept the things I cannot change – the serenity which is needed in order to change the things I can – the serenity which is needed in order to know the difference. This stuff works for me. I failed to put it into practice for a short time during dinner preparation time, and I lost my cool. Again.

DELIRIUM – 4+ MONTHS ON AND OFF

January 17, 2018 -- Mom was up and down all night with delirium caused by another UTI. Dementia and UTI together is like dementia on steroids. Not an experience I wish on anyone, caregiver or recipient of the caregiving.

January 21, 2018 -- Nobody to talk with about the emotional, legal, financial, spiritual, religious and DNR decisions which have been at hand before and which are at hand now. Mom has yet another UTI and again it is playing havoc with her dementia-rattled brain. I would like to take time to write more now, but I am just worn out from today. Mom finally dozed off last night at 10:30 and she slept until I woke her for dinner at about 4:15. I caught her for a moment this morning so that I could give her a morning dose of antibiotic, though. She was cognitively out of it for dinner, needing a lot of redirecting in order to eat what she was able and willing to eat.

Redirection, refocusing, and reassurance are three things of which my Mom is in constant need. Frankly, Dear Reader, having to focus on those while dealing with her, day in and day out, simply continues to exhaust me mentally, physically and emotionally.

I'm tired and heading to bed now, at 8:30pm. The problem is, though, that going to bed this early will have me up well before dawn. And in the morning, even before dawn, the emotional meat grinder in my head kicks in and is difficult to turn off. This is not like having a job which one leaves behind at the office when one goes home. Not at all.

February 11, 2018 -- I must clear off some text messages from a couple of friends who have shared with me some wisdom and thoughts worth considering.

From Sherrie W. -- Everyone has to be someplace! You just happen to be there. It is not forever. It is just for today!

Sleep well tonight and remember to be easy with your precious self! <u>And step back and set some distance between yourself and the emotional investment.</u>

Has no one ever mentioned to you that when you pray for patience you are put in situations where you will learn patience? That was one of the first things I learned in Program! Can you figure a way to change your mind about your life? <u>Can you just be a man, doing what you're doing but taking yourself out of the emotional investment.</u> This is what I have learned in the years of practice! It takes the onus off your precious self and lets you step back from the situation.

You get sucked into the caregiver role and then it consumes you! Be easy love! And breathe!

She has her own higher power that has been watching over her this last 45 years in Program! Higher Power doesn't leave her just because she can't remember!

She was my darling! And we had good times together! But what I really enjoyed was that she laughed at my dumb jokes.

Still miss her, as you probably do as well! Now you get to care for the shell that she has left! One more blessing to your dear self!

A most excellent day to you, precious friend and love and hugs to you and your Lady!

My goodness what precious images of that lovely lady! (I had emailed some pictures to Sherry)

She is your mom, but she was my play mate. And I get to share all that love and care with you! How wonderful is that?

If I were there I would stroke her hair as well!

And you sir are a rock star! Blessings and love continue to surround you as you go about your days!

A wonderful day to you dear one with all the love and hugs and blessings that you can handle and then pass them on to your precious lady!

If I was there, I would visit her! Could not have done that before but I get stronger every day! Blessings to me as well!

You lift my heart with your reports on your doings and also chronicles of your precious mom!

(My reply to Sherry) – My narrative and stories about Mom have worn thin with a lot of people, so I only share with you and a couple other trusted friends. This journey continues. For you. For me. For us all. For my Mother. Beautiful.

Never would I tire of hearing about the lady! The stories and photos are precious to me!

A Text from Rabbi Buz:

The strong man cries with no shame. Forgive her. She knows not. Not your fault. She is in your charge...to watch...and to hold. Strength...and courage...

March 1, 2018 -- What needs to be changed is my thinking, my perspective, my faith that I can continue to do this job one day at a time, with G-d's help always, no matter the circumstances. Dear Reader, I have worked diligently, unrelentingly and daily to change my thinking and keep it changed, so that I can bring my best to this work every day. I have succeeded a lot, and I have fallen short a lot. And I have not quit! I encourage you, whoever you are, to not quit. See it through to the end.

Yes, I must carve out time to get away, enjoy some separation from tending to my Mom's needs 24 hours a day, have some sort of social time for myself, and whatever I can come up with, outside of the house, in order to maintain some sort of emotional, mental and physical balance.

Mom is coming off yet another UTI, with the last of the 5-day antibiotic regimen completed two nights ago. Sadly, she has been delirious and confused the last couple of nights, sleeping only a scant few hours. I got her to the doctor's office today to see if perhaps there is another sort of infection or issue causing the increased behaviors of dementia. The doctor had some blood drawn, as well as some chest x-rays done, to see if there was anything to be found. I will hear back from him tomorrow or within a few days.

Delirium. I told the doctor about Mom's odd behaviors the past couple of days and nights, and I used the word "delirious" to describe it. He used the word "delirium" and that hit me hard. Delirium would be the root cause, or a root cause, of the challenging behaviors, but it is not treatable or curable by any regimen of antibiotics. The doctor talked with me for a few minutes about the idea that this may very well be part of the new normal. Tears came to my eyes. I do not know if he noticed.

This afternoon, after chewing on what he had said, it got a bit easier for me to accept my duties and my Mom's condition. I do not know why it got easier, but it did. Maybe knowing the cause of her increased confusion and delirious and insane behaviors lately is easing the process of acceptance and surrender. Maybe it is cracking open that door within my faith in G-d, allowing me yet another opportunity to truly trust in His care and my own abilities to adapt to this changing situation. Maybe He is providing me yet another opportunity to not run away from the material challenges because, after all, no matter where I run off to, I take myself with me. Maybe I think too much along this line of thought, but when one is involved in caregiving, or any other consuming duty, 24 hours a day, it is not surprising that it is front and center in my thoughts.

All of the above philosophical and spiritual pondering aside, what is also on my mind is that my perspective about being at home more, and getting out less, especially by myself, is what currently requires my attention. Mom is getting weaker, more confused in general, has less stamina and delirious episodes aside, requires and probably deserves, more down time at home while awake, and more sleep. That all means that I will be home more than I may desire to be.

There is, to be sure, much around the house that I could be working on, particularly in decluttering and cleaning out lots of stuff we no longer need and which someone else could use. Lots of stuff here is going to ARC, which has a collection office down the street from our home. It has been very challenging to get myself to return to that task, though I did get a lot of it done a year or so ago. I think I've written about the depression I believe has been going on with me, but perhaps it has served its purpose and it feels like it is dissipating.

Hard to get much of anything done when one is lethargic and just does not care about much of anything other than getting through another day. I've got a dozen good sized boxes downstairs in the den, and it is time for me to fill them and get them out of here. One day at a time. One box at a time. One feeling at a time. All that stuff plays out and rings true for me. Maybe for some other caregivers as well. Time takes time, and while I certainly have not done all this work at all times gracefully, I have not quit. I have not quit. Stalled? Yes. But quit? No.

May 5, 2018 – Mom was up much of the night, and completely up at 6:00am. Delirium once again. And when Mom is up, I am up. Once again.

I DID NOT QUIT
BUT I MOVED MOM OUT OF THE HOUSE

(Edit on February 20, 2019 – There is a gap of several months in my writing. Most of March and April 2018. Then, again, from May until August. This part of Mom's journey, remaining in her own home, came to an end. It was time to move my Mother out of her/our home and into a place where she can receive the care she needs and deserves. Again, Dear Reader, I have not read back through this piece until now, so I will wait until I see if I clarified things a bit in the pages to come. As I work on this, this afternoon of February 20, 2019, my nerves and emotions are pretty much numb.)

May 8, 2018 -- I had a lengthy phone conversation with Aaron H***** (I have not asked for permission to use his last name here) who is a social worker referred to me by Mom's doctor's office. Since he and I have the same name, Dear Reader, you will need to read closely to keep the following, disjointed entries straight. Events happened rapidly.

From: H**** Aaron
Sent: Tuesday, May 8, 2018 4:16 PM
To: Aaron Ainbinder
Subject: follow from phone conversation

Hi Aaron,

I spoke with the medical director through UHC Medicare Advantage (Secure Horizons) and they have decided that your mom does not meet the physical skilled criteria required under Medicare for a rehab stay. This is unfortunate news but I hope we can still figure out a plan.
I have outlined a few places where your mom can go for a respite stay, if need be, so you can have time to clear your head, rest, and clarify your goals for care. These are in your general area and closer to the house:

(Three nursing home facilities were listed in his email to me)
Additionally, if you would like to reach out to Jenn G***** at Care Patrol, she assists with transitional management and can help find a permanent place for your mom and help find something that works within your budget and goal for care (free of charge). Her number is 720-***-****
Please let me know how else I can help you out. Reach out at any time.

Sincerely,
Aaron H******

Reply from me, at 9:53pm, is below. In a page or so, Dear Reader, you will see why the time is pertinent.

Reply From Me:

Very kind of you to take so much time today, Aaron, both on the phone and in gathering the information you emailed below. Clearing my head is definitely in order, lest I make any decisions while lacking clarity due to caregiver fatigue. Though I said I surrender today, and I meant it at the time, I continue to view nursing home placement for my Mom as a last resort. When the dementia of hers is totally off-leash, with symptoms resembling delirium, my task with her is at its most difficult. Rather than lengthen this email with alternatives to nursing home placement that have already come to my mind, I think it best to clear my thoughts some first. I still hold onto the hope that by strengthening myself spiritually, and increasing my time away from duty, I can continue to keep my Mom in her own home. Perhaps some form of home hospice, mid-day for a few hours, a few times a week?

Thanks again for the info below. I will begin checking it tomorrow.
Take care,
Aaron Ainbinder

Email from me to Aaron H. – The Care Coordinator
Wednesday 5/9/18 -- 11:12am

Hi, Aaron;

I was fooling myself last night, or in deep denial about my capabilities. I just talked with Jenn G*** and she will have someone call me back. Time to get Mom into skilled care, perhaps at Shalom Park.
Take care, and I'll keep you posted.

Aaron

5/9/18
12:05pm

Hi, Aaron: Thank you for letting me know. I received your voicemail, too. I won't tie your line up with a call, but I'll check in later today to see where we're at. I'll keep Dr. T***** in the loop so you can just focus on working with Care Patrol.
Take care.
Aaron

August 22, 2018 -- The above email exchanges took place in early May, some 3 ½ months ago. It has taken me this long to be able to come back to my writing on this treatise. The email above is from Wednesday, May 9th at noon. I will fill in some details below, but here is a snapshot of what transpired: I took Mom to visit a group home assisted living house on Thursday, May 10th. Rose met us there at about 1:00, took notes and asked some clear-headed questions. I was anything but clear-headed. The next day, Friday May 11, 2018, I drove my Mom to the group home and moved her in. I do not foresee her returning to her/our house.

When I called Care Patrol, the placement company, I had in mind to find a nursing home for my Mom. A couple of places, primarily Jewish or at least with a large Jewish community of residents, was what I had in mind. After talking with Beth, from Care Patrol, I realized that nursing homes were out of our financial arena. Beth recommended a group home for Mom. In a book called "Being Mortal" by Atul Gawande, which I highly recommend that you read, Dear Reader, I had read about group homes for the elderly. And I had forgotten about them over these last few years.

Beth found a nice place for Mom. Group homes are about half the cost of a nursing home. They are private pay for the most part. The place we chose is called "Abby's Assisted Living" and it was a perfect fit for my Mother. Eight residents; full-time staff who live in the house and work in shifts; 7 other people of my Mom's vintage for her to be around; caregiver employees who are relaxed at all times! It was a perfect fit at just the right time. To be honest, Dear Reader, if I could rewind the time, I would have moved Mom into the place many months earlier than it worked out.

On the evening of May 7th that I saw Mom's situation in a very different light, and with different eyes. That evening, when I looked in on her while she was in bed and her eyes were wide open, I saw in my Mother's eyes and on her face such loneliness, isolation and sadness. She had exhibited delirium quite a few times in the last four or five months. UTI's caused some of them, but not all of them. Her doctor confirmed this via urine sample testing. On May 7th it finally became clear to me that keeping my Mother in her own home, with the caregiving situation (and the caregiver) being in the state it/he was in, was no longer in Mom's best interest. It had probably not been in her best interest for some time, but I did not see it.

I believe that I was granted clarity to see, on the night of May 7th that my core belief about keeping a parent in their own home until the end of their life, had run its course. My core belief was, I saw, valid up to a point. Mom and I had passed that point. Without a caregiving support team, so to speak, of family and friends, Mom had declined to a point that the isolation here at home was, in fact, detrimental to her. She was not a happy camper at all. The time had come for me to shelve my ego, my pride and my desire to look like the good and dutiful son who is giving his all to keep his Mother in her home, rather than putting her in a nursing home or some other type of care facility.

Edit on August 5, 2019 – I have been asked if I view the above issue as a failure. The answer is "No, I do not." Once again in hindsight, as wisdom often comes, it may have been, or probably would have been, better for Mom to have been moved out of her/our home prior to when it actually occurred. My core beliefs and values may have clouded my judgement. I will never know. I, and others, can only speculate and to what good purpose? As you will read in the following paragraphs, I stayed true to my values and beliefs to the best of my ability. When the time came to make a change, I was granted that insight and took action.

Know this, Dear Reader – ego, pride and desire to look good was never once in my conscious thinking during these years of caregiving. I took on this job without ever considering not doing it. The thought of moving my Mother out of her own home after the initial stroke of March 29, 2013 never entered my mind. My insight on May 7th, the gift such as I see it, was that I had done all that I could do for my Mother. I had done my job here at home. It was time to make a change, and that change was in Mom's best interest. The best way to continue to Honor my Mother, which I hold to be a sacred duty, was to find a place where she would be happy, content and well-cared-for. I would still have a responsibility and a job to do on her behalf, but not here at home. Being prone to long-winded typing, I will leave it at that.

For the first few months, I picked Mom up a few days a week and we went to the JCC swim pool. I would pack a couple of peanut butter and jelly sandwiches to take with us, as well as fruit and some cookies. We enjoyed a little lunch in the lobby of the JCC after swimming, and then I would take Mom back to Abby's. Mom adjusted immediately and peacefully to the change in her life. I did not talk about our house at all, and not once did Mom ask about going home. She enjoyed our excursions to the pool, enjoyed the friends we saw there, and then enjoyed being taken back to where she was now living.

One oddity I noted was that my Mother's episodes of delirium ceased after I moved her out of the house. I had explained to the staff about these delirium happenings, and they never had to deal with them. That is something which I will never understand. I can speculate about it, but I prefer to not go down that road. It is what it is, and it was what it was. My Mom was content and that is all that matters to me. Urinary tract infections seem to have kicked aging and dementia into high gear. Mom aged so much in these last months at our home. In the pictures that follow, you will notice that her mouth droops a bit. Strokes, even mini strokes, will do that.

Below are a few pictures and descriptions of Mom's time at Abby's Assisted Living. Rose and Mary and Patty Jo and a few other old friends came to visit Mom pretty regularly. So did both Rabbi Yossi and Rabbi Engle and his son, also a Rabbi Engle. The staff at Abby's took a real shine to Mom, as her pixie dust spreading of "Blessings and Love" filled their hearts.

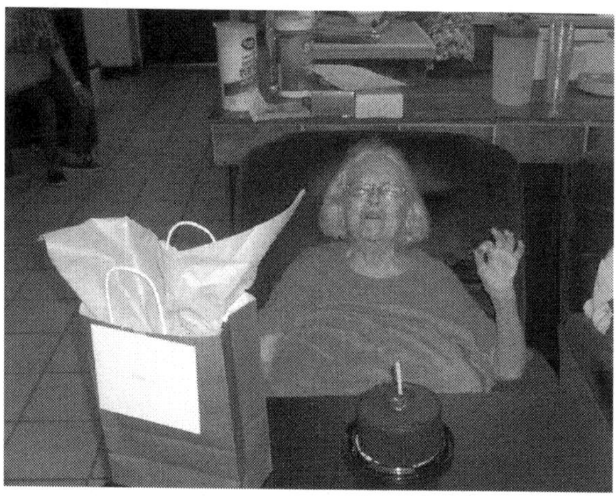

Party for June Birthdays
June 21, 2018

Patty Jo, Rose and Mom

Patty Jo dances with Mom

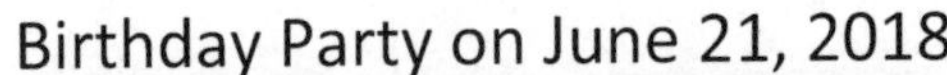

Birthday Party on June 21, 2018

Jo Martin, Gay Carlson and Mom

The ladies have known each other for decades. The joy on Mom's face when they came over was priceless.

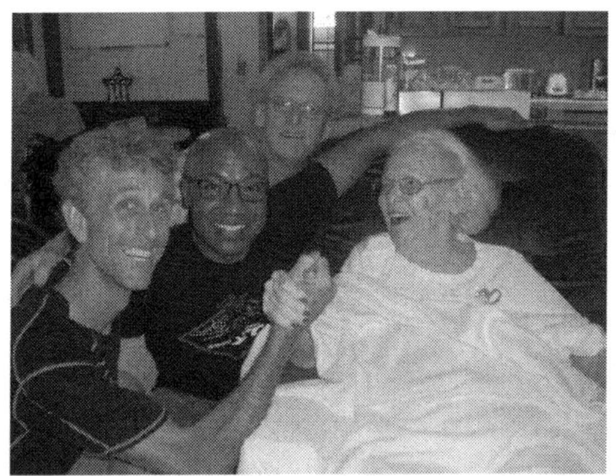

August 11, 2018

Wayne, Robert, Aaron and Mom

Wayne and I had played music at the group home.

Mom holds a Shofar from Rabbi Yossi

September 7, 2018

Wayne and I played music at the home for an hour or so on August 11th. Robert is a dear friend of ours. The shofar that Mom is holding was brought over by Rabbi Yossi Serebryanski. A shofar is a ram's horn which we Jews blow on our High Holiday of Rosh Hashanah. Rabbi Yossi was kind enough to visit Mom, blow the notes of the holiday for her, and allow Mom to hold it for a bit.

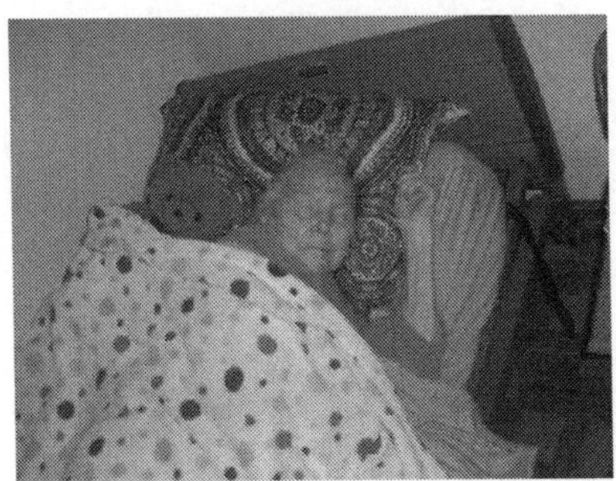

October 12, 2018

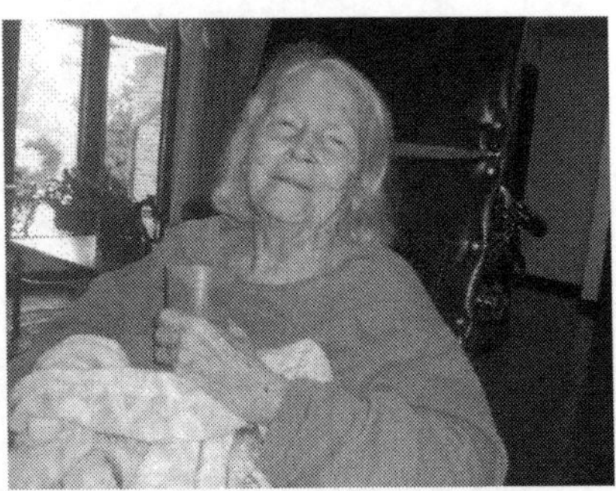

September 27, 2018

Rabbi Yossi Serebryanski
and Mom at our home
December 7, 2015

Chanie Serebryanski,
Mom & Chaya Mushka
October 21, 2015

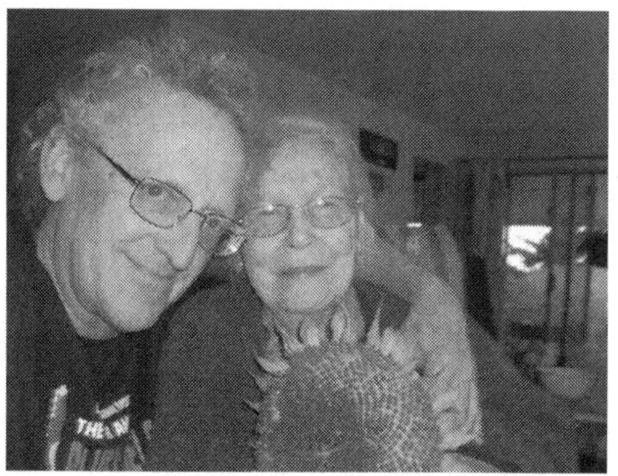

August 28, 2015
With a giant sunflower we grew

THE LAST MONTH

Rabbi Israel Engle & Family
Mom's Next Door Neighbor
for 30 Years
October 7, 2018

Sherry Weaver and Mom
Friend of Mom's
for 46 Years
October 17, 2018

September 29, 2018 -- My Mother appears to be fading quickly. She had another stroke two weeks ago, and this one initially left her with right-side paralysis, though some use of her right arm has returned, and her face is not as droopy on the right side as it was for the first couple of days. Mom's speech, however, has been greatly affected and it is very difficult for her to talk, though she is able to answer simple questions that I put to her. Her awareness, or cognitive abilities, also appear to have been greatly compromised, even compared to where she was, which was already quite compromised by dementia. Aside from the physical ramifications of this last stroke, Mom is very, very fatigued. She is tired out. I believe that it is quite likely that her time is short, but as one of the home's employees said today, "G-d has the last word."

I visit her every day now, for 20-30 minutes before she gets put to bed around 2:00 in the afternoon. Mom has dinner brought to her bedside, since moving her is quite the challenge. My Mother is of short stature, but is of a hefty build. She needs to be lifted from her wheelchair so that she can be put on the commode, then lifted again back into the wheelchair. Then lifted again to be placed and situated in bed. Those lifts require strength from the person lifting.

On Friday, Saturday and Sunday, the home has two ladies working, neither of whom are big enough to lift my Mom. So I have been going there to do the lifting. I remember from my time in special education, that lifting someone from a wheelchair must be done carefully, so as not to injure my back. The training that I had is coming in real handy.

October 2, 2018 -- What a payoff I receive sometimes. I got to enjoy about an hour and a half with my Mother today, arriving at her place around noon. I've gone there at 2:00 for the past couple of weeks, since her stroke, to help with getting her to the bathroom and to bed. By that time, Mom is pretty tired out. Getting there earlier today paid off. I brought some flash cards with animals on them, we fooled around with them for a while. One of the other ladies at the house joined in. Mom would participate for a few cards, then start to doze off, then come back around for more. It was beautiful, and the time passed too quickly.

I helped transfer Mom from her wheelchair, onto the commode in the bathroom. That takes some doing, particularly today as her legs just had no strength. The right leg was not working at all. Once she was seated, and the staff from the home had walked off, my Mom looked up at me and, with a look of love and peace on her face, simply said, "Thank you." I closed the door and let her have some privacy until the home helper returned. I hope that I will always be able to recall to mind the look on Mom's face. Pure love.

HOSPICE CARE – THE HOME STRETCH
NOTHING TO FEAR

October 12, 2018 -- We are in the home stretch now, the home stretch of my Mother's life. I've not written much here lately, as circumstances have been cascading and changing at a rapid pace. Two days ago I arrived at Mom's group home for a visit, and a hospice nurse, named Jim, was there. We had an opportunity to talk at length, and I am grateful that things worked out that way. My gut has been telling me that there is very little time left for my Mom. And that is exactly what Jim asked me, "Aaron, what is your gut telling you? You know your Mother better than anyone else here."

In the last week or so, after I helped put Mom back to bed in the early afternoon, I would just sit by her bed and watch for a while as she slept. I noticed her breathing. Deep labored breaths, followed by panting, then a few normal shallow breaths, then no breathing at all for 5-8 seconds. Then it began again. As Jim, the hospice nurse and I were quietly talking, and Mom was sleeping, I again noticed that pattern and I pointed it out to Jim. He had been there a number of times in the morning, to help a CNA (certified nurse's assistant) get Mom up and to the bathroom and/or shower. He had not seen this pattern of her breathing, and it captured his attention to see it firsthand.

Jim is showing himself to be a kind, gentle and yet direct and honest hospice nurse, with 30+ years of experience in that field. I had made it very clear to him that there was no fear of death, for my Mother or with me. He told me that what he was seeing was symptomatic of someone in Mom's condition nearing the end of their life. Days? Maybe a couple of weeks? Perhaps longer? G-d does not, of course, let us know the date or time of our death, but based on Jim's knowledge of Mom, and what he was seeing, he was very clear that her end was most likely a matter of days or maybe a couple of weeks. But, he clarified, one never knows and some people hang on for longer. What is in my Mom's favor, so to speak, is that her spiritual and religious beliefs and ways would most likely make it easier to make the transition, as death is so often referred to. Transition. Passing. End of Life. Death. There is nothing to fear, in my humble view.

Mom has been spending about 3 or 4 hours a day in a wheelchair, since lifting her is quite the challenge. I also shared with Jim that I never, or rarely, saw Mom look comfortable in the chair. In the last few days she had, in fact, been quite uncomfortable and was clearly in pain. Mom has always had a very high pain tolerance, so when she grimaces or cries out in pain, it must be something quite serious. Unfortunately, with the Wernicke's Aphasia, dementia, and now the almost complete inability to speak, due to this last stroke, she is unable to tell me, or us, what hurts. Jim told me that when he has helped get Mom up and into her wheelchair, she has been able to let him know that she wanted to stay in, or go back to, her bed.

Our plan now is to allow her to stay in bed, taking care of all of her personal needs and bringing all of her meals to her bed. Mom is unable to chew food, nor does she remember that she needs to chew or swallow, so she is eating pureed food and oatmeal for breakfast. Even helping her to drink some juice or water, as I have done, requires reminding her to swallow. And remember that with her aphasia and dementia, she does not always recognize what is said to her. The staff at this group home have their work cut out for them while my Mom is still with us. Another symptom which Jim noticed is that Mom's right hand is very swollen. Her right arm and right leg are both paralyzed from this last stroke. Until 2 days ago, Mom was able to move her right arm a bit at times. Yesterday and today, I've not seen her be able to move it at all. The right leg is completely without function. Her voice is breathy and very, very weak. She is still, however, able to say some of the Shema Hebrew prayer with me. Thank you, G-d, for this incredible opportunity to be of service, with love, to my Mother.

These are beautiful days.

These are painful times.

These are sacred hours.

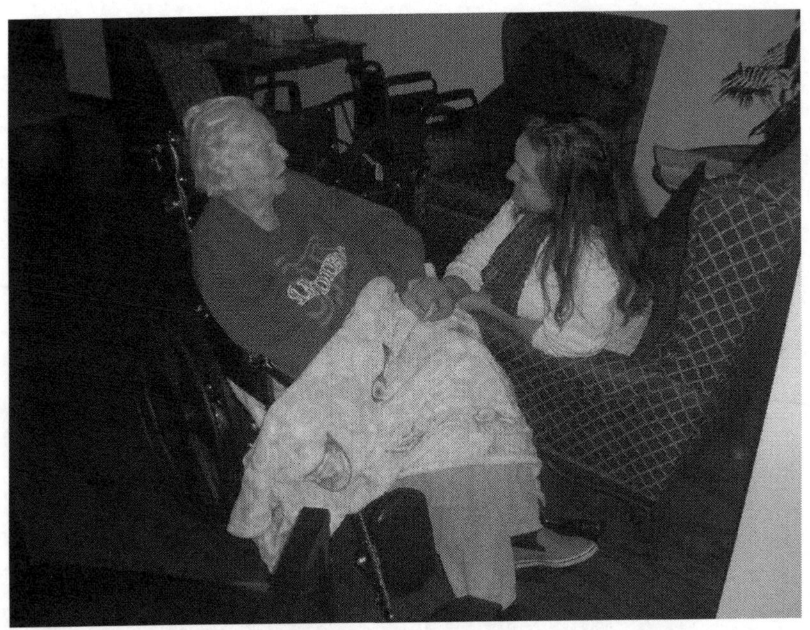

Rose and Her Marcie – Marcie and Her Precious
October 11, 2018

These are beautiful days.
These are painful times.
These are sacred hours.

October 16, 2018 -- Notes from two days ago: Sometimes the look of love on her face is far beyond what could be captured by a camera. The love, tenderness, compassion, release, gentleness in Mom's face and in her touch. She fluffed the ringlets on my head, and touched my cheek. Easier said than done sometimes, to detach. Detach to the notion that this is Mom's path to travel. All I can do is bear witness and empathize. And cry. Healthy empathy.

I had sat at her bedside for a while as she slept. Mom woke up for a few minutes, smiled at me, and I leaned over to kiss her forehead. I had been sitting and reading some psalms, and crying. I cry now as I type this. I wept a bit ago as I was saying my Jewish morning prayers here at home. Not just tears, but weeping from deep in the gut, deep in the heart and soul. Just letting it flow here, Dear Reader, and I hope you do not mind the honesty. I know that in time, the grieving will diminish. And even now it is not present all the time. But it is present at times, weaving its way through the days and the nights. Psalm 147 says that G-d is the healer of the broken hearted, and the One Who binds up their sorrows. In the meantime, this grief and this grieving process is exhausting.

It would be easier, perhaps, if I had some close family to share with and travel this with, but such is not how things are. I am very grateful for the few AA's with whom I am able to talk. Recovery experience is so beneficial, both to them and to me. Nobody is being asked to take my burden or rescue me – whatever that may mean or look like. They just know how to share, to love and to care. Then we each go on about our day, the better for the contact. It's a recovery thing.

October 17, 2018 -- Evening – The waiting is the hardest part today, and these days. I have heard and read about people being on a death watch when someone's end appears near. This is the first time I have experienced such a thing. I wrote yesterday about "...and then we go on about our day." Sometimes that is proving difficult to do, unless coming home and sleeping for a couple of hours is what going on about my day looked like today. And yesterday. And the day before. I've then gotten up and had a bit of dinner and gone off to shul (synagogue) for afternoon and evening services. I find that being around and praying with my community is comforting, and I also get to be of service to someone else who is saying Kaddish (a Jewish prayer marking the passing, or the day of the past passing, of someone of their relations) and doing so takes me out of my own head for a while. Still sort of a selfish motive I suppose, but so it is. Last night I headed to the gym. Tonight I intended to do so, but some quiet time at home seemed a better choice.

I find myself quite scattered these days, and I suppose that is understandable, all things considered. Even in my sleep, Mom is on my mind and she is the first thing in my thoughts when I awaken. And throughout the day my mind's eye sees her laying on her bed, alone, sometimes asleep but sometimes with eyes open. And alone. I wonder where her thoughts are and what her mind's eye sees. Dementia and age and stroke and loss of language will forever keep this as an unknown.

I've not slept a night through in all these years since her first stroke in March of 2013. Sleep comes for an hour or so, then I wake up. This happens five or six times a night. It is probably due to my being on alert for her while she was home, so that if she got up I would get up to assist with whatever she needed and did not take a fall. The stress of Mom dying soon, coupled with limited restful sleep is just leaving me kind of scattered. Many others have gone down this path, to be sure, so I am not thinking that I am the first. Perhaps even you, Dear Reader, have been down this road or are traveling it today. If so, know that you are not alone. Keep the faith. You will get by.

I sat on the back patio the other morning, with a cup of coffee and a cigarette, and the thought came to me that Mom will never again sit on her/our back patio. She will never again plant flowers in the pots outside the front door, or pick beets with me, or put mayo on the bread for our sandwiches at dinner, or attend an AA meeting, or call her AA ladies, or go to synagogue, or light Hanukkah candles with me, or any of the myriad things which she has been blessed to enjoy in her life. That is all over now. I will not expound on my thoughts about this. Whoever might read this thing I am writing will have their own memories and thoughts to traverse and ponder. Enjoy your memories. Cry when you feel to. Feel it all.

October 23, 2018 -- There is nothing like a Mother's touch. I sat with Mom twice today, for an hour or so each time, this morning and again this afternoon. She is unable to speak, other than an understandable "No" "Yes" and "Thank you" which is understandable, perhaps, only by myself since I know her so well. At some point this afternoon, as I was leaning close to her to hear what she might be trying to tell me, Mom reached up and gently touched my cheek, her fingertips resting on my face for a couple of minutes. The look in her eyes is beyond description. There was love, there was some concern and perhaps confusion beyond the dementia, there was some fear, there was her lower lip quivering like part of her was crying. The only tears were in my eyes, though Mom's eyes looked moist. I type this at home now, a couple of hours later, and I cannot put into words the feeling in my heart and mind. I am somewhat numb and stunned.

Healthy empathy is, at times, very difficult to achieve and adhere to. One of the hospice nurses mentioned that we all have a tendency to project, onto the patient, what we believe that we would be feeling and thinking should we be in their situation. I find it almost impossible to avoid such projection, knowing my Mother as well as I do. She is in her bed almost all the time now, alone most of the time and even when someone is in the room with her, she is almost totally incapable of expressing her needs, her pain, her discomfort or her desires and thoughts. Actually, thoughts are completely impossible for Mom to express. This last stroke has taken away just about her entire ability to speak. What she is able to say is done in a whispery voice and in words which are challenging to understand. Yes and No responses are understandable, but little else. For someone in my Mom's position, isolated in her room and in bed, the loneliness must be crushing. At least that is what my projection, such as it may be, has me thinking.

This heaviness is mine to bear, and mine to bear witness to in what appears to be this last stage of my Mother's life. I wish I had a family member to call and to share this with. I wish I could call a friend tonight to share today's happenings with, but I do not think it right to share too much heavy conversation with the few friends who have remained in touch with me and Mom. My friend, Wayne, shared with me that it is egocentric of me to presume what others can handle or want to hear. Though I believe him to be correct in this, and it may just be my ego or pride or fear of losing their friendship, which is keeping me from picking up the phone tonight. It is just after 10:00 now anyway. That is what my pride is telling me, anyway.

All I can do is be there with her and share a part of her journey, bringing some light to her as best I can. When I visit tomorrow, I think I'll bring a Dr. Seuss book to read to her. The book of Tehillim (Psalms) I have been reading to her may be contributing to the heavy heart she has. Maybe....but again that might just be me trying to figure everything out, which is not figure out-able.

Added into the mix are the physical issues which Mom is dealing with, the details of which I prefer not to share. I have been involved in helping the staff with them, and Mom's physical discomfort is due in large part to the effects of right arm and right leg being paralyzed. This paralysis is apparently causing other parts of her body, and its functions, to be quite disrupted. My Mom cannot move herself around very much in the bed. Even moving herself from lying on her back to lying on her side is impossible for her to do. *Imagine the state of mind being in such a predicament would cause, even to someone with a brain damaged by strokes and dementia. My Mother is injured, but she is not stupid.*

10:37pm – pride be darned, I just texted my friend Wayne, letting him know that is seems sometimes that all I can do is to ask G-d to guide me towards healthy empathy for my Mother. Wayne and I have talked a lot about our Mothers and their dementia, and our feelings as caregiving sons. He is a wise friend, and he can empathize with me, based on a loving heart and his own similar experiences.

October 25, 2018 -- Evening (Thursday) – Tuesday night, I lay in bed reviewing the day and as I just now re-read what I wrote here above, it is real clear that it is not constructive when I bring my heaviness with me when I visit Mom. Some heavy heart and words are appropriate, but I have been bringing too much. I had a good talk yesterday with one of the hospice nurses who had just finished working with Mom. I mentioned to her my thoughts about bringing a Dr. Seuss book, and also a Charlie Brown book, when I visit next time. I told her that I thought I was contributing to Mom's concerned looks, such as I wrote about above. The nurse told me that in her years of hospice experience, very old memories are often easiest for the patient to access, and that if Mom had read those books to me when I was a kid, she would probably enjoy my reading them to her. In fact, I told her, the two books I had pulled out are two books from when I was a child.

I visited Mom today around 11:00, and I also brought some persimmon fruit with me, which I had defrosted from last year's crop. They are only available this time of year, so I have bought a lot of them and then peeled and froze them. Mom has enjoyed persimmon these last few years, and she sure enjoyed it today. I also put on a Sammy Davis, Jr. CD. The music is more upbeat than the quieter stuff I have been playing for her on the boom box I brought from home. One of the staff came into her room to feed Mom lunch. Pureed and nutritious though it may be, my Mother has always been a good eater and we have always enjoyed homemade foods here at home. My intuition was correct, that Mom would enjoy some familiar and sweet food. I will bring more tomorrow. Today, it served well as dessert for her. Then she fell asleep for a while.

I sat quietly by Mom's bedside, reading some Tehillim (Psalms) to myself while she slept. After 10-15 minutes, Mom woke up and greeted me like I had just arrived. I took the books in hand, beginning with Charlie Brown. When I showed Mom the cover of the book, which has Charlie Brown walking and holding a baseball bat and glove, the expression of joy from the lady was priceless. The hospice nurse was wise and correct in sharing her experience with me. I opened the book to a random page, held in front of Mom so she could see the pictures, and I read to her, pointing to each frame (I think they are called frames) as I read the words on the page. There are four frames on each page. Mom laughed and smiled and laughed some more. Absolutely priceless joy! After two or three pages, Mom started to fall asleep again. I took up the Dr. Seuss book, turning to the story called "Too Many Daves" and as I showed her the colorful pictures, she fell deeply asleep. I read the story anyway, perhaps just for my own enjoyment. I have not read that story for many, many years.

I then sat back down, in the large wheelchair by her bedside, and just watched my Mother sleep, a nice smile on her face some of the time, irregular breathing some of the time, and peaceful breathing some of the time. Mom woke up one more time, just barely conscious, and reached out for my hand to hold. She fell asleep one more time, holding my hand. I sat there for another 10 minutes or so and, seeing my Mom deeply sleeping after having her lunch and some sweet fruit and some Charlie Brown, I gently removed my hand so as not awaken her. I quietly left the room, turning off the light and looking again at her face. There was the most peaceful, content and beautiful smile on that peaceful, content and beautiful face, resting with the sleep of a life well-lived for many, many years.

October 26, 2018 -- Evening – It is very difficult for me to concentrate on much of anything this evening. My visit with Mom today was strange and unsettling, as her behavior was strange and unsettling. Many times, her eyes opened wide, which is not usual at all, and she exclaimed "Wow!" while looking either above her or to either side in front of her, all while she was laying in her bed. She would then look over at me and reach out her left hand, which is not only next to where I was sitting, but it is the only hand and arm which is working. Her right arm is completely paralyzed now. When Mom looked over at me, her eyes and face were not frightened. It was more a look of bewilderment and amazement. Very unsettling, especially as this occurred several times. Perhaps eight or ten times, though I did not keep count.

I kept the notion of healthy empathy in mind, so even though the time with her was peculiar, to say the least, I have not tried (much) to figure out what was going on in her head. Perhaps it was manifestation of dementia. Perhaps it was her having glimpses of the other side, so to speak. I will, of course, never know and am conscious about not projecting what I think it might have been. It just was. Strange – just now I had something cold and wet gently touch the top of my right hand. This happens now and again here at home, usually outside on the back patio. Our old friend and neighbor, Jean Blodgett, always comes to mind, as well as a calm and peaceful feeling. This is the first time it has happened inside the house. We have a line of lilac bushes along the fence of the back yard, and Jean always enjoyed coming over to get some lilacs when they were in bloom. *"Hello, Jean. Mom is heading your way."*

Yes, Dear Reader, I know that this is some peculiar writing this evening, but as I have mentioned before, I am not editing myself as I type, nor am I trying to come across as some guru caregiver who has it all figured out, dialed in, and is hip, slick and cool at all times. And I am finding that these last pages of what appears to be the last chapter in my Mother's life, has got me kind of squirrely. And that is o.k. This too shall pass, and I am embracing these days while they are here, odd as they are at times

October 27, 2018 -- Evening – Try as I might, and try as I do, it is very difficult for me to remain upbeat, positive and happy when I am visiting my Mother. One of the things here at home, while Mom was still here, which was very hard on her was my level of sadness, intensity and being uptight. This was particularly true in the last year or so, and even with the aphasia and dementia, Mom was able to let me know quite clearly how she felt when I was off base. I have generally been an easy-going guy most of my life, but this caregiving pushed me to, and beyond, my limits. Sadly, all too often it carries over into the now. Mom gave me one of her looks today, when I was just a wee bit too sad…….it was a look impossible to describe, but picture her with her eyes rolled back and up, and an upside down smile on her face. It was kind of like, "Ughh….Too much!" I fessed up, wiped my tears away and laughed out loud at myself. This seemed to help Mom, me and the general feel in her room. My Mother is a very understanding and forgiving Mother.

I got home late afternoon and an email had arrived from Stephanie Connell. Stephanie was a dental hygienist who Mom saw for about 10 years. The two ladies got along really well. I remember Mom telling me about what it was like when Stephanie was pregnant with, I believe it was, her first child. Very pregnant dental hygienists have a bit of a challenge leaning in to work on someone's teeth. I'll leave it at that, Dear Reader, and you can form your own mental image of the scene.

Email dated today, October 27, 2018

Hi Aaron.
I got to see your sweet mom today. I could be crazy but I swear she recognized me. Maybe it's all in my mind. She reached up and grabbed my hand and didn't let go for 30 minutes. She slept a lot of the time but when she was awake she told me "thank you" over and over. What a blessing she has been in my life. I'm so glad I got to go see her.
I hope her last days/weeks/months are comfortable and you get to spend as much time as you want enjoying her company. Keep in touch as things change for your mom!

Steph

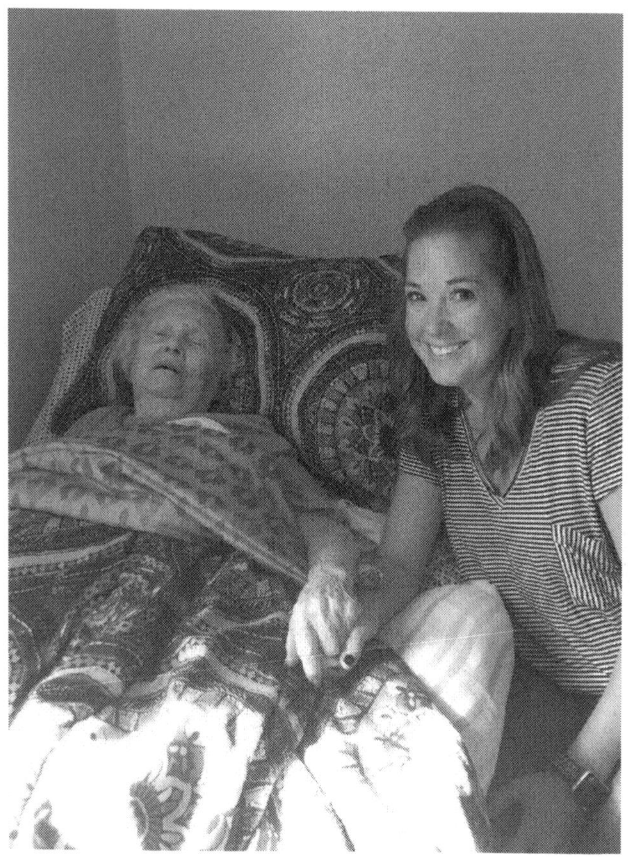

Stephanie Connell and Mom
October 27, 2018

November 2, 2018 – I spent an hour with Mom early this afternoon, and she was not a happy or comfortable lady. Having noticed Mom's physical discomfort and outright pain over the last few days, I asked the manager at the group home to ask the hospice nurse to come see Mom and evaluate things. Mom has always had a very high pain tolerance threshold, so when she is grimacing or making moaning sounds of pain, there is no question that something is going on.

I went back to the home at 4:30 and was there until shortly after 6:00. The hospice nurse arrived at 5:00, evaluated my Mother, and agreed that her pain needed to be addressed. Liquid morphine by mouth, a bit less than a pediatric dose, was used. The nurse also found a, shall we say, digestive issue which was in need of attention. I prefer not to go into details or specifics, but it was not an easy procedure for Mom or any of us. When we were through, I fed Mom some of her favorite taste – chocolate ice cream. And then she was fast asleep. We shall see how Mom handles the dosage of morphine and adjust it as needed. I will be back there at about 1:00 tomorrow, unless the house calls me earlier.

So much change in a few years.

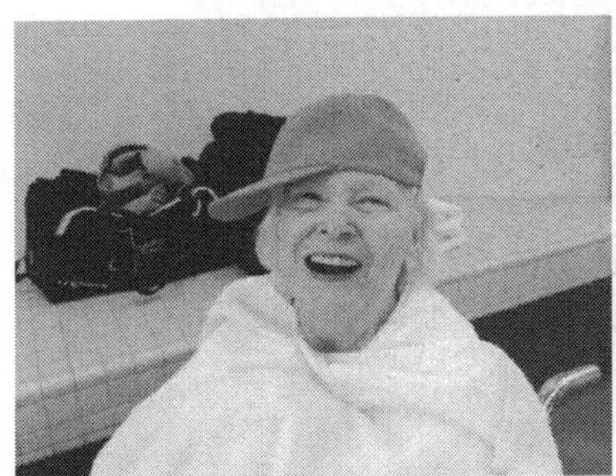

Mom after a swim
January 7, 2015

Mom and Aaron
October 17, 2018

Calling for pain medicine intervention has been the last thing I, and Mom, had wanted to do. But for her to be in great discomfort at this stage of life just made no sense. It was an emotional call for this caregiver to make, and yet my heart is calmed somewhat by the mental image I have of Mom asleep and looking more comfortable when I left an hour ago. Getting to the hospice/morphine stage is a stark picture of where this journey has taken us. I am told that with morphine, Mom will probably be eating less and sleeping more. We shall see.

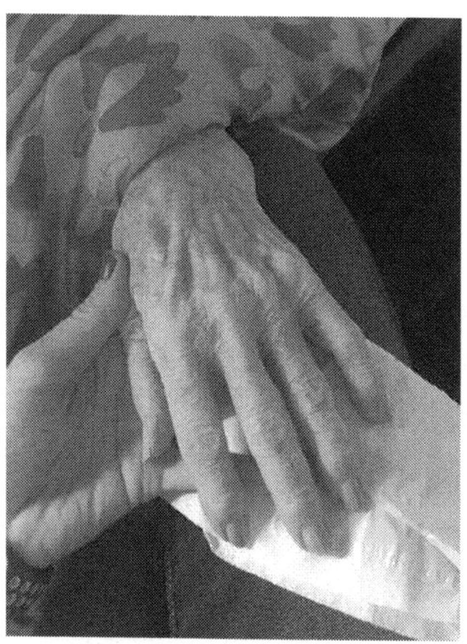

Stephanie Painted
The Lady's Nails
November 3, 2018

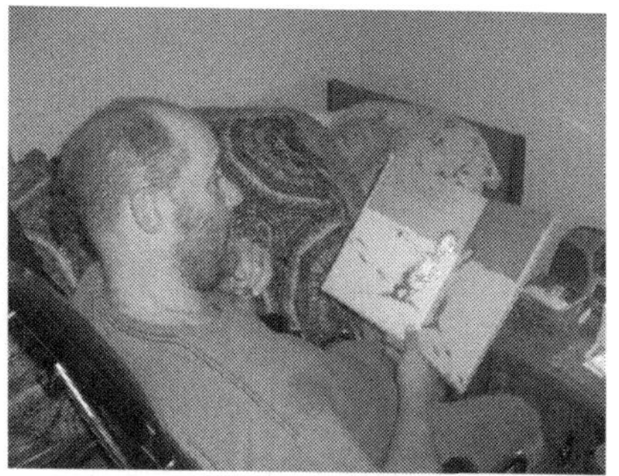

Zeke Reads Dr. Seuss
To The Lady
November 8, 2018

Zeke is a friend of mine, a practitioner of Hare Krishna, and a gentle man. He came to visit Mom and me. He quietly sang to her with his beautiful voice. And he read Mom a story from our Dr. Seuss book. I just sat, listened, and cried some. Later that afternoon, I believe it was on the 8th, anyway, I called my sister Amy, in Canada, so that she could say "Hello" to Mom. Remembering that Mom is not deaf, I did not ask Amy if she wanted to say "Good Bye" to Mom. I did the same with my brother, Larry. Mom was not able to speak, but I held the phone up to her ear so that she could hear their voices.

Friday Evening
November 9, 2018
1 Kislev 5779 (Jewish calendar)

Most likely, this is the last Shabbas (Jewish Sabbath) which my Mom will live to see. She is not conscious and has not been able to eat or drink since Tuesday evening. I have been going to the group home in the morning for the last few days, so that I could not only be with my Mother at that time, but also so that I could assist the Hospice CNA in tending to Mom's morning needs. Changing her garments, cleaning her, helping to turn her on the bed so that bed sores can be mitigated, is all done easier with two people. Added to this scenario is the fact that my Mom is in a great deal of pain. For some unknown and unknowable reason her right arm is very painful for us to move, when the situation requires. Tending to her needs while she is in bed requires turning her over onto her right side for a few minutes, then turning her onto her left side. No matter how gently I manipulate her right arm, the pain level must be excruciating.

My Mother has always had a high tolerance for pain. For her to wince or cry out means that the pain level is very, very high. All that I could do for her is to offer comfort as best as I could. This morning, though Mom appears unable to cry, her lips were quivering. I must assume that it was pain, discomfort and perhaps sadness and misery. But I must also remember that other than the pain, which was apparent, I am projecting what my emotions might be if I were her. There are also digestive issues, so to speak, which, as her body is shutting down, are not resolving and which are probably causing a great deal of discomfort.

I have great admiration for the hospice CNAs who have been doing this by themselves. It has been a learning experience to see how one changes an adult diaper, the absorbent pad beneath the patient, and the shirt, all while an unresponsive patient is in bed. If I had known that the task was such a complicated thing to do, or if I had even considered it, I would have offered to be there more often. Live and learn, eh?

After seeing the whole situation this morning, and after talking with the CNA, I got on the phone to the hospice office. Jim, the hospice nurse who has been caring for Mom, arrived about 20 minutes later, assessed the situation and increased the amount of morphine for my Mom. He also pointed out the mottling on her right foot, which he had told me to expect would occur. Mottling is pooling of blood as her circulation begins to shut down. In the 30 minutes or so, from when Jim first pointed it out to me, the mottling had gotten noticeably darker and covered a larger area of her toes and foot. The extra morphine Jim administered – liquid and in her mouth – helped to settle Mom's pain quite a bit. She will now get a full dose every four hours. May G-d bless Jim in the work that he does, and in all other areas of Jim's life. He is a caring and compassionate man, and he is bringing all of his 30+ years of experience to aid my Mother.

A couple of hours after writing the above, a horrifying thought just came to my mind. What if my Mom wants to eat and, as I witnessed Wednesday morning, is not able to remember what to do when food was put in her mouth, and yet is very hungry and we are causing some of her pain by just starving her by not feeding her? I trust, of course, the experience of the hospice nurse and others, but what if we are incorrect in our thinking? Mom is unable to communicate with us. Please, G-d, lead me to clear thinking on this. When I get there, early tomorrow morning, I may ask for a bit of chocolate ice cream to see if Mom wants it when I put it up to her mouth. And what if the damage to her brain is already done, due to lack of food and water? Though she choked on water several times, are we causing her pain by not finding a way around this, and just using strong pain medicine instead?

I do not really believe what I typed just now, but it is a possibility that came to mind. I wonder if other caregivers, family caregivers, have had such thoughts at times like this. When a person, a patient, cannot communicate, all we can do is draw on experience and presume that we are acting correctly and in their best interest. But what if our thinking is not correct? It is my belief, my gut belief, that Mom had another stroke last weekend. She has not been able to speak since then, and her cognitive abilities, such as they remained, disappeared overnight.

Aaron and Mom
November 8, 2018

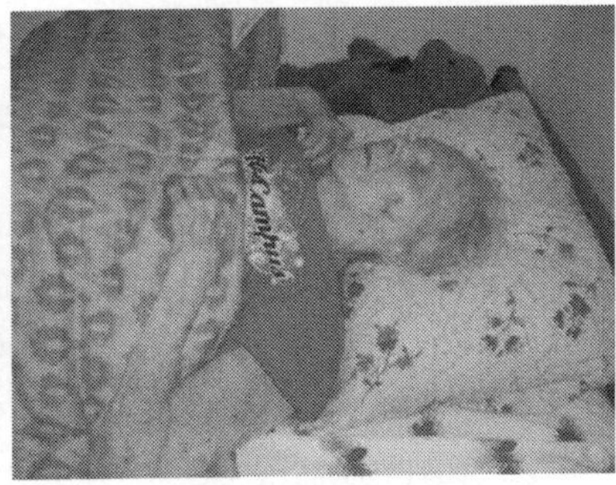

The Lady
November 9, 2018

Circa 2012

November 10, 2018 -- My Mother died this morning. I can shut off my cell phone tonight for the first time in 6 months. On Wednesday afternoon, three days ago, Mom reached over, took my hand and said, "Thank you, Honey." To my knowledge, those were the last words that my Mother said.

88 years of age
46 years of continuous sobriety
17,017 days of continuous sobriety

I had set my alarm for 5:30am so that I could be at the group home by 7:30 to help the hospice CNA with Mom's morning needs. At 6:00 something hit me and I sat in my chair in the living room and sobbed. The grief I felt was from deep down in my gut, and the sobbing was equally powerful, though I had felt nothing like it just a moment before. At 6:30 I got a call from Maria, the manager of the group home. I asked her if my Mom had died. The answer was "Yes." She told me that Sonia, a fabulous care worker at the home, had gone up to check on Mom at 6:00 and that Mom was not breathing. She had died. I learned an hour or so later, when a hospice manager arrived, that when Sonia checked on Mom her body was still warm. Time of death was at, or perhaps just before, 6:00am……Just Before The Stroke of Six……

December 10, 2018 – Evening -- Shloshim ended. Shloshim ended at sunset tonight. The circle of care and duty for my Mom has, in some ways, closed. Jewish rituals, after the death of a loved one, allow for some semblance of structure for the mourning family member. Seven days of Shivah after burial. Sadly, for me anyway, there was not a way to properly sit Shivah here at home. That is all I will say about it. 30 days of Shloshim, which include the Shivah period. Eleven months of mourning for a parent. I leave it to you, Dear Reader, to read up on our Jewish practices if you wish to. This is not the place for me to expound on the matter.

There is still the next 10 months for me to be saying Kaddish for Mom, but the initial duties after the death of a parent have come to an end. Burial. Shivah. Shloshim. I have the love and support of people Mom and I together used to be around at the JCC. And since the AA memorial meeting this past Sunday, I feel the love and support of those members of AA whom I have come to know over the years.

On Sunday, the 9th, we had a one-hour AA memorial meeting at the 1311 York Street club. We just call it "York Street" and I believe that it is the oldest AA club west of the Mississippi. It is the place where my Mom got sober. I have learned that Mom had no memory of the 6 years prior to her getting sober. That bit of information is relevant to family. To expound on that here would not be appropriate for me to do, but it is of great importance to me and my siblings.

The meeting at York Street was powerful, emotional, healing, healthy, filled with the language of recovery, and filled with love. Lots of love. I wish I could share that world with my siblings, but they have no interest in that world. None of them have asked me about the memorial meeting. It hit me a week or so back that prior to my getting sober, Mom had nobody in the family who spoke her language of recovery. Now I know what that feels like. Now I can truly empathize with how lonely Mom must have been in that area. And recovery is a huge area in the life of someone who is in the program. I do not mean this as a put-down or judgement of my siblings, as we all have our ways and our limitations. I just am so grateful that I found my way into recovery, even though the price of admission is very, very steep. If nothing else, my Mother had someone who understood her. I have come across a couple of notes from Mom, in her AA books, which makes mention of her own gratitude that one of her children finally understood her world of recovery. Thank you, G-d.

December 12, 2018 -- Since Mom died, I am finding it extremely difficult to remain focused on any one task. Grieving. Empty. Running on fumes. Lacking a sense of direction. Still doing this deal solo. Feeling disassociated from the world around me. These are some of the thoughts which come to mind right now. And yet, I do not despair of things changing in time, as they no doubt will. It is already a bit easier to navigate a day than it was a week or two weeks ago. A couple of weeks ago, or maybe it was just last Monday, I met with an attorney downtown who is handling the legal aspects of what I must do regarding Mom's estate, such as it is. My power of attorney became moot when she died. In order to file her income taxes in a few months, I will need a court order of some sort. Likewise when I transfer title of her car and the house. Mom's Will is simple and straightforward. Sibling relationships are a bit complicated, but the attorney is working with me on maintaining the privacy of those who have asked for privacy. And none of my siblings have inquired about the legal or logistical aspects of after-care for Mom.

I am writing from my heart and, again, without editing myself to try to sound good or to sound like anyone other than who I am. And right now, I am a man who is grieving the loss of his Mother, after 5 ½ years of caregiving for her. My relationship with Mom was very close, very special and spanned many decades of close contact. Yes, my siblings knew her longer, as I am the youngest of 4 children, but I am the only one who has lived with continuity of contact with Mom and who has lived here in Denver all my life, other than for 2 years in New York and one year in Oregon. Mom and I knew each other in our respective drinking years, and also in our respective years of recovery from alcoholism. We learned how to work our way through friction, and we made a conscious choice to do so in as healthy and direct a manner as possible. The tools of AA's 12-step program have proven to be invaluable in that area. Indispensable, really, for two alkies in recovery who have chosen to break the chain of broken relationships which have plagued our family for several generations. It can be done when two people want it badly enough, are willing to put ego aside, and to own their own mistakes. It works. It really does. And I am so glad that when Mom died, things were clean between us.

Mom's last words to me, on Wednesday afternoon, were "Thank you, Honey." As noted a page or two back, as far as I know, those were the last words she spoke, before G-d took her, early on that Saturday morning, a month and two days ago. None of my siblings have asked me what the last days or weeks were like for Mom. Nor have they asked what it was like on the morning that she died. I have pictures of it all, and I mean all of it, and I cannot imagine sharing them with my family. It was a chunk of very sacred time with Mom before she died, and certainly was so the morning that she passed. I helped the Hospice CNA get Mom cleaned up, changed into fresh clothes, and ready for the funeral home to pick her up. I closed my Mom's eyes when we were through. And I got to assist in lifting the gurney, with Mom on it, into the back of the mortuary vehicle. Tonight, as I type this, I can close my own eyes and picture it all, scene by scene, day by day, in the weeks leading up to her death, and for certain the day that she died. I am a very blessed and grateful man for being graced with the experience of those times, as well as the years since Mom's initial stroke on March 29, 2013. Thank you, Hashem (how we Jews usually refer to G-d) for the opportunity. Thank you, Hashem, for my Mother. I am going to stop typing now and head to my bass guitar for a while. I need to play my music.

January 23, 2019 -- It is time for this writing of mine to come to an end. It has been more than a month since I have had it in me to come back to this writing. My life and my focus has shifted from caregiving to the grieving process and all that that seems to entail, which is new to me. Rather than continue writing, with the necessary topic and focus being on my personal grief, sense of loss, both of my Mother and my purpose these past almost 6 years, I think it is time to wrap this up. Others have written about grieving and loss of a loved one, and I have been fortunate to have been given a couple of books along those lines.

And you, Dear Reader, who has read this far, might someday find your own caregiving journey come to an end, resulting in the beginning of your own journey into and through the grieving process. Since it appears to be a deeply personal and personalized process, I deem it appropriate for me not to proceed beyond the solo full-time caregiving focus which I have endeavored to stick to.

I will share this, though: These years since Mom's initial stroke have been navigated by me with the assistance of just a scant few friends, both of mine and of my Mother's. In the time since Mom died, about 2 ½ months now, nothing has changed in that arena. I did receive a stack of condolence cards from people I know, and I appreciate them having taken the time to write and send them. I have written Thank You cards to them all.

As far as regular contact resuming with the people we/I used to know? Nothing has changed. Just a week or so ago it dawned on me that a chunk of my depression and deep grief was rooted in a faulty expectation that had developed in my thinking. The expectation was that after Mom died, people would surface or call, and be around for comfort and support and consolation. This has not happened. Nothing has changed with friends or such family as I have. I try my best not to judge anyone, keeping in mind that everyone has their own stuff going on and is doing the best that they have in them to do. I truly believe this, and yet the hurt, loneliness and pain of grieving alone just surfaces from time to time. Dropping any expectations of others is helping to alleviate the feelings of abandonment and hurt. Mine has been a journey of solo full-time caregiving, and the grieving seems to be continuing along the same lines. I ask G-d daily, many times a day, for the strength and courage to continue on this part of my life's journey. There is a void now which is huge. I am very mindful to refrain as much as possible from judging others; to keep going through this process of time passing; to refrain from harming myself in a foolish act of despair (yes, Dear Reader, suicide comes to mind more often than I am comfortable with); and to trust that I am on the path I am to be on. This, too, shall pass. Everything does.

I wish you well, Dear Reader, and it is my fervent hope that what I have written and shared in this book/treatise is helpful to you in some way. People have asked me why I have written this treatise/book. I have two primary purposes on that:

First, as I have mentioned several times already, I hope that some other solo full-time caregiver reads this and, if nothing else, knows that they are not the only one to find themselves in such a position. Hopefully, some experiences which I have shared will be helpful to them.

Second, I hope to sell a zillion copies of this work, so that I can form some kind of philanthropic foundation which would help other caregivers so that they are not in financial difficulties when their duty comes to an end. A couple thousand dollars a month, banked for the caregiver, might be an incentive for others to care for their elders at home. Not working a paying job for, in my case 5+ years, puts a real strain on finances. I did not find help in this area, but perhaps down the road I can help someone else – or many someone elses.

Whether you are also a solo full-time caregiver, or if you are blessed to have a caregiving support network of family and friends, I hope and pray that my sharing benefits you and lends you strength, courage and hope, that you can see your job through to the end, whatever that end might look like and whenever that end might come. If nothing else, please know, Dear Reader, that you are not alone. Neither you nor I are the only ones to walk this walk. We are not the first, nor will we be the last.

Please do not quit the task that you have taken on.
Hard as it has been, I did not quit.
I owed my Mother that much at least.
Rest in peace, my dear Mother.
Shalom

פ״נ
MARCIE RULA
חיה מלכה בת
הערשעל פייועל
JUNE 12. 1930 ~ NOV. 10. 2018
נפ׳ כ׳ כסלו תשע״ט
ברכות ואהבה
ת נ צ ב ה

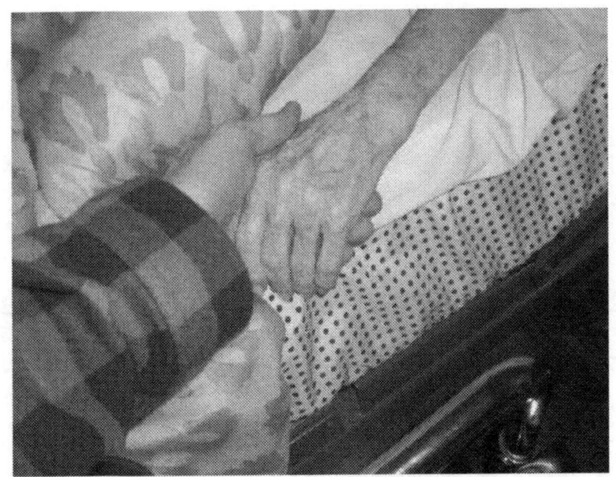

GAM ZU L'TOVAH

Marcie Rula (Mom) and Maximo Corrada
circa 2008

"Take my hand, Marcie. Let me show you around Heaven. You have a lot of friends waiting to see you again."

IMPORTANT CAREGIVING THINGS TO REMEMBER AND DO NOT FORGET

Caregiving is, or should be, participatory.

Plan ahead, and have everything with you that you will need.

If you are the full-time caregiver for someone that is unable to effectively communicate or cannot be safely left alone, write this information out and tape it to the back of your driver's license. In case, G-d forbid, something happens to you while you are out and about with the care recipient, this is where the emergency responders will look first.

It's all about the care recipient, not the caregiver.

Tuck in your nails when helping the recipient get dressed. Old skin is thin.

Slow down.....everything that you do and say

Make certain that what you ask the care recipient to do is achievable, and help them to succeed at it

Do not talk about something while you are doing something else. For example, while helping the care recipient make a bowl of breakfast cereal, do not talk about the plans for the day.

Remember that the care recipient is not stupid. They are injured.

Leave lots of "buffer time" in getting to activities or outings. Lots!

Do not discuss things that are upcoming unless really necessary to do so

How important is it...really?

Surrender to the flow of each day.

Surrender to the fact that social engagements will be challenging to accept, keep and attend.

A person who has had a stroke needs a lot of rest and sleep, particularly after engaging in any sort of activity -- mental, physical or otherwise. Their brain needs to recharge and rest.

Do not over-schedule your days

Do not over-narrate

Do not over-correct

Do not assume that what you say is understood
Do not assume that what is said to you is what they mean
Know when to stop
When you run out of patience and are short-tempered, keep quiet and step away for a bit. The care recipient is not doing it to you, they are just doing it.
When engaged in an activity, ask the care recipient if they are o.k., but do not instill apprehension. This takes practice and a high degree of mindfulness.
Don't hover over the care recipient
Always involve the care recipient in as much decision-making as is appropriate for their particular situation
Limit to two the number of choices that you present
Routine is of paramount importance.
Stay aware of the agenda-driven caregiving
Stay aware of ego-driven caregiving
Stay aware of impatient caregiving
Always strive to maintain the care recipient's dignity.
Sometimes the aged ones just need time to sit and reflect as they wish.
Unless you know the person well, prior to taking on the role of being their caregiver, know that it will take some time to get to know them and the makeup of their personality and their character traits. Take the time. It will make you a better caregiver.

Dementia Trail
Song Written by Aaron Ainbinder
July 24, 2017

Riding down the dementia trail
He's gotten old
She's gotten frail
Make no sense
Most of the time
And nothing rhymes with dementia

Riding down the dementia trail
Alzheimer's brain
Has begun to fail
Knows no season
Or date or time
And everything rhymes in the Alzheimer's mind

Where is the younger man that he once was
Where is the woman that she used to be
Where is my Mother when I look into her eyes
Who's that woman, looking back at me

Imprisoned on the dementia trail
There ain't no way
To post that bail
How much does
A memory weigh
And nothing rhymes with dementia

Dementia Trail (Page 2)
Song Written by Aaron Ainbinder
July 24, 2017

Riding down the dementia trail
He's gotten old
She's gotten frail
Make no sense
Most of the time
And nothing rhymes with dementia

Where's the Southern gentleman that John once was
Where is the teacher that Marcie used to be
Where is my Mother when I look into her eyes
Who is that woman, looking back at me

ONE FOOT
Song Written by Aaron Ainbinder
July 13, 2018

She's got one foot in the other world
The old gal's getting sleepy
One foot in the world to come
And all I can do is hold her hand.
And gently stoke her hair.
All I can do is hold her hand.
Just let her know I'm there.

Her eyes have gone grey
Her hair a silver night
Her soul is at peace now
Her world is all right
Long years lay behind her
Not long lies ahead
She's got one foot in the world to come
And now spends her days in bed

I held her hand and I began to weep
She patted my hand and then fell asleep
One foot in the world to come
All I can do is hold her hand.
Be with her for a time.
One foot in the world to come
And one hand in mine.

She's got two feet now on the other side
The gal's no longer sleepy
She's got both feet now in the world to come
Never again to hold her hand
Or gently stroke her hair
I'll never again get to hold her hand
But the memory will always be there.

RECOMMENDED READING

I recommend that other caregivers read the following books. I have never met any of the authors noted below, but I hope to some day. Each of them wrote on areas which I drew from as I grew into my caregiving duty for my Mother. She benefitted immensely from what I learned from these authors and, of course, so have I. My heartfelt thanks go out to them all. To be of service to others. That is what, I believe, G-d wants of me. And maybe you, too, eh?

My Stroke of Insight
By Dr. Jill Bolte Taylor

Being Mortal
By Dr. Atul Gawande

Move Into Life
By Anat Baniel

Everyday Holiness
The Jewish Spiritual Path of Mussar
By Alan Morinis

Made in the USA
Columbia, SC
20 April 2020